Going Stealth

Going Stealth

TRANSGENDER POLITICS AND
U.S. SURVEILLANCE PRACTICES

TOBY BEAUCHAMP

Duke University Press | *Durham and London* | 2019

Designed by Julienne Alexander
Typeset in Garamond Premier Pro by Copperline Books

Library of Congress Cataloging-in-Publication Data
Names: Beauchamp, Toby, [date] author.
Title: Going stealth : transgender politics and U.S. surveillance
practices / Toby Beauchamp.
Description: Durham : Duke University Press, 2018. | Includes
bibliographical references and index.
Identifiers: LCCN 2018023454 (print) | LCCN 2018028966 (ebook)
ISBN 9781478002659 (ebook)
ISBN 9781478001225 (hardcover : alk. paper)
ISBN 9781478001577 (pbk. : alk. paper)
Subjects: LCSH: Electronic surveillance—Political aspects—
United States. | Electronic surveillance—Social aspects—United
States. | Electronic surveillance—Sex differences—United
States. | Gender nonconformity—Political aspects—
United States. | Gender identity—Political aspects—United
States. | Transphobia—United States.
Classification: LCC HV7936.T4 (ebook) |
LCC HV7936.T4 B43 2018 (print) | DDC 363.2/3—dc23
LC record available at https://lccn.loc.gov/2018023454

Cover art: Angela Piehl, *Headdress*, 2011. Colored pencil on
black paper, 30 inches x 22 inches. Courtesy of the artist.

CONTENTS

ACKNOWLEDGMENTS

I HAVE MANY TO THANK for the care and feeding of this book, and my person, over the long period of its development. In its earliest incarnation as a dissertation, this project found guidance in an ideal constellation of faculty mentors. Then as now, Caren Kaplan's enthusiasm, insightful critiques, and commitment to ethical, collaborative research profoundly inform my work as scholar and teacher. I strive always to emulate and pay forward the balance of generosity and rigor that she models. Gayatri Gopinath provided steadfast mentorship during grad school and beyond, and she offered crucial support during the challenging period when I was grasping for the early kernels of this project. Colin Milburn was an utterly dependable source of cheer and encouragement and a generous reader whose observations unfailingly pushed me to think in new ways.

Among the many other supportive faculty members I first met at UC Davis, I thank Kathleen Frederickson, Beth Freeman, Cathy Kudlick, Juana María Rodríguez, Eric Smoodin, and Julie Wyman. It was my incredible good fortune to be part of the Graduate Group in Cultural Studies at UC Davis, which taught me the lasting value of truly collaborative work. Among my fellow Cult Studs, I am especially grateful to Santiago Castellanos, Marisol Cortez, Sandy Gómez, Cathy Hannabach, Valerie Kim-Thuy Larsen, Sarah McCullough, Christina Owens, Terry Park, and Magalí Rabasa; and to Davis grads from other departments, including Clara V. Z. Boyle, Ryder Diaz, Ryan Fong, Carmen Fortes, Matt Franks, Catherine Fung, and Vanessa Rapatz. At the UC Davis LGBT Resource Center, I particularly thank Sheri Atkinson and remember Angelina Malfitano with a tang-y appreciation. My work with Queers for Public Education—and related collective endeavors oriented toward the public good—indelibly shaped my political sensibilities.

The UC President's Postdoctoral Fellowship Program provided crucial material and intellectual support as I began the long task of turning a dissertation into a book. I will always feel lucky to have spent those postdoctoral years at UC San Diego with exceptionally generous colleagues including Lisa Cartwright, Kirstie Dorr, Fatima El-Tayeb, Kelly Gates, Nitin Govil, Todd Henry, Sara Clarke Kaplan, Roshy Kheshti, David Serlin, Nayan Shah, and Kalindi Vora. I am grateful to Ari Heinrich for reading drafts and for sharing so much through written words. Many of the first revisions were accomplished during writing dates at Twiggs coffeehouse with Lauren Berliner, whose good humor and encouragement kept me going. Patrick Anderson provided many meaningful points of connection in both scholarship and friendship, and he remains a continual source of warmth.

I thank my colleagues in the English department and Gender and Women's Studies program at Oklahoma State University, particularly the junior faculty writing group: Kate Hallemeier, Jeff Menne, Seth Perlow, and Graig Uhlin. Many other people I met through OSU provided important support and friendship, including Irene Backus, Lu Bailey, Caetlin Benson-Allot, Jennifer Borland, Ron Brooks, Jonathan Gaboury, Cristina González, Carrie Kim, Jen Macken, Shaila Mehra, Carol Moder, Charissa Prchal, Louise Siddons, Scott St. Pierre, and Stacy Takacs. One of Oklahoma's greatest gifts to me is a friendship with Angie Piehl, whose thoughtfulness, wit, and queer camaraderie continue to delight.

It has been a joy to work alongside my brilliant, funny, indefatigable colleagues in the Department of Gender and Women's Studies at the University of Illinois at Urbana-Champaign, including Teresa Barnes, Jodi Byrd, C. L. Cole, Samantha Frost, Pat Gill, Maryam Kashani, and Vicki Mahaffey. Thanks to the Hip Hop and Punk Feminisms crew—Ruth Nicole Brown, Karen Flynn, Fiona Ngô, and Mimi Thi Nguyen—for so immediately welcoming me into the fold. Chantal Nadeau and Stephanie Foote provided much-needed mentoring during their respective tenures as department chair. I am continually grateful for Siobhan Somerville's steadfast support and warm presence, and her writing has long been a model for my own. Though it will sound hyperbolic, it is simply factual that Mimi Thi Nguyen's generosity is unmatched; for reading drafts, for calming nerves, for neighborly care, and for showing me that it is indeed possible to be rad and ethical every day, I thank her in perpetuity. The dedicated administrative staff at GWS, Jacque Kahn and Virginia Swisher, deserve my gratitude always. I hold sincere appreciation for my students, especially those in my transgender studies and disability studies courses at UIUC, for creating spaces of generosity and curiosity in which to think together. Many other colleagues across campus have enriched my life and work at UIUC, including Ben Bascom, Onni Gust, David Hays, Kathryn LaBarre, Mireya Loza, Martin Manalansan, Jennifer Monson, Ghassan Moussawi, K. R. Roberto, Sandra Ruiz, Carol Tilley, and participants in the First Book Writing Group. Jenny Davis and Laura Davies Brenier arrived at Illinois just when I did, and I am lucky to know their capacity for kindness and to benefit from their excellent senses of humor. Silas Cassinelli's good company and compassion as a writing buddy eased the revision process on many occasions. I am grateful to Deke Weaver for his gentle friendship and for inviting me into the weird and beautiful worlds he creates, and to Jennifer Allen for her own energy and for her care of mine. Naomi Paik is a righteous force of nature with an enormous heart; she brings good food and good humor into our home each week, and her straightforward pep talks make all things possible.

Colleagues elsewhere have shared with me their valuable time, advice, and many small kindnesses along the way. Any list will surely be incomplete, but I wish to especially thank Aren Aizura, Simone Browne, Mel Chen, Deborah Cohler, Deb Cowen, Lezlie Frye, Inderpal Grewal, Christina Hanhardt, Ronak Kapadia, Greta LaFleur, Eithne Luibhéid, Minda Martin, Carol Mason, Robert McRuer, Nick Mitchell, Sima Shakhsari, and Susan Stryker. Jennifer Terry opened new ways of thinking for me at a critical early stage. Erica Rand has been a willing reader and enthusiastic collaborator, as well as friend. Dean Spade gave generously of his time to read and reread drafts and to offer generative questions and insights. Comrades in the Writing Every Day group freely dispensed optimism and unconditional encouragement. For their help in researching public accommodations policy for chapter 3, I thank Paisley Currah, Lisa Mottet, Alex Sheldon and the Movement Advancement Project, and the Champaign Public Library. I am grateful beyond measure to those who invited me to present portions of the book in progress, particularly to thoughtful audiences at UC Santa Barbara, CSU Fullerton, Rutgers University, Sonoma State University, University of Kentucky, University of Pittsburgh, and Illinois State University.

Ken Wissoker's steadfast commitment to this project, and to guiding me through the publishing process with minimal anxiety, made him truly a gift of an editor. Among the many other people at Duke University Press who made this book possible, I am especially grateful to Oliva Polk for patiently answering the endless questions of a first-time author, and to Mary Hoch, Jade Brooks, and Susan Albury. Anitra Grisales helped me articulate the goals of this work in its earliest stages. I thank wholeheartedly the anonymous reviewers at Duke and at NYU Press for the time they invested to provide exceptionally thorough, generative, and encouraging criticism; this book and my brain are all the better for it.

An incredible network of people gave personal support to me over the long course of this book's development, and here too, no list could encompass all who have done so. Across many different forms of relationship and types of care, I particularly thank Nimmy Abiaka, Keight Bergmann, Laura Fisher, Yumi Lee, Lauren Jade Martin, Bob Meyers, Joan Meyers, Eli Ogburn, Ali Qadeer, Jane Reid, and Jen Walter-Ballantyne. Yasmine Orangi is a bright source of reassurance and solidarity for whom I am truly grateful. I am thankful for the time I was given with Bryn Kelly and Elissa Nelson. Several nonhuman animals contributed snuggles and companionship: Olive, Pim, and Pepper, and the still much-missed Frieda and Skye. For their deep kindness and generosity I thank the extended Degnan family, supportive throughout. I am also grateful to a set of people who are not only those most readily marked as family, but who have deliberately remained so in their caring relationships with me: my mother, Terry Beauchamp, who can at long last add this book to her treasured collection; Paula Mekdeci, Ben Coppel, and Emily Coppel; my remarkable sister Lauren Marlowe, Jordan Marlowe, and my imaginative, effervescent niblings, Emma Jane Marlowe and Logan Marlowe; and my Nana, Betty Scott, whose love and support I will carry with me always.

The friendships I cultivated in graduate school remain some of my most meaningful and trusted, providing intellectual, political, and emotional sustenance across this project's life span and beyond. More than once, Tallie Ben Daniel's encouragement and compassion have been a balm for the complicated feelings that this research provoked in me. Abbie Boggs is a model for the pursuit of critical, responsible engagement with the university and as such has provided genuinely constructive feedback at many stages; I would be remiss to not also thank her for supplying cocktails in both good times and bad. As colleague, collaborator, and friend, Benjamin D'Harlingue has quite literally been on this scholarly endeavor with me from day one; I am inspired by his political and intellectual commitment, and can only hope this book does the unit proud. Tristan Josephson, stalwart companion in transgender studies, has helped me better understand the field and my place in it. Liz Montegary is a consummate reader of drafts, a source of thoughtfulness and humor in equal measures, and the best storyteller I know. No one has borne witness to this book's rollercoaster of joys and frustrations like Cynthia Degnan, who willingly joined me for the ride. She read every word across the many drafts, endured my most anxious moments, shared wholeheartedly in the unexpected delights of this research, challenged my thinking, and ensured that I had access to good food and quiet spaces, even when the latter meant my absence from her. I am truly grateful for her honesty and boundless support, which each day help me take risks that prove transformative. There's no one I would rather share a tent with.

An earlier version of chapter 1 appeared in a different form in "Artful Concealment and Strategic Visibility: Transgender Bodies and U.S. State Surveillance after 9/11," *Surveillance and Society* 6, no. 4 (2009): 355–66.

SUSPICIOUS VISIBILITY

ON APRIL 17, 2007, the day after the shootings at Virginia Tech, a parent at Cranbrook Kingswood School near Detroit, Michigan, phoned police to report seeing a man on campus wearing a blonde wig, high heels, and lipstick. The private high school was placed in lockdown for more than an hour while campus security and local police searched the grounds and each room of the school, ultimately finding no one matching the description. A spokesperson for the Department of Public Safety told reporters that the parent who first saw the "suspicious" person "thought it was kind of strange, so she called the police" and noted, "In the wake of what happened yesterday in Virginia, it's better to be safe than sorry."[1]

Public discourse about the Cranbrook lockdown, limited mostly to local Michigan news outlets and some transgender blogs, typically conveyed a sense of regret that an individual had been unfairly targeted. But these discussions also tended to rationalize the police response by positioning the Virginia Tech shootings as an understandably and singularly anxious moment for the entire United States. The reports suggest that given this broader context, a figure that visually transgresses otherwise clear gender norms justifies heightened scrutiny from both security personnel and the general public. The hour-long lockdown and meticulous search of the campus took place in the absence of any alleged criminal act. Even trespassing was not an issue, since the school grounds are open to the public and connected to a number of public tourist sites, including museums and nature trails. Rather than suggesting that the lockdown could have been justified as a response to a specific crime such as trespassing, this additional information should clarify the extent to which suspicion attaches to particular people: the lockdown occurred not in response to just any stranger on campus, but to a very particular person perceived as strange and threatening. When asked if the person had done anything illegal, for example, one detective agreed with reporters that they had not, but added, "If you're a man, you don't hang around a school dressed as a woman."[2] The detective relies on a commonsense understanding that gender nonconformity—here, a man wearing clothing that men ought not to wear—itself indicates the likelihood of dangerous behavior, rationalizing both policing and panic by imagining that a gender-nonconforming individual fundamentally has something to hide.[3] This statement—and the surveillance practices mobilized through its logic—helps construct the gender-nonconforming figure as an inherently deceptive object of state and public scrutiny.

This book argues that surveillance is a central practice through which the category of transgender is produced, regulated, and contested. It works against the idea that surveillance measures simply spring up in times of crisis—such as after the Virginia Tech shootings or in the wake of 9/11—and also against the notion that transgender people exist as a readily recognizable population to be assessed by such measures. Instead, it aims to unravel these assumptions, taking a longer view of surveillance and security to illustrate how they produce the very categories and figures of gendered deviance that they purport to simply identify. In examining a range of practices—both formally undertaken by and spilling beyond U.S. state agencies, both explicitly citing and never mentioning the term *transgender*—I consider here how the category of transgender simultaneously coheres and further fractures through surveillance. Tracing the political and cultural histories of seemingly new surveillance practices opens space for understanding gender noncompliance through race, citizenship, sexuality, and disability; in this way, the book pushes at the edges of the category of transgender and seeks to expand the scope of transgender studies.

Although it made only a faint blip on the national radar and may seem disconnected from what is generally considered post-9/11 surveillance, the Cranbrook lockdown illustrates the central questions driving this book. The case offers an opportunity to consider public and state scrutiny of gender nonconformity in the broader context of historical anxieties about gendered deception; forms of deviance read through race, citizenship, and disability; and seemingly exceptional moments of national security crisis. Cranbrook was not the only school to increase security and policing directly after the Virginia Tech shootings; news outlets reported that schools in at least twenty-seven states had closed, canceled classes, or otherwise implemented new security measures in response to threats or perceived threats during the week following the shootings. Cranbrook officials consistently referenced the events at Virginia Tech when explaining their decision to lock down their school. Transgender-related blogs and other media discussing the lockdown generally tended to acknowledge this political context as well, while still criticizing the fact that a gender-nonconforming person was singled out as dangerous based only on appearance. A group of concerned Cranbrook community members created a website that specifically called attention to the implications of the lockdown for transgender and queer people connected to the school, and they too pointed out the air of tension already present in the immediate aftermath of Virginia Tech.[4]

Using the shootings to contextualize the lockdown, news reports repeatedly cited officials' explanations that "it's better to be safe than sorry," despite the fact that at least one law enforcement officer admitted, "We're not even sure what gender the person is—it could be a tall, muscular woman."[5] This statement serves as an important reminder that surveillance of gender deviance is not limited to those who are transgender-identified, though it may appear as most visible and overt when enacted against such individuals. Although the officer's admission suggests that a tall, muscular woman is more likely to be deemed innocent than a man dressed as a woman, neither case negates school and law enforcement officials' refrain of "better safe than sorry." The phrase depends on a conception of safety as something that requires losing—or willingly giving up—privacy. Surveillance studies scholar Torin Monahan calls attention to this logic when he notes that questions of surveillance are typically framed as trade-offs, such that more of one thing (security) necessarily means less of another (privacy). Asking how much of one we have to give up to get the other, Monahan argues, is the wrong question. He suggests instead that we pursue questions about how surveillance practices organize our social lives and produce new, or reconsolidate existing, power relations.[6] This reframing must also counter the persistent belief that privacy is already distributed equally such that anyone might choose to relinquish or retain it. As scholarship and activism in areas such as reproductive justice and disability justice maintain, and as the chapters in this book show, privacy is not a default status but an exceptional one, granted largely on the basis of wealth and racial privilege.[7]

A case like the Cranbrook lockdown cannot be understood as an isolated incident, then, but rather as a constellation of representations, policies, and material practices entangled in broad historical and social contexts. As I note above, almost every media response to the Cranbrook lockdown explained it as a result of anxiety about Virginia Tech. But certainly other factors created a general feeling of high alert, a feeling cultivated on a national scale and intensifying over the previous several years. By April 2007, Congress had not only passed but reauthorized the USA PATRIOT Act, the Department of Homeland Security was well established, and the Guantánamo Bay detention facility had been operating for five years. Furthermore, by the time the Cranbrook parent phoned local police, authorities had already identified the shooter at Virginia Tech as a South Korean immigrant who had been diagnosed with mental illnesses. Although much public discourse framed Seung-Hui Cho as shockingly exceptional, it also relied on an easy recognition of the monstrous and dangerous figure regularly woven into antiterrorism rhetoric, immigration debates, and medical classifications of abnormality.

The Virginia Tech case also rests on a complex set of racialized gender and sexual norms that contribute to both U.S. national identity and conceptions of citizenship, which resonate in the Cranbrook lockdown. As Jigna Desai and Amy Brandzel point out in their discussion of the Virginia Tech shootings, within dominant frameworks, Asian American men are already outside the boundaries of proper masculinity, "evoking the historical threat of the 'yellow peril' ready to harm white femininity with contamination and miscegenation by [their] uncontrolled nonnormative sexuality."[8] They explain that public discourse about Cho tended either to position him as a violent exception to the assimilated model minority (in contrast to the expectation of terrorism commonly attached to South Asian and Arab immigrant groups) or to fold him into a broad perception of all immigrants as potential terrorists. In these ways, Cho readily appears as a dangerous figure, failing or refusing to adhere to the intertwining norms of race, gender, sexuality, ability, and citizenship that mark out health and safety. Although public narratives of the Virginia Tech shootings build on post-9/11 security anxieties, they reverberate far more deeply, drawing on decades of Orientalist discourse and racialized gender relations. One prominent response to the shootings, Desai and Brandzel note, was a call for increased state profiling measures, not simply in routine policing practices, but specifically in the arenas of mental health and immigration, a response that indicates how these various narrative strands converge through surveillance.

The panic at Cranbrook was not produced merely through temporal proximity to an individual violent event. In part, this is because even the shootings at Virginia Tech—and subsequent interpretations of them—cannot be isolated from the longer histories that inform them. Those histories therefore also resonate in the Cranbrook lockdown, setting a context in which certain bodies or behaviors appear as strange and suspicious threats even in the absence of any actual misconduct. Moreover, to explain the lockdown as either about the tension produced by recent events or about a particular individual turns attention away from the larger forces at work. Desai and Brandzel point out that Cho's case did not prompt prolonged public discussion about what influenced his actions in the ways that young white school shooters' cases did, as with the many investigations into violent video games and youth alienation that followed the shootings at Columbine High School. They suggest that Virginia Tech did not draw this kind of investigation because delving into the broader racialized and gendered aspects of Cho's case "could force us to interrogate whiteness and the ways in which U.S. citizenship continues to rely on Orientalist discourses."[9] Centralizing the strange individual thus allows larger structures of power to escape examination.

Working against this tendency, *Going Stealth* aims to turn back the scrutinizing gaze of science, medicine, and law, attending not so much to the gender-nonconforming figure that is positioned as dangerous as to the uneven relations of power that produce that figure and its accompanying threat. It is tempting to read the Cranbrook lockdown as primarily about panic created by the Virginia Tech shootings, as local law enforcement describes it, or as primarily about anti-transgender bias, as many transgender media outlets see it. But this book argues that incidents like the lockdown can never be explained simply as basic transphobia or as overzealous security. Instead, such events should prompt critical analysis of the ways that gender deviance is produced, coded, and monitored not only in these spectacular moments, but also in the everyday. Likewise, the surveillance practices at work in this case emerged not merely in direct response to the Virginia Tech shootings, but through long histories of nationalist sentiments, racialization processes, and medicolegal taxonomies of bodily difference. This book insists that the two seemingly separate explanations for cases like Cranbrook—the particular targeting of gender nonconformity as dangerous and the explicit increases in security during times of perceived crisis—must be understood as fundamentally entwined. Although one news outlet reported that the Cranbrook school practices lockdowns twice a year, community members noted that the last real lockdown of the campus occurred in response to the events of September 11, 2001. That the sighting of "a man in a dress" might prompt the same security protocol as for the events that have come to define terrorism in the U.S. speaks to some of the links between gender deviance, racial anxieties, and national security that I am concerned with here.

Toward a Transgender Critique

Although the Cranbrook lockdown received only brief public attention, it exemplifies the convergence of the apparently anomalous gender-nonconforming person and the seemingly exceptional surveillance and security measures rationalized as necessary, or at least understandable, in times of national crisis. In the most basic sense, this book seeks to dismantle such exceptions: to examine the ways that state surveillance practices, not bound to recent moments of crisis but rather long embedded in the everyday, produce a broad range of deviation from regulatory gender norms that exceeds the category of transgender. How are transgender and gender-nonconforming populations caught up in ongoing state surveillance practices that almost never explicitly name transgender as a category of concern? In cases where surveillance and policing are overtly concerned with transgender-identified people, how might such a focus obscure other aspects of securitization or troublingly limit the scope of political responses? How can an assessment of surveillance measures help us rethink the very category of transgender, particularly in relation to racialization and citizen-making processes? How and why do U.S. state agencies produce intertwined crises of security and gender, so that the notion of gendered deception becomes a threat on a national level? If surveillance mechanisms rely on normative understandings of gendered bodies and identities, what productive inconsistencies might gender nonconformity reveal about surveillance practices?

In pursuing these questions, I show how transgender and gender-nonconforming populations are inextricable from the surveillance and security measures that work to produce and regulate them. Focusing especially on those measures that have gained new recognition in relation to the global war on terror, *Going Stealth* contextualizes these practices in longer histories of bodily classification, militarization, and constructions of deviance to illustrate the persistent relationship between the concept of national security and state regulation of transgressive gender. I ask how such regulation might be displaced onto gender-nonconforming subjects, thus appearing nonexistent or inapplicable to those perceived as (or those understanding themselves as) normatively gendered. In this way, the book challenges the very category of transgender and the scope of transgender studies, engaging the fact that bodies, identities, and behaviors may be read as gender deviant in relation to perceived or actual racial identity, religious affiliation, nationality and citizenship status, class status, disability, or sexuality. Relatedly, I analyze the ways that certain transgender-identified persons, able to comply with dominant standards of appearance and behavior (themselves grounded in ideals of whiteness, U.S. citizenship, able-bodiedness, and compulsory heterosexuality), may be legible to surveillance mechanisms not as transgender but as properly gendered and thus nonthreatening.

These inquiries create what I hope is a productive tension that runs throughout the book: I attend to the specific and overt policing of transgender-identified subjects, yet am equally concerned with the ways that such scrutiny works more pervasively, regulating gender in subtler ways and positioning a variety of bodies, behaviors, and identities—not only those explicitly identified as transgender—as gender-nonconforming. In doing so, I build on scholarship and activism that pushes the relatively new field of transgender studies to expand its scope and vision. In his lengthy discussion of the field's formation, David Valentine suggests that in the most basic sense, transgender studies has been constituted through "the idea that there is a large group of people who can be understood through the category transgender."[10] Much work in transgender studies has been concerned with documenting social histories that take transgender as a fairly bounded and preexisting category, aiming to uncover and report knowledge about the people identified within that category. In many cases, this work has implicitly taken white, class-privileged, U.S.-based transgender-identified people as its subjects.[11] Valentine notes that several scholars associated with the field have expressed wariness about taking such a neatly contained category for granted, and he writes that his own concern "is still that the increasing use of 'transgender' as a term to order knowledge produces the possibilities whereby certain subjects become appropriated into a reading of transgender that obscures the complexities of their identification and experience."[12] Nevertheless, he suggests that transgender studies might offer a more expansive way to think through multiple figurations of gender in relation to sexuality, race, class, nationality, and ability.

Dean Spade engages these possibilities when he asks us to consider how medical and legal surveillance of transgender-identified people actually functions to discipline all gendered subjects toward a normative gender that appears natural and healthy when viewed in opposition to those particular bodies and identities designated as transgender.[13] Spade is interested in the ways that medicine and law demand from transgender people normalizing measures that uphold the status quo rather than resist or change it, but he also gestures at the ways that this process enforces normative gender for all people. In other words, it may seem that only certain bodies, those that cannot or will not conform to normative gender standards, are subject to surveillance and scrutiny. It may appear that only transgender people have to alter their gender presentations, for example, while non-transgender people have gender presentations that are naturally, effortlessly normative. In this way, gender regulation can appear displaced onto only the transgender-identified, such that other bodies and identities can seem naturally gender normative and free from scrutiny. Of course, as Judith Butler explains, all gendered subjects emerge through regulatory power: "persons are regulated by gender, and . . . this sort of regulation operates as a condition of cultural intelligibility for any person."[14] Yet these regulatory norms often play out in more mundane and subtle ways than the explicit medicolegal policies set up for transgender people.

Consider, for example, an American Express national advertising campaign launched in mid-2008. In response to other companies' turns to consumer-chosen designs for credit cards, the campaign sought to showcase the professional look of American Express Business Gold cards. To this end, one commercial features a white man dressed in a suit, who approaches an airline ticket counter for a business trip to San Francisco and presents a credit card adorned with images of kittens. The ticket agent looks at him suspiciously, confirms that this is a business trip, and motions to two security personnel, who immediately flank the customer from behind. The Black male security guard asks the customer to come with them, and the white woman snaps on a latex glove. As they whisk this customer away, another white man steps to the counter, also requests a ticket for a San Francisco business trip, and presents his professional American Express Gold card, which creates no disturbance.

In this case, a person not specifically marked as transgender is nonetheless subject to gender regulation because of the ways his gender is interpreted through consumer objects. The introduction of a latex glove (notably edited out of later versions of the commercial) suggests that this person is also subject to a physical form of state violence for his gender transgressions. That the security guard wearing the glove is a woman adds another gendered layer to this scene: in response to public anxieties about inappropriate and nonconsensual physical contact during security checks, government officials have repeatedly issued assurances that physical searches will be conducted by an officer of the same gender as the individual being searched. Along with the too-feminine credit card design, the gloved search conducted by a woman positions this airline customer as breaking from normative gender in ways that provoke (and, the commercial implies, justify) serious scrutiny. Importantly, the second customer—the man with the properly professional and masculine credit card—is also part of this system, as is the at-home viewer, for whom these regulatory practices may be internalized. Here, the privileges of good citizenship are arrived at through normative gendering, which is read in part through class status and consumer practices. The policing of gender transgression, though often occurring most overtly in relation to transgender-identified people, casts a much wider net. At the same time, those transgender-identified people who can comply with the regulatory norms of race, class, ability, and citizenship through which proper, non-threatening gender is read may escape these most obvious forms of scrutiny.

A central argument running throughout this book, then, is that surveillance of gender-nonconforming people centers less on their identification as transgender per se than it does on the perceived deception underlying transgressive gender presentation. Just as the telling of a lie and the omission of information are two different forms of deception, I move between an interrelated set of terms to show how this broad link between gender nonconformity and deception manifests: through accusations of fraud, through claims that certain bodies or identities do not match as they ought to, and through demands for disclosure or transparency, among others. State and public actors may justify surveillance practices by focusing on a specific form of deception, according to which form best supports the goal of maintaining normative gender. For instance, claims of fraud—a form of deception linked to personal or financial gain by taking something from another person—appear repeatedly in debates about identification documents, particularly regarding the use of false ID to gain citizenship or voting rights, which conservative discourse frames as stealing from true citizens. Yet the rationale for intensified airport security screenings more often rests on the language of concealment, which can discursively merge concealed weapons with concealed sex or gender under the rubric of public safety that justifies airport surveillance.

Crucially, the implicit anxieties about terrorism in the American Express commercial suggest that nonnormative gender presentation is cause for alarm and suspicion on the level of national safety. Indications that something is amiss or doesn't match up increasingly signal a much larger danger, producing anxieties fueled by public safety campaigns like the directive, "If you see something, say something," circulating widely in public transit stations and airports. Against the cultural and political backdrop of the war on terror, government policy and public discourse produce an atmosphere casting full disclosure as the primary avenue to security and safety: only the duplicitous terrorist would balk at providing information to state agencies, and citizens with nothing to hide have nothing to fear from intensified government surveillance and military presence.

But the panic at Cranbrook and the anxieties conveyed in the American Express commercial—as well as the gendered and racialized contours of surveillance practices ranging from biometric identification to airport screenings—illustrate that the perception of fraud clings more tightly to some than others. Although this perception undoubtedly creates material problems for many transgender-identified people, the appearance of gendered duplicity can be exacerbated or mitigated according to the ways that categories including race, class, citizenship, sexuality, and disability mutually constitute gender and various readings of it. That is to say, state actors and policies may interpret transgender people as threats to national health and safety, often in ways that connect to broad anxieties about terrorism and immigration, but such an interpretation of gendered deception extends far beyond the transgender-identified, as the early chapters of this book demonstrate.

I have therefore had to make some complicated choices about the language used to describe gendered bodies, identities, and practices that transgress dominant standards. It is partly because surveillance practices apprehend a wide range of gendered subjects as transgressive—whether such subjects are intentionally breaking from gendered norms or not—that simply defaulting to *transgender* as a catchall term cannot suffice. Where I use *transgender* in this book, I refer to those bodies and subjects that identify or are identified in ways that exceed normatively bounded categories of man and woman. Relatedly, I use *transgender-identified* to mark the ways that people identify themselves or are identified by others, denoting a specific claim to transgender itself as an identity category.[15] In general, I avoid the term *transsexual*, which is rooted in and still typically associated with Western medicolegal classifications; where this term does appear here, it references its particular employment by certain scholars or its specific use as a codified medical or legal category. Most often, I rely on *gender nonconforming* as a broader term encompassing many (though certainly not all) transgender subjects as well as those bodies and subjects that break from idealized gender binaries or are interpreted as breaking from them because of the ways gender norms are read through mutually constitutive categories such as race, class, sexuality, religion, disability, and citizenship. Roughly, then, in this book *transgender* gestures more toward identity and identification, whereas *gender nonconforming* addresses a relation to norms that may involve but need not rest on identity and identification.[16] These broader and less rigid terms are useful precisely because surveillance measures produce and affect not only those specifically identified as transgender but a wide range of gendered practices, identities, and bodies beyond that formal category.

The term *cisgender*, increasingly used to mark non-transgender identity, poses related problems for this book. First introduced in the early 1990s, the term draws on use of the cis- prefix in the biological sciences to designate something that does not change property or orientation; applied to gender, in a basic sense it describes remaining aligned with assigned gender/sex designations and related boundaries rather than changing or crossing them as the trans- prefix indicates. Although *cisgender* has recently gained quite a bit of purchase in transgender scholarship and activist discourse, and although it can do important work in denaturalizing normative gender, I do not employ it here for several reasons. The term's reliance on biological frameworks—both the biological definition fueling the prefix itself and the implicit investment in a biological grounding for gender—limits its usefulness for a project intent on exploring the ruptures and contingencies of those frameworks themselves. Following A. Finn Enke's analysis of the term, I also question the mechanisms by which trans- is distinguished from cis-, and how this additional dichotomy may close down new avenues rather than opening them up.[17] For instance, how might the circulation of cisgender as an identity category further naturalize and stabilize the categories of man and woman, even as it may be intended to highlight their constructed nature? Might cisgender status simply become equivalent to normative gender, and, if so, which transgender-identified people might it include, if any (i.e., once identified as transgender, must one always remain in that category)?[18] Meanwhile, as Che Gossett succinctly argues, the term *cisgender* "can't really account for how the gender binary was forcibly imposed on black and native people through slavery and settler colonialism. In American society, black people have always been figured as gender transgressive."[19] Inasmuch as the term centralizes a form of gender privilege that emerges through normative race, class, sexuality, and ability, but generally fails to name these relationships, can *cisgender* properly attend to the nuances of gender difference and the complexities of gender transgression? Because these questions are central to my examination of the surveillance mechanisms that assess gendered bodies, identities, and behaviors, *cisgender* cannot serve as useful shorthand in this project. Likewise, I avoid naming particular groups non-transgender, except when doing so indicates the particular assumption of non-transgender status within surveillance practices and discourses.

Rather than attempting to collect knowledge about a particular identity category or bounded group of people, this book engages the *transgender* of transgender studies as a mode of critique. I draw here in part on Susan Stryker's explanation of a transgender critique as one that "takes aim at the modernist epistemology that treats gender merely as a social, linguistic, or subjective representation of an objectively knowable material sex. Epistemological concerns lie at the heart of transgender critique. . . . Transgender phenomena, in short, point the way to a different understanding of how bodies mean, how representation works, and what counts as legitimate knowledge."[20] Building on this, Stryker and Aren Aizura forward an intellectual approach that uses the critical lens of transgender studies to put "as much pressure on the categories of *man*, *woman*, and *homosexuality*, as on *transgender*," cautioning that "those terms are no less constructed than *transgender* itself, and they circulate transnationally in discourse and analysis with no less risk of being conceptually colonizing."[21] In these senses, a transgender critique is concerned less with producing knowledge about a particular class of people identified as transgender and more with understanding the social, political, and material conditions through which those identifications emerge and that knowledge itself is produced.

Nor is a transgender critique limited to a clearly circumscribed category called transgender. Rather, it is most useful when leveraged to unseat those categories of gender and sexuality that might be normalized and taken for granted through their assumed contrast to transgender. When taken up as an analytic rather than as a bounded identity category, *transgender* can also usefully intervene into the naturalization of race, disability, and citizenship. The term *gender-nonconforming* proves especially productive for this work, by moving away from an analysis of identities themselves (which would risk further naturalizing those identities) and toward an analysis of the production of, investments in, and breaks from those identity categories and related regulatory norms. In this book, a transgender critique enables an analysis of gender nonconformity that may or may not be (or be perceived as) transgender-identified, and it provides a critical framework for examining relationships between many different gender-nonconforming practices, bodies, and identities, and the knowledge frameworks and institutions through which they are produced.

In her classic essay "Punks, Bulldaggers, and Welfare Queens," Cathy Cohen observes that queer political work thus far has failed to enact transformational politics in large part because it has relied on a narrow understanding of *queer* that turns on sexual identity rather than on shared political commitments and connected relationships to heteronormativity. While she does not advocate eliminating identity categories, she argues that "it is the multiplicity and interconnectedness of our identities that provide the most promising avenue for the *destabilization and radical politicization* of these same categories."[22] In this book, I do not discount the material effects of surveillance on transgender people, but I am primarily concerned with tracing the ways that different surveillance practices directly or indirectly rely on a gender-nonconforming figure that, as I show, may well not correspond to a transgender-identified subject. In this way, I also follow what certain queer and ethnic studies scholars have called a "subjectless critique," which "disallows any positing of a proper subject *of* or object *for* the field."[23]

Likewise, my approach is indebted to queer of color critique, which Roderick Ferguson describes as a mode of analysis that "extends women of color feminism by investigating how intersecting racial, gender, and sexual practices antagonize and/or conspire with the normative investments of nation-states and capital."[24] A critical lens that situates queer studies as inseparable from processes of racialization and the uneven transnational circulation of bodies, capital, and knowledge, queer of color critique approaches questions of gender and sexuality not through narrow conceptions of identity but as political and cultural formations mutually constituted with race, nationalism, and global structures of power. Accordingly, while this book examines surveillance enacted by U.S. government agencies and segments of the U.S. public, it does not suggest a bounded United States operating in isolation. On the contrary, the surveillance practices examined here emerge and proliferate in relationship to racism, colonialism, and border anxieties, particularly (but not only) as they structure the war on terror.[25] Relatedly, the question of citizenship animates many of the forms of surveillance that this book considers. A contested term encompassing many interrelated definitions, citizenship can be a formal legal status, a mechanism through which to access rights, a descriptor of morality and productivity (as in "good citizenship"), or a "range of everyday activities through which people claim political and social belonging within the national territory they inhabit" (as in cultural citizenship).[26] This book engages each of these meanings, which both overlap and contradict one another, indicating one reason that surveillance measures are so frequently instituted to regulate citizenship.

Drawing on Ferguson, Gayatri Gopinath explains that queer of color critique "enables us to trace the convergence of what seem to be radically distinct and disparate ideologies as they shore up heteronormativity."[27] Applying this intellectual practice to transgender studies makes it possible for this book to investigate a wide range of regulatory mechanisms producing gender, even—or perhaps especially—if at first gender does not appear central to their workings. Thus the book critically addresses dichotomous frameworks not only concerning male/female and man/woman, or even transgender/non-transgender, but also deviant/normative, terrorist/citizen, security/insecurity, and us/them. A transgender critique, as I pursue it here, offers a way to read various anxieties about gender nonconformity with a particular focus on their relationship to racism, xenophobia, ableism, and securitization.

Navigating Visibility

If, following Michel Foucault, power is not simply repressive but is productive of knowledge and categories of identity that work to manage life and regulate behaviors, then this book understands transgender not as a predetermined category into which identities or bodies are slotted, but as a shifting discursive category produced in part through practices of surveillance. In this sense, it is not that surveillance identifies bodies or subjects that are already inherently deviant, but that surveillance is one mechanism through which gender nonconformity is produced as such. This theoretical approach usefully moves away from medical, legal, and cultural frameworks that have often sought to determine the truth of transgender identities and bodies; it asks instead how the very notion of transgender enters into discourse and why its truth becomes important.

Key to both the form and content of this book is Foucault's argument in *Discipline and Punish* that the institutionalization of examinations and inspections—through spaces such as the school, the hospital, or the military—transformed mechanisms of power beginning in the late eighteenth century. These meticulous and obligatory examinations mark a shift away from sovereign power, which made itself most visible, to disciplinary power, which Foucault contends "is exercised through its invisibility; at the same time it imposes on those whom it subjects a principle of compulsory visibility. In discipline, it is the subjects who have to be seen. Their visibility assures the hold of the power that is exercised over them. It is the fact of being constantly seen, of being able always to be seen, that maintains the disciplined individual in his subjection."[28]

Much scholarship regarding transgender people has sought to make them more visible, to investigate the truths of transgender lives and bodies, and to promote recognition and legibility of transgender individuals. Work in fields including psychology, law, sociology, and anthropology has aimed to discover and articulate what transgender bodies, communities, and identities entail. Such scholarly endeavors occur alongside transgender representation in popular culture: mystery novels, medical dramas, and daytime talk shows regularly position transgender people as hiding a dramatic secret that audiences are meant to uncover, often in the most literal sense of the word. We might say, in fact, that one of the most common characteristics of work on transgender topics is the framing of transgender bodies and identities as opportunities to make visible what is otherwise tantalizingly hidden.

Although visibility projects can create spectacles and further marginalize gender nonconformity, in many cases these efforts are intended as beneficial steps toward social change. But as Evelynn Hammonds reminds us, "an appeal to the visual is not uncomplicated or innocent. As theorists we have to ask how vision is structured, and, following that, we have to explore how difference is established, how it operates, how and in what ways it constitutes subjects who *see* and *speak* in the world."[29] These tasks are crucial to a critical engagement of surveillance practices—practices that should remind us that visibility is not a panacea but rather, as Foucault famously remarked, a trap.[30] This is in part because one's visibility to surveillance mechanisms can allow those mechanisms to work more effectively. At times this can even seem desirable, as when individuals enroll in preferred customer tracking programs or register as precertified travelers under new airline screening policies; these surveillance practices may not even register as surveillance, but rather as convenient privileges for the compliant consumer-citizen. Heightened visibility of some populations, particularly those marked as deviant or undesirable, can also allow others to feel or appear untouched by surveillance (even if this is not actually the case). All of these instances tend to focus on the problem bodies that must be overtly scrutinized and deflect attention away from surveillance practices themselves, much as Foucault notes that visibility shifts away from the workings of disciplinary power and onto those subjects being disciplined. David Lyon explains this in the context of increasingly automated and digital surveillance technologies: "Surveillance practices enable fresh forms of exclusion that not only cut off certain targeted groups from social participation, but do so in subtle ways that are sometimes scarcely visible. Indeed, the automating of surveillance permits a distance to be maintained between those who are privileged and those who are poor, those who are 'safe' and those who are 'suspect.'"[31]

With these concerns in mind, this book seeks not to uncover particular information or truths about transgender subjects, but to understand how these subjects, and the shifting category of transgender, are produced in concert with a range of nonconforming gender practices and made visible through modes of surveillance that may never even name transgender as a category of concern. If, as Foucault argues, power is exerted not in a one-directional, top-down manner but through diffuse networks, then this book is concerned with the ways that practices of surveillance extend far beyond their most obvious forms—the USA PATRIOT Act, the National Security Agency—into the more quotidian aspects of our lives. These surveillance and security practices of the everyday produce and refine normative gender even when they may appear disconnected from it, as the first two chapters make clear.

Likewise, although this book pays special attention to U.S. state surveillance, it does not assume that surveillance practices originate in the state or that the state itself can be considered a stable and unified entity. Rather, in Wendy Brown's terms, we might best understand the state as "a significantly unbounded terrain of powers and techniques, an ensemble of discourses, rules, and practices, cohabiting in limited, tension-ridden, often contradictory relation with one another," and yet despite this somewhat unwieldy and shifting set of practices, also as "a vehicle of massive domination."[32] In this framework, surveillance can be analyzed as a constellation of mechanisms that may support but also exceed state power, while also illustrating the incoherence of and fractures in what we call the state. By addressing state surveillance, this book seeks to understand how surveillance practices move through and beyond formal state apparatuses and to explore how those practices put the state itself in question. Thus as Margot Canaday writes, "the state does not just direct policy at its subjects; various state arenas are themselves sites of contest over sex/gender norms, and therefore structured by those norms."[33] Accordingly, while I examine the ways that U.S. state surveillance works to regulate gender, I also address these practices as fraught struggles over the very gendered categories that such surveillance claims to bring under control.

Because surveillance practices proliferate to pervade all aspects of our lives, extending well beyond those specific measures that state agencies lay claim to, the scope of my primary source material here is necessarily both broad and incomplete. In many cases I look to facets of surveillance clearly connected to specific government agencies, such as congressional hearings and formal legislation, that set in motion and maintain security mechanisms. But I also take seriously Foucault's caution against conceiving of the state and civil society as a dichotomous and "antagonistic pair" in which the former is domineering while the latter is "something good, lively, and warm."[34] If power has no single origin or hierarchy, but consists of "the manifold relationships of force that take shape and come into play in the machinery of production, in families, limited groups, and institutions," then my archive also traces surveillance through capillary networks of power not confined to the arenas commonly associated with the state itself, as the third chapter particularly illustrates.[35] But it is also for this reason—that power "is produced from one moment to the next, at every point, or rather in every relation from one point to another"—that the archive must always be partial.[36] I bring together a combination of formal and informal surveillance mechanisms, tracing their connections through the everyday to better understand how surveillance, the state, and the category of transgender come to seem legible and stable through one another.

I also consider transgender advocacy organizations' responses to U.S. surveillance practices, responses that reflect a tension between these organizations' different political frameworks. Aligned with a mode of scholarship that promotes visibility and recognition, some organizations have urged a rather patriotic compliance with state policy while seeking to reform security measures to more accurately and sensitively address transgender-identified people. This strategy emerges out of a larger investment in existing institutions such as the legal and penal systems, understood here as granting rights and protection, provided they can be taught to properly account for and include transgender-identified people. Although intended to alleviate particular harms, these inclusion campaigns rest on claims of good citizenship that both presume equal access to that status and help legitimate surveillance practices by working within the frameworks they provide. As Jasbir Puar argues, the queer subject is often incorporated into normative white citizenship through the production of a contrasting racialized figure of terror, creating figures that appear both exceptional and binarily oppositional. But crucially, these figures can work together to deflect attention from the ways that queerness is thoroughly entangled in and produced through the biopolitics of war, militarism, and security.[37]

Working against that problem, other transgender advocacy and activist organizations begin not by attempting to fold more genders into surveillance systems but by questioning instead the very terms on which those systems operate. Structured by frameworks of racial and economic justice—and understanding these as central to transgender politics—these groups follow what Dean Spade has described as a "trickle-up" model of social justice, which prioritizes the needs and leadership of those most vulnerable.[38] Through this lens, greater recognition of transgender people from police, prisons, or biometric screening technologies exacerbates rather than mitigates harm: many transgender and gender-nonconforming people are already made visible—and thus vulnerable—to surveillance mechanisms, as this book shows, and campaigns for greater recognition tacitly support the continuation of those systems.

Two organizations' approaches to hate crimes legislation can illustrate these different advocacy approaches. The National Center for Transgender Equality (NCTE), perhaps the most prominent transgender-specific lobbying and policy organization in the United States, offers a resource manual titled "Responding to Hate Crimes." Last updated in 2009—the year that U.S. federal hate crimes law was expanded to include sexual orientation, gender, and gender identity—the manual provides extensive information about the parameters of hate crimes laws, responding to harms considered hate crimes, and working with law enforcement. In the section regarding law enforcement, NCTE begins with a short paragraph noting restorative justice programs before describing at length how to best interact with law enforcement personnel: for instance, the manual encourages readers to remind police officers that "criminal law protects and applies to transgender people in the same way that it protects and applies to non-transgender people."[39] Also in 2009, the Sylvia Rivera Law Project (SRLP)—a New York–based collective providing free legal services for low-income transgender, intersex, and gender-nonconforming people—released a statement regarding the federal hate crimes law expansion. Explicitly marking the disproportionate targeting of marginalized communities, the statement denounces such legislation as a "counterproductive response to the violence faced by LGBT people," noting that "this system itself is a main perpetrator of violence against our communities" and recommitting SRLP to creating "systems of accountability that do not rely on prisons or policing."[40]

The statement by SRLP explicitly recognizes that greater transgender inclusion and legibility in the criminal legal system intensifies harm for many and reinforces the status of law enforcement as our primary recourse for addressing violence, and it emphasizes a vision for responding to harm that does not depend on this system. The NCTE manual briefly mentions restorative justice programs as "relatively rare" in the United States, and foregrounds instead a detailed set of suggestions for assisting and educating law enforcement that naturalizes reliance on "law and order." By presuming a universal and equally accessible protection granted by the criminal legal system, the manual elides the profoundly uneven ways that criminalization and incarceration play out; it positions that system as a remedy in itself, if one in need of education regarding transgender-identified people. *Going Stealth* explores the contours of these different advocacy frameworks as enacted by a variety of organizations and considers the relationship of such responses to specific surveillance practices. Efforts toward more recognition of transgender identities and bodies within surveillance systems may reduce harm for certain individuals, yet they also facilitate the workings of surveillance, bringing those identities and bodies more efficiently under biopolitical management. To return to Hammonds's concerns with visibility, then: "in overturning the 'politics of silence' the goal cannot be merely to be seen: visibility in and of itself does not erase a history of silence nor does it challenge the structure of power and domination, symbolic and material, that determines what can and cannot be seen."[41]

In light of these interventions, this book seeks not to forward visibility for transgender subjects but to consider how that visibility works as a part of biopower to produce the very category of transgender. Rather than arguing for or against the veracity of the information that national security measures purport to offer up about gender-nonconforming people, I reflect here on the effects of that focus on truth and accuracy. In this sense, the book's form works hand in hand with its content: each chapter begins with a relatively recent and fairly overt instance of surveillance that may seem singular, often appearing as a direct response to the events and aftermath of 9/11, and works outward to excavate its historical and political underpinnings. I trace genealogies of discursive figures, classificatory frameworks, and security technologies with a particular eye to how an understanding of post-9/11 events as exceptional, new, or isolated occurrences can efface these nuanced histories. Across its chapters, the book moves from little discernible visibility of transgender subjects—by considering surveillance practices that almost never refer to the term *transgender*—to what we might consider hypervisibility—by examining practices that, I argue, come to seem entirely about an explicitly transgender subject.

The first chapter takes up U.S. government regulation of identification documents, which has garnered increased public scrutiny since 9/11, particularly regarding the introduction of the Real ID Act and related policies aimed at identifying terrorist suspects. Noting that the medical and legal scrutiny of gender nonconformity—and the medicolegal production of transgender subjects—regularly converge in the administration of identity documents, this chapter explores the broader history of such documents, including their racial and nationalist foundations. Analyzing the longer arc of efforts to identify through documentation, I demonstrate how gender-nonconforming bodies and identities point to internal contradictions in the government's control of identity, even as state-assigned documents aim to produce legible and fixed gender identities, and even when security policies seem utterly unconcerned with transgender people. This chapter also considers several transgender advocacy organizations' responses to the new forms of document regulation; I show how the strategies proposed by some of these groups bolster U.S. nationalism and fail to attend to the broader policing and classification of bodies deemed deviant or dangerous, particularly in terms of race and citizenship status.

Government efforts to screen, identify, and track people have perhaps been most noticeable and contested in that space at which travel, borders, and bodies regularly converge: the airport. In the context of wide public apprehension about the potential for recently installed X-ray screening systems to impinge on travelers' bodily privacy, chapter 2 examines the particular concern that certain bodily technologies, such as the prosthetics used by some transgender people and people with disabilities (among others), may be misinterpreted as weapons rather than as medically necessary technologies. Drawing on disability studies, I sketch a cultural history of the X-ray itself to understand its emergence in militarized contexts as a technology that simultaneously heals and harms. And I consider how those areas of the body understood as especially private—the genitals in particular—are historically suffused with public anxiety in ways that overtly link gender, race, and national security. In this way, I intervene into the frameworks used by some transgender and disability advocacy groups, which call for stronger privacy measures and more accurate screenings by which to distinguish safe bodies from dangerous ones. Analyzing the airport security screening as a particularly fraught microcosm of these interconnecting debates, I argue for a more complex understanding of privacy, health, and violence.

In chapter 3, I take up that space of bodily privacy that is perhaps the most commonly discussed site of surveillance for gender transgression: the public bathroom. Rather than focusing on accessibility concerns, I address the regulation of bathrooms and the bodies that move through them as a method for producing citizenship and determining national belonging. This chapter considers legislation regulating gendered bathrooms in the context of anti-immigrant policies and discourse. I suggest that public bathroom scrutiny (which increasingly names transgender people and their bodies as threats) is one component of the U.S. government's investment in the physical body as proof of good citizenship and spatial belonging, and I therefore argue that the surveillance practices represented by the bathroom bills are part of a renewed emphasis on biometric identification following 9/11. At the same time, I demonstrate the ongoing role that the space of the bathroom plays in creating U.S. national identity through structures of race and gender, in turn positioning its regulation as fundamental to the national project and the maintenance of good citizenship.

The final chapter turns to an instance in which the explicitly transgender figure appears utterly central to surveillance. Here I consider the case of Chelsea Manning, accused of undermining national security by sending classified U.S. military and government materials to the whistle-blower website WikiLeaks in 2010. Manning's legal defense rested in part on her apparent struggle with gender identity, suggesting that the emotional burden of hiding a transgender identity influenced her decision to leak sensitive documents. Examining the trial transcripts—which reflect the concealment not only of military actions but also of the conditions of Manning's pretrial incarceration and even the trial itself—I argue that court and media scrutiny of Manning's gender identity deflects attention from U.S. military actions while simultaneously rationalizing intensified surveillance over Manning as an exceptional, deceptive individual. This chapter shows how overt attention to transgender identity can work to obscure and thus enable broader surveillance practices.

Most of the research and writing of *Going Stealth* took place during the George W. Bush and Barack Obama administrations, but I completed the final revisions after Donald Trump's election in November 2016. In the book's brief conclusion, I carry forward the central contentions that current surveillance practices are not unprecedented and that these practices do not simply identify a ready-made set of transgender-identified people. These arguments remain in the Trump era, even as our political context undergoes significant changes. In looking ahead, I examine the Trump administration's rescinding of federal guidelines that govern treatment of transgender students in public schools and the announcement that the 2020 U.S. census will not collect data specific to LGBT identities. The book closes by returning to the seductive appeal of visibility and by considering the political possibilities that may yet arise in the enduring relationship between surveillance and gender nonconformity.

I have at times wryly remarked that this is a transgender studies book that is not terribly interested in transgender people; instead, it considers surveillance practices through a transgender critique to explore that category's edges and its complicated interactions with racialization, citizenship, disability, and militarism. But I also write with a deep investment in transgender politics and with an interest in the particular material and ideological relationships that transgender people and social movements may develop with government policies and practices. Too often, the state's regulatory gaze can appear either as an impervious and inescapable force or as the key to a liberating form of recognition. By examining the normative assumptions used to analyze and interpret—as well as to produce—gendered bodies and identities, *Going Stealth* illustrates ruptures in surveillance frameworks and complicates aspirations of legibility and visibility. In this way the book aims not to clearly define the category of transgender or to perfectly trace the workings of surveillance practices, but rather to refocus our energies on the fraught negotiations between them. It is in these struggles and fractures that new political possibilities can emerge.

CHAPTER ONE

DECEPTIVE DOCUMENTS

ON SEPTEMBER 4, 2003, shortly before the two-year anniversary of the attacks on the World Trade Center and Pentagon, the U.S. Department of Homeland Security (DHS) released an official advisory to security personnel. Citing ongoing concerns about potential attacks by Al-Qaeda operatives, the advisory's final paragraph emphasizes that terrorism is everywhere in disguise: "Terrorists will employ novel methods to artfully conceal suicide devices. Male bombers may dress as females in order to discourage scrutiny."[1] Two years later, Congress signed into law the Real ID Act, which proposes a major restructuring of identification documents and travel within and across U.S. borders. Central components of this process include a new national database linked through federally standardized driver's licenses and stricter standards of proof for asylum applications. In response to both the advisory and the Real ID Act, many transgender advocacy organizations in the United States quickly pointed to the ways that such policies would target transgender people as suspicious and subject them to new levels of scrutiny.

Criticizing what they read as instances of transphobia or anti-transgender discrimination, some prominent organizations offered both transgender individuals and government agencies strategies for reducing that discrimination. While attending to the very real harm that government policies for identification documents cause for many transgender-identified people, these organizations' approaches tend to leave intact the broader regulation of gender, particularly as it is mediated and enforced by state agencies. Moreover, they tend to address concerns about anti-transgender discrimination in ways that are disconnected from the central questions of citizenship and race that have long structured government surveillance through identification documents. This chapter puts current debates over transgender-specific identification documents in the broader context of national anxieties about race, gender, sexuality, and citizenship that form the impetus for state-regulated identity documents. I show how gender-nonconforming bodies and identities reveal inconsistencies in the U.S. government's control of identity, even as certain state-assigned documents produce transgender identity as a recognizable category. This process of recognition and legitimation marks other forms of gender transgression as deviant against the legal classification of transgender. In considering different transgender advocacy organizations' responses to increased state regulation of identification documents, then, I demonstrate how many of these strategies reconsolidate U.S. nationalism and facilitate the increased policing of deviant bodies and identities.

Producing Contradictions

Although documents such as passports and birth certificates are commonly understood simply to report observable identifying characteristics such as race or gender, they actually construct these characteristics through the process of codification. For instance, we might consider a very early example in which government agencies specifically formalized identity documents as tracking measures: the standardization of manumission papers in the eighteenth-century United States occurred as a response to enslaved people's efforts to circumvent patrols by forging written passes and emancipation documents. The new combination of printed forms and physical descriptions marked a distinct shift in power over identity construction, "from the realm of oral culture, individual assertion, and community practice to the apparatus of the state and the capital-intensive technologies of literacy and printing."[2] Recalling Foucault's model of power as productive, this process shows how state power might use formal identity documents to produce free or unfree subjects: documents generate a certain truth about individuals, and so they do not merely attest to one's identity but also create it.

The production of national identity through records such as driver's licenses and passports becomes particularly clear when we consider the ways that dominant groups use those documents to regulate race, gender, and sexuality. For instance, the documentation of enslaved people's mobility responded not only to white desires to monitor those people that the law designated as commodities, but also to white anxieties about racial purity.[3] Similarly, passport applications have historically emphasized questions of paternity, including requests for data about children classified as both legitimate and illegitimate. The collection of this information indicates the extent to which the surveillance of identification documents links race, gender, and sexuality, as marital and parental data help determine citizenship status, a process that Mark Salter also links to colonialist fears of miscegenation: "National belonging is policed by acknowledgement of the father, a clear echo of imperial and postimperial worries about racial integrity."[4] The desire to track paternity in relation to nationality is persistent: as recently as 1961, U.S. passports still assumed a heteronormative male-assigned applicant, with standardized lines for data about his wife and minors, which were simply marked out with an X for women applicants or those without children.[5]

Identification documents need not always be so overt in the ways that they create classificatory schemas through which to sort populations. For instance, in her analysis of the formation of a passport system in early twentieth-century Canada, Radhika Mongia shows how state actors' desire to selectively discriminate among immigrants led to extensive debates about how the passport system could "effect racial exclusion without naming race."[6] To accomplish this feat, the Canadian government framed anti-immigrant legislation in terms of the protection of women, a strategy grounded in fears of miscegenation and racial impurity that in turn required white women to be safeguarded. Race, gender, and sexuality thus converge as rationale for a passport system that helped the government generate and collect information about certain immigrant groups that were then sorted into categories; at the same time, this system also shored up the category of white citizen-subjects. In this way, "the passport not only is a technology *reflecting* certain understandings of race, nation/nationality, and state, but was central to *organizing* and *securing* the modern definitions of those categories."[7]

Because identification documents help produce the very categories they appear merely to record, they are far more malleable and problematic mechanisms than government framings of them typically suggest. The Chinese Exclusion Act of 1882, one of the earliest uses of formal documents to regulate the U.S. population, illustrates this point. We can trace today's U.S. passport system back to this act, in part because it "constituted the first serious attempt in American history specifically to exclude members of a particular group whose relevant characteristics were knowable only on the basis of documents."[8] The legislation required a new system of identification and sorting, to determine which Chinese immigrants were in the country legally (having entered prior to this legislation) and which were not. Notably, the act depended on paternity and marital status as key factors for determination of citizenship, with women and children receiving the classification assigned to their husbands or fathers.

But the provisions for identification proved difficult to maintain. The strategic use of "paper sons," by which Chinese immigrants reported false family ties to obtain citizenship papers, demonstrates one of the many ways in which documents could be manipulated. The inclusion of photos on identity documents served as a preventative measure against illegal selling and trading of IDs, yet in order to gain entry into the United States, Chinese immigrants often altered their identification photographs. As a result, what government officials initially considered clear evidence of identity came to expose the subjective nature of visual identification, prompting officials to more strictly regulate the types of allowable photos and the conditions under which they could be taken.

Current debates about the role of identity documents in immigration regulations and antiterrorism measures incorporate the notion that false documents reflect a fundamentally deceptive personality and that this personality trait is shared across certain marginalized groups, ideas that can be traced back to some of the earliest uses of identification documents in the United States. Government officials came to believe that Chinese immigrants and their photographs shared "a particularly treacherous artifice: on the surface both appeared honest, but this apparent honesty concealed a deeper duplicity."[9] While U.S. state agencies formally considered identification documents an effective method for restricting both immigrants and the criminal behavior they associated with immigrant populations, these documents were shown again and again to be fallible and subjective. The alteration of photographic identification demonstrates the failure of these documents to provide airtight evidence of identity, a failure that, for officials, reflected the inherent dishonesty of those holding the documents. In this way, immigrant registration papers offer an early example of the ways that state regulation of documents is inconsistent and porous, even as state agencies continually revise attempts to contain identity (and populations) through such regulation.

More recent struggles over voter identification processes in the United States exemplify the many complexities and contradictions still embedded in government-issued identification documents. In June 2013, the U.S. Supreme Court struck down Section 4 of the Voting Rights Act, which had required states and counties with a history of discriminatory practices to be approved at the federal level before making changes to their voting laws. Progressive media outlets and racial justice organizations, among others, argued that this legal change creates (or, perhaps more accurately, re-creates) severe vulnerability for many people in terms of both the denial of their right to vote and the broader effects of gerrymandering.[10] Within two days of the Court's decision, six of the nine states directly affected by the ruling had already put forward new voter ID legislation, rationalized as a method for reducing voter fraud.[11]

Restrictions based on identification documents most severely affect marginalized populations, for whom obtaining state-recognized identification can be a significant burden, if it is possible to begin with. Many people who rely on public services—often including poor people, veterans, people with disabilities, people of color, and seniors—do not have approved identification such as a driver's license, passport, or college ID, and encounter substantial difficulties when they attempt to obtain such documents. Several witnesses in the 2012 case against Pennsylvania's voter ID policy explained that even their requests for their birth certificates were futile; one witness said of her failed birth certificate request, "They say I don't exist."[12] Such cases highlight the material effects of state agencies' reliance on documents to prove identity, showing how that reliance creates hardships for particular groups. At the same time, these debates also throw into relief government agencies' own inability to comply with their policies for documentation. For instance, the identification requirement in Pennsylvania obliges that state to provide free photographic voter ID for any resident without another approved form of identification. Yet the state "can only loosen its rules but so much without breaching federal and state security concerns," creating a contradiction in which Pennsylvania must provide the voter ID card to anyone who needs it, yet cannot do so unless applicants provide other official documents attesting to their identity, such as birth or marriage certificates.[13]

Moreover, if identification documents help produce identities rather than merely recording them, then the voter ID cases helpfully illustrate how documents produce certain groups as recognized, legitimate citizens, while other groups appear simply not to exist. In this sense, missing or incorrect identity documents suggest not only fraudulence but also a certain impossible sub-

Figure 1.1 Portion of cover art from True the Vote's 2012 observer training manual for Virginia.

ject. Consider, for example, materials published in 2012 by True the Vote, an organization emerging out of a local Texas Tea Party group in 2008, which describes itself as training "average, everyday citizens to research the voter rolls in their home districts and to report inaccuracies to their County and State, to identify instances of vote fraud," and to act as observers at polls.[14] As part of the organization's nationwide outreach during the 2012 elections, True the Vote's Virginia observer training manual featured a cartoon drawing of a broad-shouldered figure with facial and body hair wearing a dress and carrying a purse, pictured next to a voter ID card for a figure with a feminine name (Mary Jane Jones) and no facial hair (figure 1.1). The drawing urges trainees to "Prevent voter fraud!," which is signaled here by gendered disguise.

The National Center for Transgender Equality (NCTE), self-defined as "the nation's leading social justice advocacy organization" that is focused on "ending discrimination and violence against transgender people," constructed a formal response to this page of the manual.[15] The organization asserts that "until this point, the concerted effort by right-wing, tea party groups to restrict voting rights with new Voter ID laws only inadvertently affected transgender voters. Only days away from Election Day, the discovery of True the Vote's training manual marks a shift by right-wing groups to explicitly target transgender people and deny them a right to vote."[16] Given the heightened scrutiny of identification documents of all sorts, it is not unlikely that some transgender people experienced difficulty at the polls; as

I show in the next section of this chapter, state-regulated identity documents pose particular problems for many transgender and gender-nonconforming people. But the manual works on a more pernicious level than the direct targeting of transgender people that NCTE's interpretation suggests.

The image intended to read as a man in a dress symbolizes deceit in this case, but it does not necessarily or deliberately create suspicion about transgender people per se; nor does the manual necessarily use this figure because it is explicitly transgender. Rather, the figure stands here as the subject that cannot be correct, particularly when contrasted with the voter ID card at its side, which signifies the legitimate citizen-subject. Pitted against the government-approved document that connotes fundamental truthfulness, the gender-nonconforming figure functions as a recognizable and basic symbol of something gone wrong, in need of further inspection. This is not to say that the image is entirely disconnected from transgender populations: it may well exacerbate already existing suspicion directed at many transgender people, at the polls and elsewhere. Yet many transgender-identified voters may feel the image's effects not because it is explicitly anti-transgender, but because of the ways that voter ID efforts overall create greater vulnerability for marginalized groups, particularly along lines of race and class. In fact, given that voter identification restrictions historically and currently centralize race—while also denying that race is a factor—then particularly if the image's gender-nonconforming figure reads as white, we can understand it less as a way to target transgender people as a specific group than as a strategy for conveying and playing on racial anxieties about voter fraud without explicitly referencing race.

In this context, NCTE's claim that previous voter ID programs only inadvertently affected transgender people elides the ways that race and class marginalization work with transgender status to increase risk of scrutiny (and denial of voting access) and to complicate how state agencies produce and interpret gender through identification documents. Efforts to raise suspicion about false identities and documents need not explicitly mark out transgender people in order to significantly affect them; likewise, as the True the Vote manual illustrates, efforts that can appear to specifically target transgender-identified people may do so unintentionally, and may have their broadest effects on those populations already most vulnerable, whether transgender or not.[17] The ways that medicine and law produce transgender as a recognized category offer some insight into this category's relationship with race, class, and citizenship, as well as the administrative conflicts it reveals.

Normalizing Gender

The relationship between transgender identity and government-ordered identification documents provides a particularly clear example through which to understand how medicine and law converge to produce and regulate identity categories, as well as how such categories fluctuate, pushing back against the regulatory mechanisms that create them. The production of "the transsexual" through Western medical discourse can be clearly traced through sexologist Harry Benjamin's *Standards of Care for Gender Identity Disorders*, first published in 1979. The *Standards*, continually revised and circulated by the World Professional Association for Transgender Health (WPATH), define the criteria by which health care professionals should assess their clients in order to determine whether they are "true transsexuals" (in early versions of the document) or experience gender dysphoria (in later versions).[18] Clients fitting the profile can then be formally diagnosed and allowed to proceed with medical transition in the form of hormones, surgeries, and other medical procedures. Central to this standardized definition of transgender identity, however, is the expectation that transgender people will, through the process of transition, eliminate all references to their birth gender and essentially disappear into a normatively gendered world, as if they had never been transgender to begin with.

Thus two major forms of surveillance operate relative to transgender people in medical and psychiatric institutions. The first is the monitoring of individuals in terms of their ability to conform to a particular medicalized understanding of transgender identity and observable behavior.[19] But more salient to my discussion here is the second component, which is the construction of medical transition primarily as a method to rid oneself of any vestiges of nonnormative gender: to withstand and evade any scrutiny (visual, auditory, social, or legal) that would reveal one's transgender status. Medical science relies on a standardized, normative gender presentation as its benchmark, monitoring transgender individuals' ability to pass seamlessly as non-transgender. Medical surveillance thus focuses first on individuals' legibility as transgender, and then, following medical interventions, on their ability to conceal that transgender status.

But medical science itself determines normative gender through a particular form of raced, classed, and sexualized body. Western medicine has consistently linked race, gender, and sexuality such that the norm of white heterosexuality becomes a marker against which deviance is constructed. Scientific studies from the early nineteenth century on helped designate particular bodies—typically those that were racially or sexually mixed—as degenerative threats to Western norms and national security.[20] To be classified as normatively gendered is also to adhere to norms of racial and economic privilege. Under this logic, marginalized gender identities can approximate the norm in part through clinging to ideals of whiteness and class status. Likewise, concealing gender deviance is about much more than simply erasing transgender status. It also necessitates altering one's gender presentation to conform to white, middle-class, able-bodied, heterosexual understandings of normative gendering.

The notion of concealment via medical intervention structures legal gender as well, a link made clear by the fact that most state and administrative agencies deny changes of gender on identity documents without proof of irreversible medical procedures. United States law depends on medical evidence to verify gender identity in almost every case involving transgender-identified people. Importantly, Dean Spade argues that medicine—and thus also law—continues to rely on an ideal of success in diagnosis and treatment plans for transgender people, where success is typically defined as "the ability to be perceived by non-trans people as a non-trans person."[21] Spade's work points to the ways that medicine and law work together to correct individuals whose bodies or gender presentations fall outside of the expected norm, promoting the concealment of transgender status in order to reestablish that norm.

The discourse of concealment haunts transgender populations across a number of cultural sites. The impossibility of fully erasing one's sexed and gendered history is evident in the fact that many U.S. states either refuse to change gender markers on birth certificates or allow only a partial change in which the original gender marker is merely crossed out and replaced.[22] Legal gender in these cases cannot be changed, but only cloaked. At times, even proof of irreversible surgery cannot overcome the characteristic of fraud attached to transgender persons: in 2012, a district judge in Oklahoma refused to grant legal name changes for two transgender-identified women, writing in an order that "a so-called sex-change surgery can make one appear to be the opposite sex, but in fact they are nothing more than an imitation of the opposite sex."[23] Citing DNA as evidence that one's sex and gender can never really change, the judge concluded that "to grant a name change in this case would be to assist that which is fraudulent," and he worried that it could lead to dishonest marriages, undermine state laws against same-sex marriage, or hinder DNA-based criminal investigations. The decision was reversed in an appeals case later that year, but the language in the initial denial illustrates the extent to which transgender bodies and identities may be considered inherently duplicitous.

Similarly, cultural representations of transgender people often depend on the popular notion that with enough scrutiny, one's true gender can be revealed at the level of the body. Consider the abundance of talk shows, reality television programs, and episodes of medical and crime dramas that run on the presumably simple premise of uncovering—often in the most literal sense—a transgender person's "real" gender or sex. These frameworks tend to link gender concealment with harmful or dangerous deception in the cultural imagination, for example in numerous cases revealing the transgender person's birth-assigned sex not only to the audience but also to a shocked and horrified sexual partner. The constant repetition of this narrative structure locates violence not in the institutional practices of media, medicine, or law, or in the rigidly gender-normative behaviors and relationships they uphold, but instead in individual transgender people's fraudulent bodies and identities.

Echoing this perspective, legal cases dealing with violence against transgender people often revolve around the victim's responsibility to disclose their transgender status or birth-assigned sex. Such cases imply or outright claim that the individual's dishonest concealment of their sex was the root cause of violent actions taken against them. This approach is clearly demonstrated, for instance, in the narratives constructed around transgender teenager Gwen Araujo's murder (and sexual relationships) in 2002. Legal arguments, news media, and made-for-television movies converged to situate Araujo's murder in the context of a "trans panic" defense, centralizing the shock of discovery and frequently faulting Araujo for not revealing her assigned sex.[24] In this and many other instances, the interplay of medical, legal, and cultural representations of transgender populations helps associate transgender identity with secrecy, precisely because it is understood that the secret can and should eventually be discovered.

With such a pervasive cultural emphasis on concealment, it may come as no surprise that the slang used by many transgender-identified people to describe nondisclosure of transgender status is "going stealth." Those living stealth are unknown as transgender to almost everyone in their lives. The term itself invokes a sense of going undercover, of willful secrecy and concealment, perhaps even of conscious deception. The resonance of militarism in this term suggests the extent to which going stealth entails a certain complicity with state agencies, which demand compliance with specific legal and medical procedures and ostensibly offer in return official documentation that helps make stealth status possible.

Yet by granting medical and legal changes of gender, government offices also maintain detailed records of these changes, producing a paper trail of past identity markers that threatens to expose one's stealth status. At the same time, these documentation practices can inadvertently create new spaces through which transgender people might slip: hundreds of state agencies and jurisdictions across the United States produce a variety of policies governing gender changes, put into practice by many different individual state officials. A driver's license clerk in one office may allow a gender change merely based on the applicant's claim that the current gender marker is a clerical error, while a clerk in a neighboring office may insist on filing documented evidence (such as a birth certificate or a physician's letter) to change the marker. Other factors such as race, citizenship, criminal record, and location can further facilitate—or limit—the possibilities of skirting these types of inconsistent administrative practices.

The very linguistic construction of "going stealth" depends on the constancy of *going*: of continuing to conceal one's transgender status, even if that concealment can never be airtight. Although the legal procedures used to document transgender people's gender status frequently conflict with one another, they collectively work toward stricter regulation of legal gender. Some state agencies and programs refuse to change the gender marker on birth certificates, while others do so only with documentation of specified surgeries. Other institutions first require amended birth certificates in order to change the gender marker on other documents, and in some cases state and city regulations contradict one another in their medical requirements for documentation changes.[25] These inconsistent requirements and contradictory methods for determining gender and administering identification documents can create a host of difficulties for transgender people, given the ways that such documents are central to housing, employment, travel, access to public benefits, and other daily life activities.[26]

Such difficulties reflect not transgender people's inability to fit into categories, but rather the fundamentally normalizing function of state-regulated identity documentation. The creation of an official third gender category exemplifies this point. Although sometimes imagined as a helpful answer to the administrative problems I have outlined so far, such a category shows how state classification systems produce and reinforce normative gender, frequently in ways that support surveillance practices. For instance, Nepal's Supreme Court established a third gender category in 2007 for government paperwork including citizenship certificates, voter registration, and the national census. The U.S. news media widely reported the new category as intended for those who "do not wish to be identified as male or female" and suggested that it would simplify bureaucratic processes and basic life tasks for such individuals.[27] Similarly, U.S. news media reported Pakistan's 2009 creation of a third gender category on national identity cards as one intended for hijras, transvestites, eunuchs, and hermaphrodites, and typically included interviews lauding the category as a step toward rights, respect, and recognition as human beings.[28] This kind of formalized category might well ameliorate some of the problems created by state institutions built on a binary gender system. At the same time, the introduction of a catchall third gender category meant for those who do not fit into the first two groups reconsolidates the normative status of male and female as standard options, from which other identities deviate.[29] This is not to speculate that the third gender category is always understood this way in practice throughout Nepal or Pakistan; rather, U.S. news reports on the new policies demonstrate how such categories circulate transnationally in ways that can strengthen and naturalize a Western gender binary. Notably, U.S. news media almost never link the third gender category in these two countries to the gendered administrative conflicts pervasive in the United States, an omission that might help locate gender deviance elsewhere, beyond the modern Western state.

At the same time, the establishment and recognition of third gender categories can come to seem indicative of a modern, liberal sense of tolerance grounded in rights discourse. This point was clarified for me as I spoke about identification documents at a variety of U.S. universities and academic conferences: not infrequently, audience members—including faculty, undergraduates, and community members—expressed surprise that Pakistan in particular had implemented a state-recognized third gender category. These reactions suggest, in part, a general conception of Pakistan as an oppressive state with outdated gender norms, a notion apparently at odds with the country's formal recognition of gender-nonconforming people. But they also suggest a contrasting (and failed) expectation that the United States should be a forerunner in that recognition. Moreover, these responses point to how tightly identification documents and state-regulated categories are ideologically linked to the notions of both rights and national progress.

It is perhaps no surprise, then, that a 2011 California law easing the requirements for legal change of gender is titled the Vital Records Modernization Act. A fact sheet jointly issued by LGBT advocacy organizations Equality California and the Transgender Law Center explains that the former process for changing legal gender "was first established decades ago," creating an "outdated state policy" that conflicts with "current medical understanding of what is required for obtaining identity documents that reflect the appropriate gender."[30] In this way, the new law comes to represent more advanced thinking about gender, which aligns with modern medical standards to expand rights for a marginalized group. The California state government's treatment and formal recognition of transgender people likewise become a measure of its progress toward liberal ideals of tolerance and rights. Like the third gender categories, this law certainly has material benefits for many transgender-identified people harmed by the dichotomous gender system structuring most institutions and government programs. But these benefits arrive through classification schemas and record-keeping practices that both discipline individuals and regulate the health and security of the population overall. The very fact that the California law concerns vital records (a government registry holding records of life events such as birth, death, and marriage certificates) and is part of the California Health and Safety Codes reflects the ways that identity documents are deeply embedded in surveillance practices.[31]

This dual-function system in which care and discipline operate at once with surveillance and broad classification—the intertwined workings of disciplinary and populational power that Foucault terms biopower—means that the restructuring of formalized gender categories does not merely change individuals' access to state institutions or benefits but also merges with state surveillance practices that take up and reinforce those categories. For instance, in 2013 Australia created a new gender marker of X as a third option alongside F and M on government records. While this category undoubtedly alleviates some of the problems created by the former system, it also produces a new gender category through which state agencies can apply normative standards, collect data, and track groups of people. It makes sense, then, that the Australian attorney general's press release on the policy change ends by explaining that "increased consistency in the way the Australian Government collects and records gender under the Guidelines will strengthen Australia's identity security system."[32]

Identification documents thus come to play a major role in security efforts, particularly in the kind of "anticipatory surveillance" so central to the war on terror and related programs implemented by the U.S. DHS.[33] Government officials explain increased tracking and closer scrutiny of documents as preventative measures that distinguish between safe and dangerous people. The monitoring of U.S. Social Security records offers an especially clear example of the ways that state agencies' own contradictions are magnified through gender and race to position certain groups as particular objects of state surveillance, even if they are not explicitly named as such. That the Social Security number has been considered and rejected as a form of national ID card several times since the early 1970s is telling of the ways that it has long functioned as a surveillance mechanism, particularly in relation to race and class.[34] Its use in this capacity has been reinvigorated by post-9/11 efforts to prevent both terrorism and undocumented immigration.

The monitoring of Social Security numbers, benefits, and the data used to issue both of these reveals state agencies' own conflicting policies of classification as well as their drive to ferret out these inconsistencies. Since 1994, the Social Security Administration (SSA) has sent "no-match" letters to employers in cases where an employee's hiring paperwork contradicts employee information on file with the SSA. Ostensibly in place to alert otherwise law-abiding employers to the possibility that they are unwittingly hiring undocumented immigrants, the no-match policy intensified dramatically after 9/11, with 2002 seeing more than eight times the typical number of letters mailed than in 2001.[35] The no-match letters and related data can now also be accessed by the DHS, which sends employers guidelines about how to correct the problem and avoid legal sanctions.

These policies help construct unregulated immigration and terrorism as interlocking concerns and illustrate how surveillance of gender contributes to the violence of these policing systems. The no-match policy aims to locate undocumented immigrants (and potential terrorists) employed under false identities, yet it casts a much broader net. Because conflicting legal and medical regulations can prevent transgender people from obtaining consistent gender markers across all of their identity documents, transgender individuals are disproportionately affected by the policy, whether they are undocumented immigrants or not. The NCTE website notes that the organization "receives calls regularly from transgender people across the country who have been 'outed' to their employers by the Social Security Administration's unfair gender 'no-match' employment letter policy."[36] The no-match policy exemplifies several interrelated characteristics and effects of state-regulated identification documents: how scrutiny of these documents targets specific groups as unruly, thus normalizing other groups, yet can also affect those beyond the explicitly named targets of surveillance; how state agencies' own conflicting classification systems produce the very troublesome identities they purport to merely locate; and how these practices can appear newly instituted in the wake of 9/11, yet build on much longer histories of classification and surveillance.

The Threat of Ambiguity

It is in this cultural landscape of long-standing but intensified medical, legal, and social surveillance that the DHS advisory appears. By warning security personnel of the gendered pretenses that terrorists might use, the advisory neatly fuses the threat of terrorism in disguise with perceived gender transgression, marking particular bodies as deceptive and treacherous. Three days after the advisory's release, a *New York Times* article reported the Pentagon's recent screening of the classic 1965 film *The Battle of Algiers*. The film examines the early years of the Algerian War of Independence, as the guerrilla insurgency resisted colonial French rule. The *Times* piece suggests that the Pentagon screening was held in part to gain tactical insight into the U.S. war against Iraq.[37] *Algiers* is a film filled with depictions of guerrilla warfare tactics, including those that rely on the links between gender and national identities. Algerian women pass as French to deliver bombs into French civilian settings, while Algerian men attempt to pass as women in hijabs, their disguises undone when French soldiers spy their combat boots. Though neither the DHS advisory nor the Pentagon's study of the film explicitly reference transgender populations, both nevertheless invoke the ties between gender presentation, national identity, and bodies marked as dangerously deceptive.

That the advisory does not specifically name transgender populations in its text does not make it any less relevant to those populations. The focus on nonnormative gender presentation certainly raises questions about how this framing of security affects transgender-identified people. But it also raises questions about how state institutions might view gender nonconformity as an act not limited to—perhaps not even primarily associated with— transgender identities. In the context of security rhetoric related to the war on terror, transgender individuals may not be the primary target of such advisories, particularly if those individuals are understood to be conforming to normative presentations of race and citizenship. Transgender people who conform to a dominant standard of dress and behavior, for instance, may be legible to the state not as transgender at all, but instead as properly gendered and safe.

But not all gendered bodies and identities are so easily normalized. Dominant notions of what constitutes proper feminine or masculine behavior are grounded in ideals of whiteness, class privilege, and compulsory heterosexuality, and individuals might be interpreted as nonconforming depending on particular racial, cultural, economic, or religious expressions of gender, without ever being classified as transgender. For example, racialized physical difference has been understood in both medical and cultural contexts as a signifier of gender and sexual difference. Comparative racial anatomy in the nineteenth-century United States drew on public displays and scientific studies to classify African and Black women's womanhood as abnormal precisely through racialized readings of their genitals.[38] Similarly, race regularly marks certain bodies as threatening and others as threatened: white panic about the supposed sexual danger white women experienced at the hands of Black men served to justify public lynchings of Black men throughout the United States, particularly in the late nineteenth and early twentieth centuries. The genital mutilation and castration frequently involved in these practices emphasizes the links between racialization, anxieties about masculinity, and violent sexual deviance. Joy James draws on this history to analyze contemporary racialized state violence, arguing that state practices of surveillance and discipline read sexual and social deviance through racialization processes. She explains, "some bodies appear more docile than others because of their conformity in appearance to idealized models of class, color, and sex; their bodies are allowed greater leeway to be self-policed or policed without physical force."[39] These examples demonstrate that gender normativity is not limited strictly to gender itself but works through other identity categories as well. Thus individuals need not be transgender-identified to be classified as gender-nonconforming. Bodies and identities may be perceived as abnormal or deviant because of gender presentations read through systems of racism, classism, heterosexism, and, particularly in the case of the DHS advisory's focus on Al-Qaeda, Islamophobia.

Amplified attention to immigration and national security in the early 2000s, justified by the war on terror's racist rhetoric, spurred the passage of the Real ID Act in 2005. The 9/11 Commission, created to detail the events of September 11, 2001, and assess the United States' response to terrorist attacks, endorsed the Real ID Act as a way to strengthen national security through identity verification and border fortification. The commission determined that "for terrorists, travel documents are as important as weapons," an assertion that helps explain how the major changes proposed in the Real ID Act were approved so swiftly.[40] The legislation establishes minimum standards for U.S. driver's licenses and nondriver ID cards, with the intention that eventually any ID card that is not compliant with these standards will be invalid at the federal level, including activities such as air travel, access to government buildings, and access to federal funding such as Social Security.[41] Stricter standards are to be used to verify identities, citizenship, names, and birth dates. Draft regulations also specify that Real ID cards and all supporting documents used to create them (e.g., birth certificates, Social Security cards, court-ordered name changes, etc.) will be linked through a federal database and stored there for seven to ten years. Although a number of states and organizations ranging from the American Civil Liberties Union to the conservative Christian American Center for Law and Justice have publicly opposed the legislation, and despite several proposed alternatives at the congressional level, the Real ID Act remains in place.

John Torpey distinguishes between passports and identification cards by noting that while passports regulate movement and support state control of borders, ID cards typically affirm an individual's identity for state records and distribution of state benefits.[42] The Real ID Act combines these two functions in many ways: it imposes stricter standards for asylum application and provides funds for border security projects, in addition to collecting and sharing data about U.S. citizens overall. In a 2007 congressional hearing on the Real ID Act's ability to ensure safety, Senator Arlen Specter (then R-PA) echoed the logic of the Social Security no-match letters, stating that "one of the issues that we are struggling with [in immigration legislation] is, beyond securing borders, to have employers know who is legal and who is not legal. And we are wrestling with the costs of foolproof identification."[43]

But the government's own definition of "foolproof identification" works hand in hand with the constant potential for documents to be forged, inaccurate, or otherwise inconsistent, as is evident from former special agent Michael Johnson's statement in a 2006 congressional hearing on the U.S. passport system and antiterrorism legislation. Johnson, who served in the U.S. State Department's Bureau of Diplomatic Security for eighteen years, explained that most passport fraud is committed not by those seeking to immigrate but by individuals already within U.S. borders. His testimony contends that the passport "provides ironclad proof of an individual's identity. The value of this document to an individual trying to conceal his identity or blend into American society is obvious, given the post September 11 scrutiny placed on non-US citizens inside the United States."[44] In this logic, ironically, the purported accuracy and stability of documents like passports are precisely what make them desirable objects to falsify. Similarly, the very value of an "ironclad" ID here lies in its own potential to be cracked open. The notion that identification documents can be simultaneously ironclad and undermined is particularly clear in government officials' anxiety over the possibility of multiple identities, in which one person might hold two or more different identification cards, as when the 9/11 Commission warns that terrorists can easily evade current travel restrictions "by tossing away an old passport and slightly altering the name in the new one."[45]

But this anxiety, and lawmakers' leverage of it to pass more restrictive parameters for identity documents, is not new. Nor can it be understood as distinct from state regulation of gender. For instance, increased concern over fraudulent identities proved a major argument in favor of continuing the compulsory national identity documents instituted in Britain during World War II. Efforts to maintain individual identity converged with efforts to regulate sexual practices and gendered relationship structures, as postwar attempts to shore up the nuclear family took the form of public outcry against bigamy, viewed by the British government and much of the public as a foreign practice that enabled both sexual deviance and multiple identities. In this sense, "bigamy starkly highlighted the extent to which social institutions depended on individuals living under one, and only one, identity," fueling desires not just to continue the cards, but to expand the amount of information they contained.[46] For many, compulsory ID cards recalled totalitarian governing practices associated with Nazi Germany and thus conflicted with British ideals of privacy and individualism. Yet the possibility that such cards could eradicate bigamist practices—securing individual accountability alongside normative sexuality and family structure— provided its own form of national differentiation. Moreover, because the ID cards were promoted as preventative measures against stolen identities, state regulation of identity was encouraged as a personal right and civil liberty: a method of increasing lawful citizens' security. The British government thus implied that those who had nothing to hide had nothing to fear from the implementation of national identification cards.

The Real ID Act and the discourses surrounding it echo much of this rhetoric, which helps explain how and why Congress passed the legislation with little debate (and unanimous final approval from the Senate), four years after 9/11. In fact, Real ID was tacked onto an emergency spending bill to fund the wars in Afghanistan and Iraq. In the context of U.S. nationalism that seeks to eradicate the foreign, the act most overtly targets the figures of the immigrant and the terrorist, categories that frequently overlap in both public discourse and government policy. To address the threat that these figures pose, the Real ID Act increases state surveillance of identity by requiring and storing a single identity for each individual. But the administrative systems in place mean that maintaining a singular, consistent, and legally documented identity can be quite complicated. For instance, common-law name changes do not depend on a court order that would then be filed with a Real ID card, creating a gap in the paper trail that state discourse frames as airtight. Similarly, this chapter demonstrates how administrative processes make a single gender marker across all records difficult if not impossible for many transgender and gender-nonconforming people. This is especially clear, for example, in the ways that different state agencies define change of sex differently, with some requiring one surgery and some another, while other agencies require nonsurgical medical evidence or other forms of medical approval. Ironically, then, state agencies' own contradictory methods of designating legal gender and sex render Real ID cards ineffectual. Although the Real ID Act creates and enforces singular, static identities for individuals, it also exposes the fluidity and confusion characterizing state policies on identity documents. Thus "the very multiplicity of these documents may ... disrupt the state's ostensibly monolithic front."[47] In this way, state regulation of ambiguous gender actually reveals ambiguities within state practices and agencies.

Moreover, such policies point to the ways that the practices of concealing and revealing transgender identity actually depend on one another, unraveling the notion that these actions are binary opposites. To conceal one's gender status within the parameters of the legal system requires disclosure, since administrative agencies keep on public record the steps taken toward changing one's legal gender marker. Those same records are later invoked when individuals seek to prove their transgender status through medical and legal documents that ostensibly serve to obscure or even disappear such status. These interdependent relationships illustrate that concealment necessarily entails disclosure, and vice versa.

That the Real ID Act, created as part of a war funding bill and approved in a climate of exceptionalized (if not actually exceptional) militarization and nationalism, seeks to maintain individual identities and make them more accessible to state agencies speaks to the ways that multiple, ambiguous, or shifting identities register as menacing and risky on a national scale. Alongside more overt statements like the DHS advisory, the Real ID Act and SSA no-match letters function as significant administrative policies that link gender ambiguity to national security threats. Like other new security measures, the Real ID Act can appear benign and even beneficial for those citizens with nothing to hide. But the notion of concealment remains strongly associated with the category of transgender and with perceptions of gender nonconformity, fueled by cultural associations of transgender deception and by medical and legal processes that aim to normalize transgender bodies while also meticulously documenting gender changes. As transgender activist and advocacy organizations respond to and resist new state security measures, then, they do so in the context of these cultural and legislative constraints.

Nothing to Hide

Dean Spade notes that despite the significant problems that the Real ID Act poses for the most marginalized LGBT people, many high-profile and well-resourced gay organizations initially failed to take it up as a central concern. In assessing this fact, Spade notes that "choices about what to put on the 'gay agenda' are actually choices about who the constituency of the gay rights movement is and about the ultimate visionary goals of this movement."[48] The Real ID Act, DHS advisory, and no-match letters did emerge as major concerns, however, for many advocacy and lobbying organizations with a specific focus on transgender politics and for many grassroots-based queer and transgender organizations. And although all of these groups shared an opposition to the policies' harmful effects on transgender individuals, their different strategic responses reflect the choices that Spade references.

Organizations with a primarily legislative focus on inclusion did not tend to consider these security measures' implications for state regulation of gender presentation more broadly, particularly as the policies might resonate for people perceived as gender deviant who are not transgender-identified or linked in any obvious way to transgender communities or histories. Nor did these organizations address the ways that particular groups of transgender-identified people may be targeted differently by such policing. For example, in a 2006 public statement to DHS regarding the no-match letter policy, NCTE recommends that gender no longer be one of the pieces of data used to verify employees, arguing that employers are not legally required to submit gender classification to SSA, and therefore any exchange of information about employees' gender is "an invasion of private and privileged medical information."[49] In an effort to protect transgender employees, the NCTE statement suggests limiting the amount of information that can be shared between SSA and DHS. But it also implicitly supports no-match letters as a form of regulatory state surveillance, by stating clearly the importance of avoiding fraud through Social Security number confirmation. The statement does not oppose state surveillance measures more broadly, but rather seeks to optimize them, offering recommendations on behalf of transgender employees "in order for the employee verification system to be efficient and equitable."[50]

An argument based on privacy rights may benefit some gender-nonconforming employees, but in assuming equal access to privacy and legal recourse for all transgender people, this strategy fails to address the ways that privacy is compromised or nonexistent for many. Because the medicolegal system governing transgender identity tracks gendered changes to identification documents, transgender people's medical and legal information is never really private or privileged. Likewise, many groups of people—such as those who apply for disability benefits, use certain social services, or are incarcerated—must routinely make their medical information available to state agencies, whether they are transgender-identified or not. In addition to this absence of medical privacy in the everyday, NCTE's argument must also be considered in the specific context of post-9/11 surveillance practices. Diminished rights to privacy are particularly evident in the wake of the 2001 USA PATRIOT Act, legislation that provides much of the ideological and legal foundation for more recent surveillance measures. This legislation builds on earlier policies such as the 1996 Antiterrorism and Effective Death Penalty Act, which in part removed certain restrictions on state surveillance of suspected terrorists and dramatically increased government scrutiny and deportation of immigrants, and the FBI's COINTELPRO activities in the 1960s, which monitored and eradicated domestic organizations and individuals considered subversive national security threats, ranging from Black and American Indian resistance groups to antiwar organizers. The USA PATRIOT Act further limits privacy rights by expanding the federal government's ability to secretly search private homes; collect medical, financial, and educational records without showing probable cause; and monitor internet activity and messages. Passed as part of the anti-immigrant nationalism and overt racial profiling that followed 9/11, the act bolsters particular understandings of the relationships between citizenship, race, privacy, and danger that underpin surveillance measures like the Real ID Act and SSA no-match policy. This context, absent from the NCTE statement, demonstrates the frailty of any claim to privacy, particularly for those transgender and gender-nonconforming people who are immigrants, poor people, and people of color.

Other advocacy organizations more explicitly rely on the network of legal and medical policies governing transgender identity to offer protective strategies, by advising transgender individuals to make themselves visible as transgender to authorities that question or screen them. In response to the DHS advisory, the National Transgender Advocacy Coalition (NTAC) released its own security alert to transgender communities, warning that given the recent advisory, security personnel may be "more likely to commit unwitting abuses."[51] The organization suggests that transgender travelers bring their court-ordered name and gender change paperwork with them, noting that "while terrorists may make fake identifications, they won't carry name change documents signed and notarized by a court."[52] The organization recommends strategic visibility as a safety precaution, urging those who might otherwise be going stealth to openly disclose their transgender status to state officials and to comply with any requested searches or questionings.[53]

Calling the potential violence and violations against travelers "unwitting abuses" suggests that authorities enacting these measures cannot be blamed for carrying out policy intended to protect the general public from the threat of hidden terrorism. Such a framework neatly sidesteps any broader criticism of the routine abuses, especially against immigrants and Muslims, that have been justified in the name of national security. It implicitly supports the policing of individuals or groups perceived as dangerous, so long as they are not transgender-identified. The advice for transgender people to make themselves visible as such is couched in terms of distinguishing the good, safe transgender traveler from the dangerous, deviant terrorist in gendered disguise. Moreover, by avoiding any larger critique of state surveillance or policing, NTAC also positions itself as a good, safe, even patriotic organization.[54]

Torpey argues that "our everyday acceptance of 'the passport nuisance' and of the frequent demands from state officials that we produce 'ID' is a sign of the success with which states have monopolized the capacity to regulate movement and thus to constrain the freedom of ordinary people to come and go, as well as to identify and constrain possible interlopers."[55] But the framing of this as merely capitulation to the state's monopoly on power belies Foucault's model of power as dispersed and fragmentary, never simply exerted in one direction. On one level, state institutions coerce the calculated reveal of transgender status that NTAC encourages. Yet on another level, that reveal functions as an example of the confession, which Foucault explains as a ritual understood as critical for the production of truth. He argues that "the obligation to confess is now relayed through so many different points, is so deeply ingrained in us, that we no longer perceive it as the effect of a power that constrains us."[56] Moreover, he suggests that the confession is made all the more powerful and privileged through the careful concealment of what is to be confessed.[57] Thus while ostensibly forced by state agents and institutions, the confession that NTAC urges affords the confessor a sense of pleasure as well, of presenting oneself as patriotic and willingly compliant.[58] In this way, the relationship between the figure of the compliant transgender traveler and state surveillance programs exemplifies Foucault's concept of "perpetual spirals of power and pleasure," such that the concealment and unveiling of transgender status in response to state pressure form a seductive circle of evasion and discovery.[59]

The recourse to strategic visibility remains grounded in assumptions that invisibility was ever possible. Which individuals and groups can choose visibility, and which are already visible—perhaps even hypervisible—to surveillance mechanisms? For whom is visibility an available strategy for either social advancement or personal safety, and at what cost? Moving well away from the approach taken by NCTE and NTAC, other queer and transgender organizations accounted for these questions as they addressed the Real ID Act and related surveillance measures. The Audre Lorde Project (ALP), a community center based in New York City and focused on support and mobilization in communities of color, held two community meetings about the war on terror and released an open letter in January 2003 that explains why the war on terror is an LGBTST issue and urges fellow organizations to oppose the war. This letter directly addresses the question of visibility by highlighting the increased violence, racial profiling practices, and surveillance measures after 9/11.[60] More than a decade later, the organization continued to explicitly address the Real ID Act as part of anti-immigrant policies that it articulates as central to LGBTST struggles. For the tenth annual NYC Trans Day of Action for Social and Economic Justice in 2014, ALP released a "Points of Unity" statement demanding, among other things, safety in public spaces including public transit, an end to police violence and harassment, and the "full legalization of all immigrants."[61] This last point names the Real ID Act alongside other policing programs and the increased power of DHS, maintaining solidarity with all groups targeted by these policies and specifying transgender and gender-nonconforming people of color as particular targets.[62] These approaches clarify that not all transgender people can occupy the role of the good, safe transgender traveler that NTAC recommends, and that increased visibility simultaneously places one under greater scrutiny and surveillance. Those made visible as abnormal or unruly and in need of constraint or correction may experience increased vulnerability, such that visibility wields more damage than protection. The statements by ALP explain that some bodies and identities would be read under the DHS advisory's warning as gender deviant, dangerous, or deceptive even if they did produce paperwork documenting their transgender status. While this documentation may lessen suspicion of some, it compounds scrutiny of others.

The Transgender Law Center in San Francisco also released a set of recommendations for transgender people, including one statement jointly issued with NCTE in 2005, which discusses new security measures including the DHS advisory and Real ID Act. They note that although these measures were originally conceived in response to "legitimate security concerns" regarding terrorists' use of false documentation, they ultimately create undue burdens for transgender individuals who seek to "legitimately acquire or change identification documents."[63] Like NTAC's concern that nonthreatening transgender travelers could be mistaken for terrorists, the response from NCTE and the Transgender Law Center omits critical engagement with the rhetoric of terrorism used to justify state regulation of gender, race, and citizenship more broadly. Instead, the organizations' statement asks for rights and state recognition on the basis of legitimacy, a classification already infused with the regulatory norms produced and maintained by medical science and government policy. In the case of transgender people specifically, formal legitimacy is based on legal documents that typically require some medical evidence for change of gender marker. In almost all cases, medical professionals depend on a formal diagnosis of gender identity disorder or dysphoria, which itself turns on the language of correction and normalization. Circularly, then, legitimate status requires identity documents, while identity documents simultaneously require legitimacy.

Organizational responses like those produced by NCTE and the Transgender Law Center are unable to address the ways that pervasive surveillance of gender is inseparable from that of racial difference. New shifts in—and renewed attention to—racial profiling practices in the aftermath of 9/11 offer important context through which strategies of visibility must be considered. Within the framework of these organizations' statements, for which bodies is legitimacy attainable, and for which is it already foreclosed? The Sylvia Rivera Law Project provides an analysis of this approach based on its commitment to a nonhierarchical liberation movement in which gender is "inextricably related to race and class."[64] The organization argues that the current political climate of "us vs. them" contributes to the polarization of communities that could otherwise work in coalition, as some targeted groups attempt to divert surveillance and policing onto others.[65] Assimilation—going stealth, or claiming status as a good transgender citizen—becomes a tactic for escaping state surveillance or persecution, and understandably so. But these assimilation strategies are regularly used in conjunction with the scapegoating of other marginalized groups, such that the good citizen and the normatively gendered person are produced against the terrorist, undocumented immigrant, and gender deviant. In fact, these two seemingly contradictory groups mutually constitute and require each other: "docile patriots" and good citizens claim normalcy precisely through distinguishing themselves from other marginalized groups figured as dangerous intruders.[66] The terrorist figure thus makes possible the construction of a national identity and image of citizenship, providing a necessary contrast against which the citizen is formed in opposition.[67]

The repeated advice to reveal one's transgender status, proving that transgender people are good citizens with nothing to hide, suggests a different interpretation of going stealth. Here, such a practice means not simply erasing the signs of transgender identity, but rather maintaining legibility as a good citizen and patriotic American, providing evidence of legitimate transgender identity that erases any signs of similarity to the deviant, deceptive terrorist figure. Yet because normative, nonthreatening gender is read through ideals of whiteness, economic privilege, able-bodiedness, and heterosexuality, this form of going stealth is an option available only to certain people; in fact, going stealth in this way requires the simultaneous maintenance of a nonnormative and suspicious category that can produce the safe citizen as its contrast. The specific reliance on identification documents as a primary measure of legitimacy intensifies that polarization. This is not only because approved documents are not available for certain groups, or because even approved documents might compound scrutiny for other groups (such as documentation showing that one's country of origin is on a terrorism watch list). More fundamentally, an investment in identification documents as evidence of credibility reconsolidates nationalist policing of deviance and illegitimacy. As documentation produces new and refines existing categories of legitimacy, it also shores up those nonnormative categories that make the normative possible. In this way, identity documents produce and refine classification schemas that support biopolitical regulation of bodies and populations as well as the categories of race, gender, sexuality, and citizenship.

CHAPTER TWO

FLYING UNDER THE RADAR

ON DECEMBER 25, 2009, a passenger aboard a commercial airplane attempted to detonate a plastic explosive en route from Amsterdam to Detroit. The passenger, Nigerian citizen Umar Farouk Abdulmutallab, had concealed the explosive device in his underwear; according to FBI reports in late 2012, he had worn the explosives-rigged underwear for three weeks prior to the flight in an effort to be comfortable enough to pass easily through airport security. When the device failed to detonate as planned, he suffered second-degree burns to his hands, inner thighs, and genitals. News media accounts linked Abdulmutallab to Al-Qaeda, and he was soon commonly known as the underwear bomber. By October 2011, he had pleaded guilty to eight charges, including attempted use of a weapon of mass destruction, and was sentenced to life in prison.

The attempted bombing and its attendant anxious discourse about dangerous bodies' threats to national security and public safety functioned as leverage for U.S. state efforts to increase formal surveillance measures. In particular, security agencies called for more thorough screening procedures for air travel. The Transportation Security Administration (TSA), an agency within the Department of Homeland Security (DHS), installed new advanced imaging technology (AIT) machines in many U.S. airports. These machines, some using X-rays and others using radio waves, allow security officials to see beneath travelers' clothing, producing sketch-like images of the physical body and any objects attached to it. More recent versions of the scanners include pink and blue scan buttons that require TSA agents to input each traveler's gender in order to begin the scanning process.[1] Thorough, individual pat-downs serve as an alternative to the scanners for travelers who voluntarily opt out and as a second round of screening for travelers whose scans appear suspicious or produce what TSA terms "anomalies."[2]

Much public apprehension accompanied these screening procedures. Anxieties about privacy underlay a significant portion of the public conversation, including questions about what the scanned images look like, who can view them, and how they circulate; about the health effects of repeated X-ray scans when traveling; and about maintaining bodily privacy while being patted down by a TSA officer. Echoing these concerns, prominent transgender advocacy organizations such as the National Center for Transgender Equality (NCTE) and the Transgender Law Center released statements warning that the new screening processes could incorrectly target transgender people as terrorist suspects by revealing prosthetic breasts, genitals, or binding materials that might be misinterpreted as explosives. Like several other organizations, they called for more accurate screening processes, or failing that, for transgender people to clearly identify their prosthetic materials as medically necessary and therefore safe.[3] Notably, these organizations focused on the effects of the screening technologies but almost never addressed their apparent catalyst, the case of the underwear bomber in the broader context of the war on terror. This is a curious omission: after all, the question of what precisely is in one's underwear is—however crude— arguably the most basic form of policing for those bodies perceived as gender-nonconforming. These amplified security measures—pat-down procedures and X-ray scanners new to most U.S. airports, if not to state security practices more broadly—emerged in a specific cultural and political moment concerned with the dangers to national security and public health that could be concealed with, or perhaps as part of, the genitals.

Paying close attention to the questions of privacy and health in state agencies' preoccupation with dangerous genitals and bodily prosthetics, this chapter considers the X-ray scanner not primarily in terms of its ability to accurately distinguish bad bodies from good ones, but in terms of the broad effects produced by the circulation of AIT images, especially regarding the interplay of race, gender, and disability. I position the medicalized technologies central to airport security debates in a broader cultural and political context to argue that efforts to objectively distinguish between bodies that are worthy of care and bodies that are inherently harmful displace the violence of state policies and practices onto individual bodies marked as threats. Analyzing the discourses of vulnerability and violence that circulate through the airport scene, this chapter demonstrates how the common recourse to medical legitimacy taken up by many transgender advocates helps naturalize not only ideals of normative bodily health, but also security screening practices themselves.

On Medical Necessity

Given the key role medicine has played in producing the category of transgender, it is perhaps no surprise that prominent advocacy organizations establish prosthetics as a major site of contention in airport screening procedures. Likewise, their concerns about TSA's treatment and interpretations of transgender travelers' bodies—for instance, whether the presence or absence of certain body parts in AIT images will incite suspicion because they conflict with agents' perceptions of the gendered body in front of them—follow from the notion that modern medicine helps produce transgender bodies as such. This pervasive belief appears in a range of scholarship suggesting that transgender identity emerges primarily in relation to medical developments that enable physical sex reassignment, positioning the transgender-identified person (and body) as unique to modernity, produced through a modern West's sex/gender categories and its technological and medical advances.[4] As I explained in chapter 1, contemporary medical and legal institutions continue to rely heavily on the presence of medical technologies as evidence of legible transgender identity.

Much discussion of transgender people and medicalization focuses on the processes through which transgender-specific medical care, including surgeries and hormones, can or should be accessed. Typically, such care is available only after a formal diagnosis of gender dysphoria (formerly gender identity disorder). Many critics of this process argue that transgender identity is not a disorder and accordingly should be removed from the *Diagnostic and Statistical Manual of Mental Disorders*, allowing access to hormones and surgery through informed consent, as with most non-transgender-specific medical care. Those favoring the current process often contend that the diagnosis provides a measure of legitimacy that makes health care available to transgender people, particularly for those populations with the least access to care, including youth, poor people, and incarcerated people.[5] Advocates have accomplished several expansions of transgender people's access to medical care by arguing that care such as surgeries and hormones is medically necessary, following a broader framework in health coverage that supports physicians' decisions for diagnosing and treating illness, disease, or injury.[6] In other words, naming certain medical technologies as medically necessary treatments for a clinically diagnosed condition can justify the coverage and administration of such care. In some cases, the medical necessity argument has won crucial access to medical care. For example, since 2011, U.S. federal prisons and federal halfway houses have been required to provide incarcerated persons appropriate evaluation and treatment (including hormones) for gender dysphoria; similar requirements for carceral institutions on the state level are still under debate. Likewise, several major cities and public university systems in the United States, along with Medicare, now cover certain transgender-specific forms of care deemed medically necessary.[7]

The rhetoric of medical necessity need not turn only on the notion of treating a physical or mental disorder. In fact, the term is sometimes explained in ways that locate disorder in social systems rather than in individual bodies: for instance, several public health and medical organizations' statements on the topic note that access to transition-related care may help alleviate the mental and physical pain caused by pervasive transphobia in the form of harassment, assault, or employment and housing discrimination.[8] This approach echoes the development of a "social model" of disability in disability studies and activism, which eschews a medical framework that "defines disability in terms of individual deficit" and instead seeks broad structural change in social and political systems that disable certain bodies and groups.[9] Yet while the concept of medical necessity can be strategically beneficial, particularly in the realm of law, it also fundamentally grounds transgender identities and bodies in Western medicine and particular forms of medical technologies. As I show below, commentators invoke these technologies as the very things that allow transgender people to pass or appear unmarked as transgender, a medicalized ability that can be interpreted as both freeing and damning. On one hand, certain bodily technologies are said to grant transgender people the ability to move more freely in public space and to escape the more overt scrutiny applied to transgressive gender presentations. On the other hand, that same supposed ease of movement can mark these bodies as dishonest and deceptively threatening, able to hide deviance and bodily abnormalities until they are actively revealed.

Consider for example a widely circulated fact sheet that NCTE released in June 2009. Addressing new airport X-ray scanners, NCTE implicitly re-affirms the idea that medical technologies not only are part and parcel of inhabiting a transgender body, but also offer the freedom to move through the world without scrutiny—except in special cases where state surveillance impinges on individual rights to privacy. The document lists prosthetics and binding materials alongside other body parts that the new X-ray machines will record, noting that "if a transgender person's [X-rayed] body looks different from what the TSA agent considers 'normal,' the passenger may be subjected to further searches and/or humiliation under the auspices of security measures."[10] The fact sheet suggests that were it not for these new imaging techniques, many transgender people would not be noticeable to security personnel as different or not "normal" because they would otherwise be able to pass freely through security checkpoints.

Of course, only certain transgender bodies can fully achieve or approximate the idealized image of normative gender. The fact sheet bypasses this point by reassuring readers—in a section titled "What Should I Do to Avoid Problems at the Airport?"—that the new X-ray scanners are "used primarily for passengers who are flagged for further screening after passing through a metal detector."[11] The document further encourages travelers to "make their own decisions" about whether to opt for a pat-down instead of going through the scanner, "based on what feels most comfortable and safe to them."[12] These statements assume that most transgender travelers would not be flagged for reasons beyond clearly marked transgender status, such as race, nationality, or citizenship status, and that these factors would not influence whether security officials interpreted their gender presentation and gendered body as normal or not normal. At face value, NCTE's declaration that "transgender people have as much right to travel as anyone else and we have a right to express any gender we want, any way we want while traveling" is admirable.[13] Yet it also privileges a mobile U.S. citizen who can take rights as a given, and for whom the choice between AIT screening and pat-down appears in the guise of freedom and personal safety rather than as a false choice between related forms of militarized surveillance. Medical necessity can serve as recourse only for certain bodies and certain bodily technologies. This legitimating rhetoric classifies particular types of bodies as in need of and worthy of care, so that the concept of medical necessity helps construct the line distinguishing health promotion from health endangerment. Like all classificatory systems, this process simultaneously extends recognition and legitimacy to some groups while it withholds them from others, either by specifically marking certain groups as illegitimate or by failing to name them at all.

Many advocacy organizations' own reliance on medical validity illustrates how that logic of care produces and reinforces conceptions of health and safety by creating specific—if constantly fluctuating—categories of legitimacy. For example, NCTE's air travel resource guide for transgender people, released in late 2012, begins with advice for packing luggage: "Gel-filled prosthetic items such as breast forms are not included in the three-ounce liquid limit for carry-ons, as they are considered medically necessary, but their presence in your carry-on luggage may result in extra screening."[14] This guidance suggests that although they technically exceed TSA's current parameters of safety, certain prosthetics can achieve medicalized approval; at the same time, those approved prosthetics may also provoke increased scrutiny to ensure that they are worn or carried in the interest of health rather than harm.

In response to multiple official complaints and public concerns about TSA treatment of various forms of disability, TSA implemented a new program clarifying the process of amplified scrutiny that leads to medical approval. Launched in December 2011 and titled TSA Cares, the program consists of a help line and related website that specifically address travelers with disabilities or medical conditions. It offers personalized phone or email responses as well as general website assistance explaining government policies and helping travelers prepare for security screenings. The TSA Cares website lists several types of disabilities and medical conditions, each linking to further details about what the related screening process entails. Notably, during most of 2012 the category "Breast Prosthetics" linked directly to an article titled "What to Expect at the TSA Checkpoint If You Are a Breast Cancer Survivor."[15] Although in practice one may assume that the information provided here applies to any use of breast prosthetics, the identification of such prosthetics specifically and only with breast cancer survivors constructs a limited range of prosthetic use, marking some bodies as legitimate users and failing to recognize others. In this framework, NCTE's assurance that transgender travelers' breast prosthetics are "considered medically necessary" appears somewhat more tenuous, particularly considering common gendered expectations about which bodies experience breast cancer and use related prosthetics. Under what circumstances and by what measures of proof can TSA approve as safe those breast prosthetics that are unrelated to breast cancer? Put another way, what imagined purposes might such prosthetics have outside of the approved context of breast cancer?

This is not really a question of practical procedure, especially since TSA subsequently included on its website an article covering "special considerations" for transgender travelers, indicating that this too is a population that the agency now recognizes.[16] Rather, it is a question of discursive effect: what understandings of normative bodies—of health, of gender, of medical necessity—are reconsolidated by defining breast prosthetics as those prosthetics used by breast cancer survivors? This question is of particular import when such definitions underwrite state surveillance practices that already sort bodies and populations according to their perceived threat to national security. That TSA's policy formally recognizes breast prosthetics use only in relation to breast cancer does not mean that in practice TSA agents deem all other uses suspicious. Rather, this policy is exemplary of how narrow the process of recognition can be and how regulatory norms shape it. In this sense, the formal inclusion of breast prosthetics use in other contexts might expand the range of legitimate uses but would simultaneously expand and refine the classificatory system that produces healthy and dangerous bodies. As TSA's policies and public materials reinforce the lines between these categories, the claim to medical necessity can become a strategy of claiming certain bodily technologies as healthy and reparative, in contrast to those framed as violent and damaging. The process of making these distinctions displaces violence onto those nonnormative bodies and bodily technologies that cannot otherwise be recuperated through the rhetoric of care or medical necessity. This process also effaces the violence of state agencies such as DHS, not only in material practices such as forced searches and detentions, but in the act of classification and the naming of certain bodies as dangerous.

More broadly, the very existence of TSA Cares signals the limits of medical necessity as a conceptual strategy for legitimacy: although the program helps distinguish between bodies that must be scrutinized in the name of care and those that must be scrutinized as threats to national health and safety, both groups are nonetheless marked out as populations requiring greater or more specific forms of surveillance than those unmarked bodies that are seemingly free from technological components or somatic anomalies. The particular screening methods in place for travelers with disabilities or medical conditions address material concerns for groups that can be vulnerable to violence and discrimination. Yet framed in the language of care, the program also helps more fully incorporate those groups into the biopolitical management of health and risk, via surveillance technologies. By positioning certain types of bodies as in need of this care, TSA Cares naturalizes the screening process overall, which comes to seem normative and routine except in those cases requiring particular forms of care. Additionally, it naturalizes a form of able-bodied health, defined as one that needs no special screening techniques. In this way the program draws a line between able-bodied and disabled, health and medical condition.

But no body fully aligns with ideal health, and no body is untouched by medicine or technology. Lennard Davis observes that perhaps now more than ever, care of the body is understood as "a requirement of citizenship," such that no body is perceived as complete without consumption of medical, technological, and hygienic products.[17] Suggesting that the categories of disability and impairment are productively unstable, Davis proposes embracing that instability to unseat classificatory distinctions between bodies along lines of health, dependence, and wholeness. In contrast, the TSA Cares program invests in these distinctions, relying on the broad title of "disabilities and medical conditions" that implies an easily recognizable category with clear and fixed parameters. Yet TSA's own continual editing of that category—which conditions can be included, how they are grouped together or separated out, and what specific bodily states constitute each of them— illustrates just how unstable and permeable such divisions are. It is not that certain bodies exist as anomalies within a stable system of health, but rather that this very system and its attendant technologies reinforce and rework deeply embedded conceptions of normative bodies that can be interpreted as healthy and safe.

X-Ray Specs

Beyond the bodily technologies under scrutiny, there is another medical technology at work in these airport scenes: the X-ray machine itself. Used by a variety of state institutions to see beyond the capabilities of the naked eye, X-ray machines enable a different form of vision and visual surveillance. Unlike photography, X-ray imaging (radiography) records variations in density and composition, penetrating some layers of matter and being absorbed by others. The most well-known form of X-ray imaging, generally used in explicitly medical contexts, makes visible the skeletal system and other objects in the body's interior that are otherwise visually inaccessible without physically opening the body.

Despite public concerns about privacy and safety when such technology appeared at the airport, radiography has long been promoted as central to national health and security, and its use in medical imaging and military contexts—beginning just after the X-ray's discovery in 1895—has frequently helped it cast off the shadow of intrusive state policing. Folded into the broader context of military preparedness structuring World War I, radiology equipment and training programs gained extensive military support in the early twentieth century. In these early incarnations, the X-ray machine was key to concepts of mobility on multiple levels, foreshadowing its installment in major travel hubs: it assisted military physicians in more efficiently assessing injuries that affected bodily mobility and also helped regulate the spread of disease and movement of infectious bodies by visually identifying them as such. World War I also saw the development of the first X-ray units that were themselves mobile, as portable units moved between army hospitals and battle sites.[18] In these cases, military use lends X-ray technology credibility as a medical advance that helps save wounded soldiers, strengthening the health of the nation itself.

The status that the X-ray machine gained through use in medical and military settings paved the way for its extension into other institutional sites, including local U.S. policing practices. For example, a variety of handheld battery-powered devices built on X-ray technology, which allow users to see through walls just as the medical X-ray machine allows one to see through flesh, were developed for military use in the 1980s but later marketed to domestic law enforcement agencies as part of a larger trend of finding civilian uses for militarized technology. In an April 2000 report to the U.S. Department of Justice, researchers from Georgia Tech describe the development and applications of one such device, the RADAR flashlight, according to their DOJ-funded study. They explain that the flashlight would serve two main purposes: identifying the presence of suspected criminals during searches, and tracking vital signs of hostages not otherwise visible.[19] Throughout, the report frames the device as a tool that will increase police officers' safety, but principal researcher Eugene Greneker elsewhere described the flashlight as "a force multiplier [as well as] a safety enhancement tool," suggesting that this X-ray-based instrument might be used for more than merely preventative measures.[20] But the potential damage such technology might cause (not only for those bodies directly targeted by law enforcement, but for all bodies and populations under state scrutiny) tends to be muffled by commonsense beliefs in the necessity of policing technology to ensure safety, beliefs supported here by the X-ray's long-standing reputation of health promotion.

Law enforcement use of X-ray equipment can offer a way of testing potentially damaging technology on a targeted population before it is implemented more broadly. Backscatter X-ray machines were in use in several prison systems in the United States during the late 1990s, more than ten years before their introduction to most commercial U.S. airports. Correctional facilities lauded the machines as a more efficient and effective way to screen both incarcerated people and visitors for concealed weapons and other prohibited items. Backscatter manufacturers and prison officials alike described the technology as safe, locating danger not in the radiation dosage, but rather in the incarcerated body that might be hiding harmful objects.[21] Not until the early 2000s, when the U.S. government began to consider extending backscatter screenings to the general public, did the FDA begin a series of health risk assessments, which similarly characterized X-ray technology as beneficial to bodily and national health.[22]

Just as with claims to medical necessity, defining and securing public health necessarily entails delineating specific threats to that health status. The X-ray machine's reputation as an objective medical technology that reveals bodily truths has long positioned it as a central tool for this sorting process. An 1896 *New York Times* article announcing the discovery of the X-ray concluded that it would revolutionize modern medicine because it enabled surgeons to "detect the presence of foreign bodies."[23] In this case, the foreign bodies in question were bullets and other material objects lodged inside human bodies. But "foreign bodies" also came to mean other things. For instance, Lisa Cartwright shows how public health campaigns about the use of X-rays to detect tuberculosis in the early twentieth-century United States visually represented the disease as a literal foreign body, in one case figuring tuberculosis as a cartoon Japanese soldier invading the otherwise healthy American citizen.[24] Produced just four years after the closing of the last Japanese American internment camp, the film carries forward white fears of an enemy within: in this depiction, the racially unmarked individual body symbolizes the American social body, and the racial other stands poised to penetrate national health and safety. The campaign positions X-ray technology as key to locating this hidden danger—and in doing so, constructs disease as a particularly racialized threat to the nation.

This cultural resonance carries over to more recent contexts, such as the use of X-ray images in immigration enforcement, formally practiced in the United States since at least the late 1990s and strongly considered in the United Kingdom in 2009 and again in 2012. In the United States, undocumented immigrants under age eighteen are treated differently from adults: they are not subject to immediate deportation and may gain asylum under a special juvenile provision. A 2004 memorandum from U.S. Immigration and Customs Enforcement (which like TSA also falls under DHS oversight) explains that dental and wrist-bone X-ray images are to be used to help determine age for those subjects suspected of lying about their birthdates in order to be classified as minors. Although the document specifies that such images must be "considered among other available and credible evidence of age" such as identification documents and do not necessarily "constitute conclusive evidence of age," a spokesperson for the agency noted in 2000 that the practice "is a widely accepted process within forensic medicine to accurately, within a given range, determine an individual's age."[25] Agreeing with this, one dentist employed by the agency explained in a *New York Times* interview how he assesses dental X-ray images, invoking biological determinist understandings of racial and gender difference: "When all four molars have erupted in a Caucasian male, this means the patient is between 18 and 21. In black males the person is between 17 and 21. In females the molars erupt about six months later."[26] This approach, framed as objective science, links X-ray imaging with taxonomies of race and gender to identify the deceptive immigrant body.

State agencies like DHS need not actually employ the X-ray machine itself to invoke its power of penetrating vision in locating threatening bodies. For instance, Camp X-ray, which housed detainees at the Guantánamo Bay detention center between January and April 2002, takes its name from the NATO phonetic alphabet and does not necessarily indicate the literal use of X-ray screenings. The camp held individuals believed to be connected to Al-Qaeda or the Taliban in rows of chain-link cages, fully visible to guards at all times. This architectural emphasis on vision as key to the identification of danger and the maintenance of national safety underwrites the camp's primary purpose beyond mere detainment: to serve as a site of information gathering later revealed to involve complex torture scenes, through which detainees were expected to reveal hidden truths about their links to and knowledge of terrorist organizations. These interviews, as guards and military officials named them, frequently relied on medical expertise for legitimacy, incorporating physicians to ensure the safety of various torture techniques and psychiatric experts to determine the processes' efficacy.[27] Thus the X-ray, even without literal use of its technology, suggests here the uncovering of information that cannot be identified or extracted by more superficial tactics. Used against the terrorist figure, it is the X-ray that deftly seeks what is concealed.

These aspects of X-ray technologies and the discourses surrounding them may seem rather far afield from the concerns expressed by transgender-specific organizations, blogs, and news media pieces. Many of these commentaries address the use of such technologies in commercial airports since 2009, and they primarily focus on questions of accuracy, repeating the basic concern that transgender bodies will be wrongfully marked as dangerous merely because they do not appear aligned with the gendered characteristics that TSA agents expect. In public statements and resource documents like the fact sheet discussed above, for example, NCTE implies that TSA policies and X-ray security screenings are new, unique, and shocking measures, rather than articulating them as an extension of ongoing surveillance over bodies that are designated as outside the boundaries of the normal. This approach tends to efface the profoundly racialized nature of bodily surveillance: the transgender traveler imagined in NCTE's publications does not seem to confront bodily scrutiny through racial profiling or anti-immigrant measures, despite the fact that such practices characterized U.S. airport security long before September 11, 2001.[28] As such, the X-ray machine appears in these discussions as a sudden intrusion into the lives of the general public, rather than as a technology thoroughly embedded in routine policing practices.

Private Parts

State agencies and media outlets produced and circulated a handful of official images demonstrating how AIT scans of travelers appear to TSA agents. The TSA website hosted two such images: one depicting the results of a backscatter machine, which uses X-ray technology (figure 2.1), and one of a millimeter wave scan, which uses radio waves (figure 2.2). Each image depicts the front and back of two different bodies that appear white against a dark

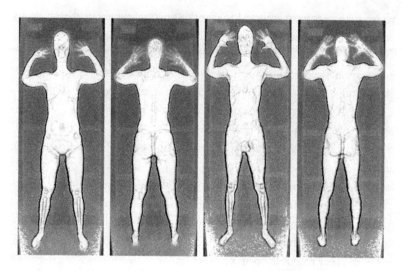

Figure 2.1 Image produced by X-ray backscatter technology and circulated by TSA (ABOVE). **Figure 2.2** Image produced by millimeter wave scan and circulated by TSA (FACING PAGE, ABOVE). **Figure 2.3** "Whole Body Imaging FAQ" circulated by the National Center for Transgender Equality (FACING PAGE, BELOW).

background; TSA's website describes the grainy backscatter image as resembling a chalk etching, and the more detailed millimeter wave scan as "a fuzzy photo negative." A third widely circulated image appeared in a February 2007 *New York Times* article addressing the introduction of new scanners at U.S. airports, and in a slightly different form in NCTE's 2009 fact sheet (figure 2.3). This image shows the front and back of a body in white and blue against a dark background, and its clarity is far greater than those images on TSA's website: the *Times* article notes that it depicts an X-ray image "before software was used to blur bodily contours."[29]

Despite the popular notion that the X-ray machine objectively sees beyond social categories to produce neutral images of bodies, it is not difficult to read sexed characteristics onto these three images. Even in the least detailed examples, such as the backscatter image, genitals are clearly recognizable, indicating for many viewers that one image is male and the other is female. In fact, genitals may come to seem the most compelling component of these images, in part because AIT seems to strip away so many other markers of social categories. For instance, the body scans purportedly do away with racial profiling: their images may appear essentially deracialized because

WHOLE BODY IMAGING FAQ

Travel Information • June 2009

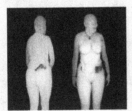

Whole Body Imaging scanners produce a three-dimensional image of the passenger's nude body, including breasts, genitals, buttocks, prosthetics, binding materials, and any objects on the person's body, in an attempt to identify contraband. These scanners may out transgender people to TSA staff and potentially subject transgender people to further screening at the airports.

they are absent the most common surface markers of race, such as skin color. As the next section of this chapter contends, racial meanings can profoundly shape these images and their interpretations, but the imagined absence of racial difference in the X-ray's gaze shifts public anxieties about such screenings onto identities and bodily components that may be more overtly present in the circulated images.

Major concerns about airport screenings—regarding both AIT scans and pat-down procedures—tend to focus on the forced exposure of bodies along lines of gender and sexuality and, to a lesser extent, age and disability. These anxieties coalesce around the question of vulnerability, and as such the model complaint cases tend to be those bodies envisioned as most vulnerable: young children, the very elderly, and those with visible disabilities. After U.S. senator Rand Paul (R-KY) refused to undergo a pat-down and was consequently denied passage through an airport security checkpoint in early 2012, his father, U.S. representative Ron Paul (R-TX), used these three categories to bolster his repeated argument that TSA exemplifies a "police state," asserting that the agency "gropes and grabs our children, our seniors, and our loved ones and neighbors with disabilities."[30] Likewise, U.S. representative Jason Chaffetz (R-UT) said of the X-ray scanners in 2010, "We don't need to look at naked 8-year-olds and grandmothers to secure airplanes."[31] These recurrent concerns frame airport screening practices as questions of gender, vulnerability, and individual privacy rather than of citizenship and structural racism. But this is an illusory displacement, as evidenced by Rand Paul's own response to TSA's policies. Contending that "regular, ordinary citizens don't need to be put through this," Paul supports instead "selective risk assessments done on people [who] are international travelers [and] people who have ties to groups that may be terrorists."[32] In this racially coded framework, normative citizenship connotes an unjustly exploited personal vulnerability, contrasted against those imagined to exploit national vulnerability, who therefore require airport scrutiny.

This defense of ordinary citizens' privacy butts up against the broader antiterrorism rhetoric that posits individual privacy as a necessary sacrifice for the good of the nation. In the binary logic summed up by George W. Bush as "you're either with us or against us," to resist or question TSA scrutiny is to disregard or even undermine national security. The TSA policies work to ease the tension between these two positions by offering travelers the choice to request a pat-down conducted in a private room, an option meant to alleviate individual apprehension about being touched or exposed through more public screening procedures. Yet this option may actually feel less safe for some people, and for reasons beyond gendered discomfort or sexual modesty. When considered in the context of indefinite detention and related security practices that increasingly operate outside of public view, many people—including immigrants, transgender people, and people of color—may feel far more vulnerable entering a private room alone with a government agent than undergoing a screening in the more public space of the security line, where other travelers could serve as witnesses to possible state violence.

Compared to the still unclear procedures for taking, transmitting, and viewing AIT images, the pat-down can seem quite straightforward. Yet because it relies entirely on individual TSA agents' interactions with travelers, it can be equally opaque. Although TSA's website does not provide an official detailed description of the enhanced pat-down that has been in practice since 2010, the procedure is relatively standardized; some airport security lines even have clearly posted statements that TSA agents read verbatim to travelers who request a pat-down.[33] But the fact that this is only the case in some locations indicates how variable the process can be. The basic ritual of the pat-down proceeds as follows: the traveler assumes a specific stance (feet shoulder-width apart, arms outstretched with palms facing up), and an agent of the same gender explains the procedure; asks about injuries, disabilities, and any desire for a private screening; and then physically searches the passenger. Public anxiety has focused primarily on the enhanced pat-down's requirement that agents touch travelers' breasts, buttocks, and (of particular concern) genitals, actions specified in agents' scripted statement that they will move their hands up the traveler's legs until they meet resistance.

Though routine enough that it follows codified standards and scripts, the pat-down process also changes significantly depending on airport, specific security line, individuals involved, and a host of other variables. The TSA itself records feedback and complaints not only about the fact of the enhanced pat-down (that is, complaints about its very existence), but also about the unpredictable ways in which it is carried out.[34] These reports range from confusion about different standards in different airports to multiple accusations of sexual assault, molestation, and racial and sexual profiling of the travelers selected for pat-downs. In addition to the many variations in how the pat-down is physically conducted, individual agents regularly add their own questions and conversation to the process, such that the pat-down is simultaneously a repetitive, uniform state practice and a unique interaction between individual bodies. The divergence that occurs between the formal physical routine codified by TSA and the spontaneous, diverse range of verbal interactions produces moments of slippage in which the TSA agent both carries out standardized state practices and disrupts those practices. These unpredictable interactions built into pat-downs can position the AIT scans as routine—indeed, mechanical—by contrast, supporting the illusion of an objective surveillance practice that is removed from the social or political.

The coerced act of choosing between these two forms of surveillance involves complicated negotiations of privacy, which is made available to some bodies through being overtly foreclosed for others. For instance, it is easy to understand the sustained focus on genitals—as a site of dangerous secrets and as a particular marker of invasions of privacy—as linked to anxieties about gender and sexuality. But these body parts in particular are always fraught with questions of race. In popular and scientific discussions about race, gender, and sexuality, genitals have been a central object of analysis in the West since at least the early nineteenth century. White sexologists and anatomists specifically studied and documented the bodies of people of color, focusing on sexual and reproductive organs as evidence of these bodies' inherent inferiority and abnormality. In the context of evolutionary theory and early eugenics movements, such studies played a key role in popular media as they attempted to distinguish civilized, advanced bodies from primitive ones. Images and descriptions of these bodies circulated as part of a larger effort to secure white heterosexuality against the threats of immigration, miscegenation, and sexual ambiguity.[35] This history informs more recent efforts, both subtle and overt, to identify the bodily truth of transgender people. That truth frequently relies on the classification of one's genitals and is sought on the grounds that the concealment of nonnormative gender and genitals threatens public health and safety. In this sense, certain "private parts" have never really been private, but have intentionally been made public as part of ongoing efforts to maintain a national health characterized by racialized sexual difference.

To argue—as Ron Paul and Jason Chaffetz do, for instance—that certain airport screenings are unacceptable because they undermine individual privacy assumes a universalized right to privacy, eliding the fact that state and public scrutiny of bodies, and perhaps of genitals especially, is a new or newly alarming invasion of privacy only for some groups. Routinely making certain bodies public produces a group of normative bodies for whom privacy seems attainable. The installation of backscatter X-ray machines in U.S. prisons, years before their broad installation in commercial airports, is instructive here. When the California prison system began using such machines to screen visitors in 1997, strong opposition emerged, ultimately resulting in a lawsuit that forced the state to terminate the practice. Critics of the X-ray scans repeatedly invoked privacy and health concerns, representing the screening process as an inherent infringement upon visitors' rights. For instance, one attorney told the *San Francisco Chronicle*, "for the state to subject us to this is just unconscionable."[36] In the same article, a health instructor who regularly visited her incarcerated son likened the compulsory screenings to "living in a police Gestapo state" and continued, "this is a hazard to the general public. I think we're guinea pigs." While these statements may well have some validity, they gain it in part through the naturalized oppositional relationship between "the general public" and incarcerated people. Because the prison is understood to void bodily privacy for those bodies that are incarcerated, as a practice built into the very concept of imprisonment, these statements need not attend to the ways that prisoners already live in a police state, as do wide swaths of criminalized populations, whether literally imprisoned or not.[37] Thus it is not deemed unconscionable to subject prisoners to the public exposure of X-ray scans, a notion clarified by a senior staff member at a maximum-security facility in North Carolina, where backscatter X-ray machines were being used to screen prisoners rather than visitors: "We wouldn't use it on our staff because it is very intrusive. . . . If a female stood in front of it, it would show her bra, her panty line; [with] a male it would show just about everything he's got."[38] Debates over such surveillance measures in the context of the prison starkly highlight the ways that bodies that are compelled to be public sustain the concept of privacy for other bodies: because bodily privacy loses purchase within the prison, it appears natural (if at times endangered) outside of it. We can see the residue of these discourses in the repeated critical description of both the pat-down and AIT scan as prison-style searches, rhetoric that sets the free, rights-bearing citizen against the incarcerated person for whom privacy is foreclosed as a matter of course.

This does not mean, of course, that all those not formally incarcerated are in fact naturally imbued with a right to privacy, for bodily privacy rests on a constellation of factors ranging from economic status to disability to age. (Reproductive justice advocates, for example, have made this clear in their analyses of the limitations of bodily privacy for pregnant or potentially pregnant people under increasingly restrictive policies governing reproductive decisions, which curtail bodily privacy for all pregnant people but particularly for those who receive public assistance, who are disabled, who are minors, or who have criminal records.)[39] Rather, these imagined clear distinctions between the inside and outside of the prison occur in part through basic understandings of the prison as a space of unquestioned and thoroughly rationalized loss of privacy, so that violations of privacy register as such only when they touch those for whom privacy otherwise appears so obvious as to go unspoken. In this sense, it is telling that anxieties about police states and public health hazards immediately and persistently saturated public discourse when airports required X-ray screening even for those who are most mobile and privileged, rather than when such technology was applied in the specific scrutiny of criminalized bodies by law enforcement or prison officials. Concerns about the public exposure of bodies thus emerge in relation to the ways that privacy is unevenly dispersed through structures of race, gender, class, and disability.

Violence and Repair

In addition to their depictions of physical anatomy, the AIT scans also show various types of objects attached to bodies. Of course, the machine itself can only record these images; TSA agents operating the scanners must then interpret them to determine whether individual bodies warrant further examination. In the three primary images that circulated as examples of AIT scans, some of the objects shown are fairly readily recognizable. For instance, the image reproduced in NCTE's fact sheet depicts a handgun on the rear hip, suggesting that this figure is hiding a dangerous weapon. Yet the figure also has a variety of other objects on the hips and waist, and these are more difficult to interpret. This is precisely the concern articulated by many transgender and disability rights advocates.[40] Within the "nothing to hide, nothing to fear" logic of the war on terror, the images' vagueness may work in favor of bodies that TSA agents perceive as normative and innocent; these travelers already have greater access to privacy and may be given the benefit of the doubt in order to maintain that privacy. But for more troubling bodies—those that are difficult to classify or are already classified as potential threats based on perceived race, nation of origin, or citizenship status, for example—vague images may intensify scrutiny. Yet to remain focused on the machines' accuracy too easily accepts the prevailing parameters of state surveillance, militarized safety measures, and good versus bad bodies.

The constant reproduction of the same handful of images entices viewers to examine the depicted bodies again and again. The TSA released the images ostensibly to clarify the inner workings of these surveillance practices, a gesture toward full disclosure on the part of state agencies. In fact, the TSA website offered these images in the context of several pages of information about what passengers can expect when asked to go through the scanners and what they can do to assist officials and ensure efficient security lines, all information intended to make the process perfectly clear. At the same time, the images themselves are rather less than clear, functioning as invitations for extensive inspection. The production and circulation of these images encourages focused examination of particular bodies that come to seem out of the ordinary or difficult to define. Furthermore, the very repetition of such images naturalizes the process of visual scrutiny and of X-ray imaging specifically. One may even feel a certain pleasure in the act of studying these vaguely defined bodies, which begin to stand in for the terrorist body, the dangerous body, the body that attempts to deceive.

Likewise, these images work closely with the racism embedded in antiterrorism policies and practices. The literal whiteness of these ubiquitous figures—ghostly white bodies set against black space, with dark shadows indicating potentially threatening objects—may visually suggest that the figure under inspection represents a normative white traveler. But because antiterrorism discourse so persistently locates violence outside of whiteness and attaches it instead to Black and Muslim people in particular, these white figures and their attendant signs of violence (weapons, indeterminate objects, and as the next section of this chapter suggests, even genitals) are more likely to signal racial categories other than white. Leti Volpp explains that particularly since 9/11, public discourse and government actions in the United States construct the category of the terrorist as one inhabited by certain racial groups, forming the constitutive outside to the category of the American citizen. Arguing that these categories are productive of and thus dependent on one another, she writes that the events of 9/11 "facilitated the consolidation of a new identity category that groups together persons who appear 'Middle Eastern, Arab, or Muslim.' This consolidation reflects a racialization wherein members of this group are identified as terrorists, and are disidentified as citizens."[41] If the scanned images produced and circulated by TSA are imagined to represent dangerous or terrorist bodies made available for inspection, then already these images and their meanings are produced through anti-Muslim racism. For many viewers, race may come to mark these bodies in ways that are at odds with their literal whiteness, even without visual reference to other surface features through which race is routinely read.

The repetition of images may also support the notion that an identifiable terrorist body exists to be sought out by certain technologies. In this sense, for the projected audience of compliant citizens, there may be plea-sure in distancing oneself from these images, through imagining that one's own body is distinctly unlike certain others and through learning to inspect other bodies that might be dangerously deceptive, as the images themselves instruct. In the case of transgender travelers and others using "good" medical technologies, this would entail distancing one's bodily technologies from their militarized histories or from questions of war and violence more gen-erally, in order to see technology linked to violence only in the figure of the terrorist. That is to say, certain types of bodily technologies can be folded into the normal as they are understood to be medically necessary and thus health promoting, in contrast to those framed as harmful to both individual and national health.

In his extended analysis of Western conceptualizations of terrorism and suicide bombings, Talal Asad points to the contradictory framework in which the modern liberal state discursively positions violence and killing as criminal and morally abhorrent when located in the terrorist figure, yet as an organized and authorized means of securing freedom when accomplished by the citizen-soldier at war. The latter understanding of violence positions it as a necessary caretaking function of the state, so that "violence is there-fore embedded in the very concept of liberty that lies at the heart of liberal doctrine."[42] Because it is cast as absolutely oppositional to the backward and corrupt violence of terrorism, the U.S. government and military's own vio-lence can appear not only legitimate but protective and beneficial. In this way, Asad demonstrates how colonialist and Orientalist discourses mask the violence that is foundational to the Western state, perhaps especially when that violence is understood as a form of care.

At the same time, Ghassan Hage examines the case of Palestinian suicide bombings, often described as "the worst possible kind of violence," against the mass killings wrought by the Israeli state.[43] He considers the possibil-ity of reading acts explicitly classified as terrorism—suicide bombings in particular—not as the most abhorrent form of violent death, as they are so commonly interpreted, but as "a sign of life" in populations otherwise ravaged by the structural and material violence endemic to colonialism: "for what better sign of life is there, in such violent conditions, than the capacity to hurt despite the greater capacity of the other to hurt you?"[44] The seemingly clear boundaries between life and death, violence and care, break down and become interdependent when understood through these broader frameworks. Extending Hage's analysis, Jasbir Puar posits the figure of the suicide bomber as a "queer assemblage" that exposes these binary systems as false, producing "a systemic challenge to the entire order of Manichaean rationality that organizes the rubric of good versus evil."[45] It is this rubric that animates and rationalizes the war on terror, in which the twin violences of war and terror can be articulated as fundamentally oppositional, the former imagined as necessary for health and security precisely because the latter transgresses the boundaries of legitimate violence.[46]

Asad unpacks the ways that the legitimating rhetoric of war intertwines violence with care in part by examining how military technologies are mutually constitutive with medical advances, noting that modern warfare has produced "improved techniques for destruction, of course, but also for the restoration of human life."[47] In this way, we can understand harmful and healthful technologies not as binarily opposed, but rather as fundamentally intertwined: the development of war-making technologies occurs alongside medical advances to treat injuries incurred in war, in a continuous cycle. Jennifer Terry explains, "plenty of medical knowledge results from bodily wounds inflicted in human conflict, indicating a mutual provocation of might and medicine that lays to waste the cherished idea that violent conflict and humanitarianism are mutually exclusive."[48]

The X-ray machine serves as an apt example for this point, in part because it is an ostensibly medical technology regularly employed in militarized contexts and thus also a militarized technology taken up in medical settings—for instance, the desire for a portable radiography machine during World War I influenced the transition from glass plates to film, and then to increasingly fast film, improvements implemented on the battlefield and later extended to civilian medical institutions.[49] But further, the X-ray's ability to heal occurs precisely through acts of harm: the use of X-rays to diagnose, prevent, and treat various ailments necessarily entails exposing the body to the damaging effects of radiation. Early physical evidence of radiation's potential for destruction and disease—including the decomposition of scientists' own bodies during the research process—was typically downplayed through public health campaigns that figured X-ray imaging as preventing rather than creating illness.[50] A version of this rhetoric lingers in the airport screening process, as TSA assures concerned travelers that the radiation used in AIT scans poses only minimal threat to individual bodies while guarding against broader threats to the nation itself.[51]

The relationship that Asad and Terry discuss, between medical advances and the violence of war, also returns us to the question of genital prosthetics, which featured so prominently in the initial rationale for AIT airport screenings. Like most medicalized prosthetics, genital prosthetics and implants developed largely in response to injuries sustained in war, and they functioned both to reconstitute manhood and masculinity for wounded veterans and to help maintain a reproductive citizenship that could continue to serve the nation through military force.[52] The demand for and refinement of these medical technologies accelerated with the introduction of new combat weaponry such as land mines and grenades during World War I, which caused explosions directly underneath soldiers' bodies and increased the rate of injury to genitals.[53] Many reports suggest that this rate continues to rise for U.S. military personnel in Afghanistan.[54] Even while advances in body armor as well as trauma care in the field may lead to a drop in the casualty rate for U.S. soldiers, the increase in particular types of injury and the concurrent development of new treatments illustrate the biopolitical function of war that is concerned not merely with "advanced technologies for death dealing," but with the maintenance of a particular form of life.[55]

Eliding this mutual relationship between medicine and war, many transgender advocates seek to clearly distinguish between the prosthetic genitals of the transgender citizen and the explosive genitals of the foreign terrorist. This rhetorical feat also involves navigating the contradictory positioning of the terrorist figure as technologically inferior to the West, even while more primitive technologies—the shoe bomb, the box cutter—evade the U.S. government's cutting-edge surveillance techniques. In the context of the war in Afghanistan, the status of genitals exemplifies this conflicted logic: U.S. officials praise their military's high-tech weaponry as superior to Taliban arsenals, yet military physicians report a rise in genital injury rates for U.S. soldiers (loss of testicles may be considered the war's signature wound), citing Taliban forces' targeting of the legs and genitals through improvised explosive devices that outwit U.S. body armor's focus on head and torso regions.[56]

Thus Abdulmutallab—or at least the discursive figure he is made to represent—can be both mocked as the underwear bomber, whose failed attempt to explode his own genitals serves to cement the foreign, racialized figure as primitive and backward, and reviled as the terrorist threat to U.S. freedom and safety, whose explosive genitals legally function as weapons of mass destruction. These complicated positionings speak to the ambivalent ways that white, heteronormative U.S. nationalism navigates racial and sexual difference. The focused anxiety about genitals in this case recalls what Kobena Mercer, following Frantz Fanon, observes as "the primal fantasy of the big black penis [that] projects the fear of a threat not only to white womanhood, but to civilization itself."[57] This threat is then managed in part through positioning the racialized figure as sexually perverse and primitive and therefore inferior, even while the persistent emphasis on and anxiety about this figure (particularly as represented through genitals) reaffirms the power of the perceived threat. Relatedly, the ways that genitals come to signify racial, gendered, and national identifications echo David Eng's concept of racial castration, a psychic and political framework through which racial and sexual difference are both produced and managed always in relation to one another. Importantly, Eng contends that these identifications not only construct racialized subjects within narrow frames but also "produce against these particularized images the abstract national subject of a unified and coherent national body."[58]

In this sense, the explosive/failed genitals of the underwear bomber contrast with the exploded/repaired genitals of U.S. soldiers, who are at once emasculated by the foreign enemy and restored by the West's modern medicine and technology.[59] Legitimated violence thus merges with medical advancement in the figure of the loyal citizen-soldier, whose genital trauma signals not perverse failure but patriotic sacrifice, not foreign threat but national progress and renewed masculinity. The determination of many transgender advocates to classify transgender-related prosthetics as medically necessary—as enabling the modern, mobile citizen—thus has little room for consideration of the underwear bomber, or the ways that those genitals (both as literal body parts and as symbolic concepts) become a site of anxious scrutiny. In fact, the logic of classification here buttresses efforts to more effectively and accurately demarcate the dangerous figure, whose body must ultimately differ from those of ordinary citizens. Obscuring that figure's historical and ideological resonances with the broader scrutiny of nonconforming bodies treated as threatening, many prominent advocacy efforts highlight instead the reparative function of medically legitimated prosthetics, which purport to fold otherwise deviant bodies into the norm by portraying them as inherently safe, legible, and nonviolent.

Reading the Anomalies

In early 2013, partly in response to sustained public concern about the use of X-ray technology in airports, TSA began replacing backscatter machines with millimeter wave scans.[60] (Notably, the machines were scheduled to be moved from airports to other government agencies, and by mid-2014, more than 150 such scanners had been transferred to local law enforcement agencies, including jails and prisons.)[61] The new machinery does not rely on ionizing radiation, and it does not produce images specific to individual travelers but instead uses a generic outline of a body (figure 2.4). Anything that the scanner records as suspicious is marked on this outline, and in these cases the traveler must undergo additional screening, such as a pat-down. If the machine does not detect any problems, a green screen stating "OK" indicates that the traveler may proceed through the checkpoint. Because every traveler's body is depicted through the generic figure, TSA describes the software as increasing privacy. Yet images of the upgraded machines show pink and blue buttons marked "scan," indicating the requirement that security agents assign each traveler one of two genders to begin the scan, a classification process that many transgender organizations and commentators critique as disproportionately affecting gender-nonconforming travelers.[62] Beyond this concern, however, the use of a standardized, generic bodily image, while potentially offering a certain kind of privacy, also supports normalization processes by which certain bodies are marked as deviant and dangerous. In fact, we might understand such images as intensifying those processes, such that the image of the generic body comes to mark the norm in the most reductive way possible. The generic "OK" body, for example, is one with four limbs and a legible gender presentation, and it is absent any additional materials or objects.

These standardized figures build on a longer history of circulating images that depict an idealized, normative body in the context of national health and safety. They echo, for instance, the Norma and Normman statues first displayed in New York's American Museum of Natural History in 1945 and circulated as replicas during the height of the U.S. eugenics movement. Julian Carter explains that the statues, created through anthropometric studies of thousands of "native White Americans," facilitated eugenicist efforts to promote the superiority of the white, heterosexual, able body as that which exemplified American health and citizenship, and could be contrasted with

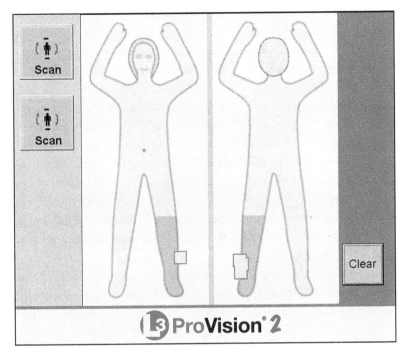

Figure 2.4 Marketing material for ProVision2 security scanner, showing generic body image and pink and blue scan buttons.

the perceived physical and psychological deficiencies of immigrants, people of color, queer people, and people with disabilities, all of which represented threats to the nation.[63] Notably, Carter contends that the figures helped forward these ideas without explicitly referencing race or sexuality at all; it was in fact their standard, generic quality, seemingly devoid of remarkable characteristics, that helped solidify whiteness and heterosexuality as the normal. This is not to suggest that current airport screening technologies are consciously designed with eugenics in mind. Rather, their attempts to standardize bodies—both through the explicit marking out of anomalies and through the creation of a generic standard framed as a benevolent, protective gift from the DHS—must be understood in the broader context of scientific efforts and interpretive practices that sort bodies along lines of race, gender, and disability toward a goal of national health and security. In this way, even though TSA frames the new software as less subjective (because each individual body is depicted through the same basic image), the generic figure produces new, further standardized understandings and expectations of bodies that are safe and normative.

The circulation of certain screened images, ostensibly intended to clarify the screening process and to demonstrate the objectivity of X-ray technology, actually makes clear that such imaging techniques are rooted in racializing and gendering processes that produce and distinguish the categories of citizen and terrorist, normative and deviant. These images circulate in political contexts that necessarily cast certain bodies as violent or as threateningly anomalous in an effort to stabilize the notion of healthy, safe bodies. In this sense, to call for a more accurate or objective mechanism of surveillance serves not to undo the profiling strategies at work but to reinforce them by seeking ever more careful scrutiny of difference and by reaffirming public understandings of what a threatening body—and the technologies it takes up—must look like.

Likewise, more refined surveillance programs attuned to the "special considerations" of certain populations can solidify expectations about how normative and safe bodies ought to appear, creating more categories of classification that can then be scrutinized anew. Mara Keisling, executive director of NCTE, argues, "any security system that relies on gender and 'anatomical anomalies' will always disparately affect transgender and gender nonconforming people. The TSA must act to bring their screening practices up to speed with social norms that value transgender people and our privacy."[64] In one sense, these statements are accurate: certainly those bodies that do not comply with dominant understandings of sex and gender will be especially vulnerable in security screenings, even if for some that vulnerability is mitigated by recourse to whiteness, wealth, or U.S. citizenship. And altering screening practices to account for transgender bodies and identities would likely decrease risk of scrutiny for many. Yet by what measures will bodies be identified as transgender, and how might they apply (or not) to nontransgender bodies interpreted as gender-nonconforming? What parameters should state agencies use to delineate safely medicalized transgender bodies from threatening anomalies? How will bodily anomalies be redefined, as bodily normality is incrementally expanded through these alterations? Like claims to medical necessity, this call to modernize airport security practices aims to incorporate (some) transgender people more fully into TSA's embrace and gaze, a move that, while potentially lessening vulnerability for some, also strengthens the efficacy of screening measures.

At the same time, perhaps there is something productive—even if unintentionally so—in the anxiety and confusion provoked by these security procedures and surveillance images, anxiety that can extend even to the most normative of bodies and identities. That is to say, there is a common narrative even from many people who are rarely or never singled out for scrutiny that they feel anxious approaching security personnel, that they fear their identification documents may not look enough like them, that they are concerned their body may be misread by the AIT scanners. As this chapter shows, certain types of bodies and identities, routinely represented as security threats, historically bear the brunt of state policing practices, making it possible for others to imagine that they are free from such practices. This is no less true at the airport, of course; one reason that new airport screening procedures draw so much attention is that they overtly scrutinize those bodies that may seem otherwise outside of surveillance systems' critical gaze. This more widespread anxiety has the potential to open up different questions about nonnormative bodies and about bodily anomalies that position them not as fixed, ahistorical, or easily read markers of deviance, but rather as active interpretations that—like the images from AIT scanners themselves—can shift according to context. And while certain people might more easily argue that the screening process has wrongfully misinterpreted them, the growing awareness that such misreadings occur at all might usefully make clear the fragility of any surveillance program's grasp on bodily norms.

Even this potential disruption can be adjusted for, though. In 2013, TSA expanded its Precheck program for "trusted travelers," allowing any U.S. citizen to apply for this preapproved status. First piloted in 2011, when it was available only to certain frequent flier members and those already enrolled in similar programs through Customs and Border Protection, Precheck requires a background check, an in-person interview, fingerprinting, and a fee of $85 for five years of enrollment. In exchange, TSA provides "a more convenient and efficient screening experience," with expedited security lanes and, during the screening process, permission to keep shoes and jackets on and to keep laptops and liquids in carry-on luggage; by June 2017, the agency announced that more than five million people had enrolled in the program.[65] Given that Precheck status also typically routes travelers through a metal detector rather than a full-body AIT scanner, it is perhaps no coincidence that TSA expanded this program during the same period that it implemented the new generic image machines: both changes can be understood as responses to public disapproval of AIT scans.[66]

Precheck represents a willing participation in surveillance that may seem at odds with the widespread resistance to invasive airport screening measures. But TSA markets its trusted-traveler program as advantageous to both national security efforts and to individual travelers who can claim this vetted status. A TSA promotional video describes Precheck as a benefit: short interviews with three enrollees (all of whom are legible as white, able-bodied, and normatively gendered) emphasize the convenience and even superiority of being preapproved, with one person explaining that her envy of Precheck travelers motivated her to enroll.[67] Moreover, TSA encourages enrollees to understand themselves as crucial participants in national security, rather than as suspects who must submit to the intrusions of the body scan and pat-down. After all, the video explains, "a one-size-fits-all security approach no longer applies," because most travelers are not actually risky and TSA must focus its resources on genuine threats. The program can be imagined as a way to avoid invasive scrutiny, even as it entails actively inviting surveillance by other means, including providing one's biometric data through fingerprinting. But this submission of data helps restore distinctions between healthy and harmful bodies that AIT machines had threatened to erode at the airport, just as they did when extended to visitors in prisons years before. These screening measures puncture the illusion of privacy for many travelers who must now, with AIT scans, confront overt physical scrutiny in the manner of prisoners or terrorists. Precheck reaffirms that bodily privacy—for instance, through permission to remain fully clothed during screening—while simultaneously undermining it through biometric data collection. The program thus layers several sorting processes: it tracks the voluntary relinquishing of data to apply, inspects fingerprints and identification records of enrollees, and determines whose bodies will undergo which type of screening at the airport itself. (It should come as no surprise that TSA's Precheck website includes information for "disabilities and medical conditions.") The promotional video concludes by noting that TSA "continues to adapt for an ever-evolving threat." Though this statement positions Precheck as evidence of more refined antiterrorism programs, it also speaks to the process by which state agencies become attuned to variations in bodies and bodily technologies, continuing to revise somatic norms and folding new differences into surveillance practices themselves naturalized as healthy and safe.

CHAPTER THREE

BATHROOMS, BORDERS, AND BIOMETRICS

IN EARLY 2013, Phoenix, Arizona, prepared to expand its nondiscrimination ordinance to include sexuality and gender identity. The revised law, which passed after a lengthy and controversial public hearing, explicitly incorporated LGBT people into basic city protections against discrimination in employment, housing, and public accommodations. In order to reframe the law from one that sought to protect certain marginalized groups to one that would actively endanger other groups, the ordinance's opponents dubbed it the "bathroom bill" and described it as primarily changing city policy governing public restrooms. For instance, the conservative nonprofit organization Center for Arizona Policy reduced the bill to one that "would allow 'transgendered' men to use the women's restroom in public accommodations like restaurants, schools, and churches—the same restroom that your child uses."[1] This tactic makes use of the basic rhetoric of dangerous deception, suggesting that the bill condones transgender fraud and assists the inherently deceptive transgender person in preying on vulnerable (non-transgender) women and children. The scare quotes around "transgendered" position transgender women as men, while also implying that many such people in the restroom are not actually transgender. In the organization's logic, then, the transgender figure signifies not only the deviant or deluded transgender-identified person, but also the perverse and threatening non-transgender perpetrator who—in a fantasized reversal—falsely puts on a transgender identity as a strategy to *avoid* scrutiny. Soon after the Phoenix law passed, the Arizona state legislature introduced two bills seeking to align bathroom use with birth-assigned sex.

Arizona represents only one of many U.S. legislative struggles over gendered bathrooms at the state and local levels. And as in Arizona, many legal challenges follow closely on the heels of new antidiscrimination laws. For instance, a broad equal-rights ordinance passed in Houston, Texas, in May 2014 covered a range of identity categories (including race, national origin, and age) and addressed employment, housing, and city contracting practices. Yet public discourse regularly framed it as essentially about gendered public bathrooms, with some opponents referring to it as the "Sexual Predator Protection Act."[2] The ordinance was overturned by popular vote in 2015. Other legislation operates preemptively, as when Utah representative Michael Kennedy proposed a 2014 bill that both defines gender based on a physician's examination of genitalia and explicitly prohibits students in Utah public schools from using a bathroom that does not correspond to their (genitalia-based) gender.[3] These are just three moments of contention about the regulation of bodies entering the public restroom, each of which illustrates the powerful anxieties that space commonly provokes. So pressing and incendiary are these anxieties that broad legislation can be reduced to the single threatening specter of the unregulated public bathroom and the deceptive interlopers it hosts.

The basic concerns present in these debates are not new in themselves. For four decades, advocates have worked to pass nondiscrimination ordinances at the state and local levels that cover transgender people's use of public accommodations, and bathrooms regularly emerge as a sticking point in these efforts. For example, St. Paul, Minnesota's policy first included transgender people in 1975, and local transgender activists recall that it faced considerable resistance for decades, with opponents "attempting to exploit fears about trans people and bathrooms" to overturn the ordinance.[4] Increasingly, though, legislative and public responses to bathroom debates reflect the anti-immigrant and antiterrorism frameworks that intensified after 9/11. In particular, this chapter shows how a discourse of deception and an investment in biometric surveillance practices shape public and legal approaches to gendered bathrooms.

Beginning with Arizona state legislators' challenge to the Phoenix ordinance in 2013, bathroom policies not only explicitly criminalize those determined to have entered the bathroom improperly, but also base that determination on specific body parts—such as genitals or chromosomes—framed as natural and unchanging. This chapter argues for understanding such bathroom scrutiny in the context of biometric surveillance, which promises objective identification of individuals through the assessment of presumably immutable physical characteristics. Biometric data are typically considered harder to falsify and therefore more objective than ID documents. While fingerprinting has long been a familiar form of biometric data collection to track and identify criminalized persons, biometric surveillance practices garnered renewed state and public interest after 9/11. Government officials vigorously pursued an array of biometric technologies as strategies to guard against terrorism and to track people crossing U.S. borders. By insisting on the primacy and factuality of the physical body for identification, criminalizing bathroom surveillance employs the basic logic of biometrics. Moreover, because public bathrooms have always been sites through which good citizenship is produced and access to public space managed, that surveillance functions as one component of the anti-immigrant and antiterrorism biometric programs intended to reinforce spatial boundaries and identify threatening outsiders in the name of public safety.

Bathroom surveillance often appears as a matter of public safety rather than as surveillance per se, and rationalizing bodily scrutiny in this way allows concepts like "the general public" and "safety" to stand unquestioned as common sense; those bodies understood as wrongly moving into certain spaces are discursively disassociated from the public because they jeopardize safety. In this way, surveillance of public bathrooms helps produce ideals of good citizenship and determine the parameters of citizenship by delimiting access to public space. The space of the bathroom may seem quite minor in relation to the vast scope—and effects—of antiterrorism and anti-immigration projects, but I show here how bathrooms can highlight the relationship between those larger projects and the everyday surveillance practices that regulate citizenship and participation in public life. If, as Isaac West observes, use of the public bathroom is "one of the most, if not *the* most, quotidian practices of citizenship," then this chapter argues that surveillance criminalizing public bathroom use is one element of a larger effort to secure citizenship and spatial belonging through the apprehension of physical difference.[5]

Civilizing Spaces

As intentional public spaces, bathrooms in the United States emerged out of growing investments in cleanliness and public health in the late nineteenth century, and they were meant to project ideals of modernization and civilized social practices. Because they were initially created for men, early public bathrooms implicitly coded those ideals (and public space more generally) as masculine. At their core, these two concepts supported one another: if civilized, respectable womanhood—an idealized gendered position built on whiteness and class privilege—entailed detaching women from the dirtiness and sexualization so often associated with excretion, and if it also entailed linking women to the domestic rather than the public sphere, then the absence of public bathrooms for female-assigned bodies aligned with both of these social standards.[6]

Yet white middle-class women entered public space in greater numbers during this period, in part via new roles in factory labor. Sex separation in public spaces, including workplace bathrooms specifically designed to separate men from women, developed "as a kind of cure-all for the full range of social concerns surrounding factory women" and as support for stricter sanitation policies.[7] Business owners and legislators framed gendered bathrooms as protective measures for white women, whom they positioned both as the virtuous, civilizing backbone of Victorian society and as especially vulnerable to the immoral world outside of the domestic realm. But because gendered bathrooms were constructed to alleviate the social upheaval provoked by white women's increased participation in public space, these bathrooms actually protected the social hierarchy that designated the public arena as white men's domain. In this way, such spatial boundaries respond to and reinforce broader investments in the purity of not only individual bodies, but also social morals and national identity. The residue of that initial moral framework for public bathrooms lingers in more recent arguments that these public spaces must be rigidly sex-segregated and policed accordingly to protect vulnerable citizens—commonly portrayed as white women and children. While the gendered public bathroom may make possible a fuller form of citizenship and greater public participation for certain groups, it does so through protectionism that reiterates those groups' unfitness for general public space, and it implicitly and explicitly casts others as threats to public safety.[8]

Figure 3.1 Lauren Quock, *White/Colored, Men/Women* (2011).
Acrylic on wood, 10 × 14 inches. Courtesy of the artist.

Sex-segregated bathrooms in the United States emerged roughly concurrently with the institutionalization of racially segregated bathrooms and other public spaces, as part of Jim Crow laws intensifying after the 1896 *Plessy v. Ferguson* decision. Work that considers these historical links often positions raced and gendered bathrooms as parallel boundaries rather than as mutually constitutive ones. For example, California-based visual artist Lauren Quock created a 2011 series titled *Modified Bathroom Signs*, which the artist's statement describes as "deconstructing antiquated definitions" to "transform sites of rejection into sites of resonance and affirmation for people who exist across the gender spectrum."[9] The series revises standardized "men" and "women" bathroom signs typical of public restroom doors in the United States, and produces new signs such as "butch," "fabulous," and "queer." The final piece in the series, titled *White/Colored, Men/Women*, remakes a 1931 race-segregated drinking fountain sign from Alabama by painting over the entire sign in black (figure 3.1). With the original raised letters now only vaguely visible, new lettering in white overlies them: *Restroom* over the words *Drinking Fountain*, *Men* over *White*, and *Women* over *Colored*. The piece works to bring race and gender together: the vaguely visible words of the original sign indicate that racially segregated public space is fading away though its fundamental remnants linger in more clearly marked gender divisions. This imagined decline of racial segregation suggests that the construction of racialized space informs current gendered divisions, with racial difference always present in gender difference. At the same time, the artwork's format relies on one sign taking precedence over another, a claim highlighted by the color scheme, in which white words about gender literally write over a black background obscuring words about race. The near erasure of the original words may imply that racially segregated spaces are relegated to the past, and the substitution of nouns suggests that gendered bathrooms have taken the place of raced ones. The date and location marked on the original sign are painted over in black but not replaced by new words, situating race-segregated spaces in a past time and a specific location, while evoking a timelessness and omnipresence of gendered bathrooms.

In making these moves, the sign cannot account for the continued racial division of public space: while perhaps not overtly marked in the same way as drinking fountain signs, the routine surveillance and criminalization of people of color in public spaces ranging from sidewalks to public schools makes clear that spatial boundaries have not simply shifted away from race onto gender.[10] This is true even in the specific case of public bathrooms, since racial segregation by neighborhood remains entrenched throughout the United States.[11] Because racial divisions of public space encompass public bathrooms, those bathrooms are informally racially segregated as part of larger patterns of raced spatial boundaries. The *White/Colored, Men/Women* piece literally glosses over these conditions, representing race and gender as related but sequential categories of difference such that gender divisions are the new version of spatial segregation.[12]

In ways that are perhaps less starkly drawn, much scholarly work also tends to conceptualize raced and gendered bathrooms as two different but parallel spaces. Philosopher Richard Wasserstrom argues that racially segregated bathrooms, like gendered bathrooms, fundamentally depend on anxieties about hygiene and purity, both materially and metaphorically: the point of separating these spaces by race was not so much to prevent different races from using each other's toilets, he contends, but to ensure that Black people "would not contaminate bathrooms used by whites."[13] This rationale both drew on and developed perceptions of Black people as inherently unclean, set in contrast to whiteness as the purest and most advanced racial category. It is no surprise that the space of the bathroom—that space hosting a variety of behaviors and bodily functions associated with dirt, waste, and disgust—plays a key role in marking certain groups as more or less civilized than others.[14] Despite drawing these connections in his discussion of racially segregated bathrooms, Wasserstrom argues against their influence on gendered bathrooms. He attributes the latter's creation instead to "the importance of inculcating and preserving a sense of secrecy concerning the genitalia of the opposite sex," an analysis that, as I showed in chapter 2, assumes as universal a sexual privacy that actually depends heavily on whiteness.[15]

These notions of gendered bodily difference are fundamental to racial and national formations, a point made particularly clear in the way that segregated bathrooms developed to help construct public space as clean, modern, and civilized. Writing about the concept of civilization in the late nineteenth-century United States, Gail Bederman describes it as an "explicitly racial concept" that "denoted a precise stage in human racial evolution": one that had evolved past primitive or barbaric characteristics.[16] Drawing on Darwinism, this logic rationalized white supremacy through claims that people of color simply had not developed in the same ways or at the same rate as white people, situating civilization itself as a racial characteristic and producing and solidifying distinct racial categories.[17] Bederman notes that gender was crucial in distinguishing civilized societies from the less advanced, with the former identified in part by clear binary gender divisions.[18] Greater differences between men and women—in social roles, behaviors, appearances, and adherence to separate spheres—indicated further advancement along the evolutionary scale. In the context of this ideological framework, the institutionalization of separately gendered spaces for public bathrooms in the late nineteenth-century United States is inseparable from the development and maintenance of dominant racial and national identity in that period.

Moreover, in the era of formal Jim Crow, while bathrooms marked for white people were typically separated into men's and women's spaces, those labeled "colored" were often unmarked by gender at all, a practice that aligns with civilizational discourse.[19] If we understand the overt racial segregation of bathrooms in this period to also inherently produce and maintain hierarchies of gender—in which only white people are civilized enough to warrant distinctly gendered spaces, and those gender distinctions likewise cast white people *as* civilized—then we must also consider how today's gendered bathrooms continue to rely on racist conceptions of a modern, civilized society, even if these spaces are no longer formally segregated by race. Even the repeated claim that criminalizing bathroom legislation makes transgender people second-class citizens—which strategically invokes antiracist and civil rights movements of the mid-twentieth-century United States—relies on an understanding of the U.S. as otherwise socially and politically advanced, by relegating racial segregation to the past and implicitly aligning transgender identity with an unmarked whiteness.[20] The second-class-citizen argument works by recalling a shameful racism of the past that is at odds with ideals of the present-day United States as a modern, civilized nation that treats all citizens equally. It warns against returning to that less civilized time in which public bathrooms marked some citizens as less than others, and it implies that the only problem with current bathrooms is a new restriction affecting transgender people. The history of segregated bathrooms and its use in more recent second-class-citizen arguments reflects complicated anxieties about citizenship as both a formal legal status and as a social status that turns on idealized understandings of propriety, morality, and legibility. Strict legal definitions of citizenship are inextricable from the development of ideals of good citizenship that arise through both state actions and "social policies and practices beyond the state that in myriad mundane ways suggest, define, and direct adherence to democratic, racial, and market norms of belonging."[21] Rather than resting on the national progress narrative built into transgender advocates' use of "second-class citizen," the invocation of citizenship in this claim should prompt consideration of how gendered public bathrooms are always sites through which struggles over citizenship and belonging play out.

Bathrooms and Citizenship

Shortly after Phoenix's nondiscrimination law passed in 2013, Arizona state representative John Kavanagh introduced a new statewide bathroom bill, which would criminalize any individual who intentionally entered gendered public spaces—such as restrooms, locker rooms, or dressing rooms—that did not align with the gender marker on that person's birth certificate. The proposed bill, SB 1432, would add such behavior to the state's definition of disorderly conduct, making it a class one misdemeanor subject to six months in jail and a $2,500 fine. The National Center for Transgender Equality and the Transgender Law Center (TLC) dubbed Kavanagh's proposal the "papers, please" bill, and broad opposition by these and other organizations led Kavanagh to withdraw his original proposal, only to introduce a revised version (SB 1045) specifically protecting business owners from being legally required to allow transgender people into gendered restrooms.[22]

Although Kavanagh and other opponents' vehement response might suggest that Phoenix's law was the first to include transgender people in public accommodations nondiscrimination policy, in fact, many such ordinances have been in place at the city and state levels since the late 1970s. Several of these policies are remarkable for their legal definitions of sex and gender, which understand these categories as processes, feelings, or expressions, rather than as obvious facts of birth or body. For example, nondiscrimination ordinances passed in Champaign (1977) and Urbana, Illinois (1979), define *sex* as "the state of being or becoming male or female or transsexual, or pregnant."[23] Ordinances in other locales can be interpreted as addressing transgender identity under other terms; the ordinance for Los Angeles, California (1979), defines *sexual orientation* in terms of "emotional or physical attachment" to another person, but also includes here "having or projecting a self-image not associated with one's biological maleness or one's biological femaleness."[24] Some ordinances explicitly name bathrooms in their definitions of *public accommodations*, while some include single-sex public bathrooms as possible exceptions to nondiscrimination policies. For example, St. Paul, Minnesota's ordinance (1988) states that "nothing in this chapter shall prohibit discrimination on the basis of sex in such facilities as rest rooms, locker rooms, and similar places." But this line need not be understood as requiring people to use gendered bathrooms according to the sex they were assigned at birth, or according to any single physical attribute. Instead, because the ordinance defines *sex* as "having or being perceived as having male or female characteristics," the exception can be interpreted as covering every person's use of the bathroom that aligns with their gendered characteristics, which, like all bodily or behavioral characteristics, might be self-defined or perceived in any number of ways.[25] In such cases, then, the exceptions for gender-segregated facilities may not tighten control over these spaces but actually open them up to more gender possibilities.

In later years, it was precisely these nuanced and expansive definitions that opponents pointed to as creating problems for gender-segregated public spaces, especially bathrooms. Such was the case in 2008 when Gainesville, Florida, amended its nondiscrimination ordinance to include gender identity. The new law defines this term as "an inner sense of being a specific gender, or the expression of a gender identity by verbal statement, appearance, or mannerisms, or other gender-related characteristics of an individual with or without regard to the individual's designated sex at birth."[26] For one city commissioner who opposed the ordinance, this was the central point of contention: "The heart of the definition is not on any type of objective or measurable criteria," he told a local newspaper. "It simply goes on how someone feels, so that is sort of ripe for abuse."[27] This commissioner's statement prefigures the connection between public safety and objective assessment of sex/gender that just five years later would become the hallmark of criminalizing bathroom bills.[28] Yet despite recurring concerns, until 2013 no other state or local public accommodations legislation encompassing transgender identity was met with the kind of explicitly punitive legal response that Kavanagh's Arizona bills proposed.

Because criminalization is fundamental to these bills, so too are questions of citizenship, through which Arizona politics and public life had already been framed. The state's highly controversial anti-immigrant legislation, coalescing in 2010 under the title SB 1070, originally made it a misdemeanor to be in Arizona without valid immigration paperwork, all but requiring immigrants and those who might be perceived as immigrants to carry that paperwork or proof of citizenship with them at all times. The legislation also dramatically increased local law enforcement's power to arrest and detain people perceived as undocumented or deportable. Although the U.S. Supreme Court struck down several components of the law in June 2012, one section remains in play: Section 2(B) mandates that Arizona law enforcement officers check citizenship status of anyone they arrest or detain, and allows them to stop and arrest anyone they suspect may be undocumented. This section of the law became widely known as "show me your papers," and several other U.S. states promptly proposed similar legislation.[29] Many immigrant advocacy and racial justice organizations criticized the law as a codified form of racial profiling.[30]

The criminalizing bathroom bill, which demands that bodies match birth certificates to justify their presence in certain public spaces, echoes and reinforces anti-immigrant legislation requiring bodies to align with documents evidencing their citizenship status. While Kavanagh's bills may be prompted by the nondiscrimination ordinance, their strategic reliance on identity documents merges with Arizona's broader criminalizing practices against immigrants. But these cases are not only about documents as classificatory tools. In each case, deceptive bodies themselves must be identified, marked as deceptive in the act of traversing particular spatial boundaries. The birth certificate and immigration paperwork act almost as afterthoughts, with documents legitimating the policing of bodies already deemed unlawful threats.[31] Moreover, since all such identification documents might be falsified, misread, or otherwise deemed unreliable, these policing practices fundamentally rely on the body as the primary and most accurate form of identification.

It is easy to imagine these connections between citizenship and gender as simply analogous, because the metaphors of travel, citizenship, and mobility are so common in descriptions of transgender identities. These discussions tend to rely on the transgender figure as a white and Western one, narrating transgender travel in the abstract or metaphorical sense: while the immigrant figure may travel between countries, the transgender figure journeys across genders.[32] Even projects seeking to highlight important connections between anti-immigrant and anti-transgender discourse often hinge on a parallelism that attempts to bring two separate sets of regulations together. For example, in 2013 the TLC produced an educational web-based slide show titled "Crossing Borders: Connections between Transgender Equality and Immigrant Rights" that seeks to clarify the overlaps between and "tactics used to divide" these two movements.[33] Several slides with the subheading "Crossing the Border" use a split-screen approach to detail similarities between nationality on one side and sex/gender on the other. In this formulation, the slides instruct that "everyone has a legal nationality" typically determined by place of birth, and "everyone has a legal documented sex" typically determined by the body at birth.[34] More pointedly, "many people are murdered for crossing the border," and "many people are murdered for transitioning," an analogy that reads gender transition as a metaphorical border crossing, if one that may incur the same material punishment as for literally crossing national boundaries.[35]

This TLC project clearly seeks to emphasize the relationship between immigrant and transgender politics, and it ultimately focuses on conditions facing transgender-identified immigrants. But throughout, the slides reference two different sets of policing practices that correspond to two distinct groups in analogous ways. In a split-screen slide explaining how immigrants and transgender people are each made scapegoats for broader social concerns, "homeland security" and threats to neighborhoods appear on the immigrant side, with "deconstruction of family values" and bathroom panic on the transgender side. The larger point made here—that particular social panics attach to different marginalized groups and can pit those groups against one another—is an important one. Yet citizenship status and gender status cannot be pulled apart in any of the slide's examples: just as the previous two chapters of this book traced specific aspects of the Department of Homeland Security that produce and rely on a gendered citizenship, we might consider how campaigns for neighborhood safety and family values regularly invoke a kind of good citizenship that is determined in part through gender attributes.[36] Similarly, public bathrooms are sites in which citizenship and gender are mutually constituted, even if public and legal discourse largely foregrounds gender and sexuality in those spaces.

Multiple media sources set Arizona's criminalizing bathroom bill in the broader context of the state's stringently punitive immigration legislation, but only in terms of bathroom bills being analogous and sequentially related to immigration laws. In a 2013 TLC blog post, attorney Abigail Jensen writes that "instead of our country's immigrant community, SB 1432 has a new target—transgender people and anyone else that police, business owners or other restroom users think isn't 'man' or 'woman' enough to be in a restroom or other sex-segregated facility designated for that sex or gender."[37] She restates this claim in the closing paragraph of her post: "First, Arizona targeted people who look different in terms of race or ethnicity. Now, trans people and anyone else who violates gender norms are in the 'bull's-eye' of the Arizona Legislature." The *Daily Wildcat*, a student-run University of Arizona newspaper, characterizes SB 1432 as "another 'papers' bill," noting that "this time it is policing gender identity."[38] National progressive news outlet *ColorLines* reports, "first Arizona lawmakers went after the immigrant community with SB 1070. Now they're going after transgender people with SB 1045."[39] In all of these analyses, the bathroom bills repackage early immigration legislation, so that two separate marginalized populations—the presumed noncitizen and the gender-nonconforming person—experience similar surveillance, but each in turn.

Arizona legislators may well have strategically copied the SB 1070 model in their efforts to weaken nondiscrimination orders. That their public statements about bathroom policies do not reference the state's immigration laws suggests that they too might view these two sets of legislation as addressing wholly separate issues of citizenship and gender, their only connection the political rhetoric emphasizing deceptive threats to the general public. But the text of the bathroom bills themselves demonstrates how they delimit the practice of citizenship precisely through creating and responding to gender anxieties. Kavanagh's initial bill, SB 1432, proposes a misdemeanor offense under disorderly conduct for entering gendered facilities at odds with one's legal sex classification. In restricting use of gendered public space, this legislation helps define citizenship by granting or limiting full participation in the public sphere. But perhaps most telling are the bill's specific exceptions, including bathroom entrance required by "job responsibilities" or to provide "aid or assistance to another person," including a child.[40] Under these exceptions, certain behaviors that the law would otherwise define as illegal gendered transgressions are excused because they align with an ideal of good citizenship. That is, the gainfully employed and the responsible assistant/parent can cross these gendered boundaries in their role as good (re)productive citizens. In its explicit efforts to address gender, the bill constructs good citizenship as a status marked by characteristics such as productivity, personal responsibility, and family formation.

A third exception in SB 1432 applies to those who are "physically disabled." Although listed alongside the previous two exceptions as if easily equivalent, disability does not signal good citizenship in the same way that (presumably able-bodied and normatively gendered) workers and parents do. On the contrary, disability has historically served as a rationale for denial of citizenship in both the legal and cultural senses.[41] In particular, disability has served as a key exclusionary category in legislation purporting to keep public space safe, especially for women and children.[42] The disability exception specified in SB 1432 therefore works differently from the other two exceptions and might be understood in several different ways. It may be an attempt at compliance with the Americans with Disabilities Act, to expand or ensure accessibility and presumably affirm citizenship through public accommodations. It may be a reflection of the common structure of public restrooms in the United States, in which the symbol for disability (and for legal compliance) typically appears on single-user, gender-nonspecific bathrooms. Or, particularly since the bill is part of a social and moral panic about sexualized threats in bathrooms, this exception may be influenced by long-standing dominant perceptions that people with disabilities are nonsexual; such perceptions could frame disabled bathroom users not as threats to children, but as themselves children, whose bathroom use requires aid or assistance from good (and able-bodied) citizens.[43] The explicit inclusion of disability might both ensure and limit access to the category of citizenship here, demonstrating how regulations like the criminalizing bathroom bills actively construct that category rather than simply protecting it.

The bill's specification of physical disability may be a strategic effort to avoid loopholes that could grant transgender people access to public bathrooms through this legal exception; after all, many legal arguments have positioned transgender identity as a disability to win legal protections, and opponents have often cast transgender identity as mental illness.[44] But this legislative strategy may not even be needed, since the exceptions as a whole already work in at least two contradictory ways regarding transgender people. On one hand, they could nullify the criminality of entering the "wrong" bathroom, provided a transgender person falls under one of the citizen-marking exceptions at the time of entry. On the other hand, they might assume and imply that good citizens are wholly distinct from those whom the bill characterizes as a threat to the general public, such that the exceptions never apply to transgender people at all. Additionally, because the law would typically be invoked only on the basis of individual complaints, it is unlikely to be applied in cases when a transgender-identified person is not perceived as a threat, such as when one's bodily characteristics are read as markers of non-transgender status, of legal citizenship, of membership in the general public. The law attempts to draw clear boundaries, but in practice, interpretations of deceptive threat would surely vary according to context, including a bathroom's location and size, the time of day, and the user demographics, among other factors. So while the exceptions in SB 1432 help define citizenship, they also destabilize that concept: they create allowances for and reiterate the presumed characteristics of good citizenship, a category that can then be put to use in any number of ways.

There is no doubt that the criminalizing bathroom bills in Arizona and elsewhere target gender, but they do not neatly substitute gender for earlier legislation's focus on citizenship. Public bathrooms emerged in the United States as spaces that helped construct the boundaries of citizenship through restrictions that explicitly named race, gender, and disability. This history informs later efforts to restrict access to those public spaces, even when the specific language of such efforts shifts away from citizenship and onto gender. Attending to the citizen-making function of the public bathroom can clarify why this particular form of bathroom bill first appeared in Arizona: not because legislators adapted anti-immigrant laws to address a wholly separate marginalized group, but because questions of citizenship are central to public bathrooms, and so these spaces are already contentious in the context of statewide struggles over identification of citizens and noncitizens.[45] We need only consider the emphasis on birth certificates to understand the extent to which anxieties about citizenship undergird these bathroom scenes, since those documents mark not only state-approved sex designation, but also legal citizen status. In the most formal sense, birth certificates purportedly confirm citizenship and thus one's legal belonging to the nation-state. At the same time, they can serve as evidence of citizenship in a more informal or cultural sense: if producing appropriate paperwork is one way of complying with state regulations and requests, then doing so performs good citizenship. These two conceptions of citizenship work in tandem, since those who cannot or do not produce the required documents appear both to resist the law's demands and to demonstrate their lack of legal citizenship status.

Moreover, the bathroom bills' focus on documentation can overshadow the bodily scrutiny that they ultimately rely on, a somatic assessment performed in order to identify safe or risky individuals, which follows a well-established method of surveillance. After all, the demand for birth certificates as evidence of proper bathroom use is primarily directed at those visually perceived as trespassing in gendered public space. And because state agencies' own conflicting policies already position that paperwork as unreliable, the desire for birth certificates is less a request for appropriate paperwork than an assessment of the body itself, with birth certificates acting as placeholders for sexed bodies.[46] The documents stand in for the physical bodies at the heart of these bathroom scenes, acting as confirmation of the deception already attached to particular bodies. This close attention to the body as objective evidence of belonging (or of danger) draws on the basic logic of biometric surveillance, which, as we will see, is likewise rooted in anxieties about citizenship.

The Bathroom's Biometric Logic

Biometric identification, an approach to the body developed through anthropometry studies and eugenics programs of the nineteenth and early twentieth centuries, eschews unreliable ID documents in favor of linking identity to unique aspects of the physical body, and it has a long history in medical and state surveillance programs.[47] Biometric programs generally treat physical characteristics such as fingerprints, irises, and facial bone structure as immutable. Once catalogued, these physical features serve as comparative data to verify identity as bodies move through different securitized spaces. Because it relies on data recorded directly from the body, biometric identification is often characterized as more accurate and reliable than a corruptible paper trail of ID documents. This assumption lay at the heart of a November 2001 congressional hearing, Biometric Identifiers and the Modern Face of Terror, which singled out biometrics as a crucial tool in identifying terrorists and regulating immigration. Senator Dianne Feinstein (D-CA) introduced the hearings by claiming that the individuals who carried out the airline hijackings of September 11, 2001, were able to do so because "we could not identify them," and by suggesting that biometric technologies like facial recognition software, fingerprint databases, and retinal scans are vital for U.S. national security.[48]

As a set of technologies and identification techniques that had already been steadily integrated into U.S. border control and immigration programs, biometrics gained renewed state and public support after 9/11, when government officials repackaged them as central to counterterrorism efforts.[49] In fact, antiterrorism and anti-immigration discourses merged in part through this support of biometric surveillance: in that same congressional hearing, senator Strom Thurmond (R-SC) called for biometric identifiers for all noncitizens entering the United States, arguing that this practice would help immigration officials identify "terrorists who attempt to cross our borders."[50] So as biometric technologies were folded into the war on terror, their role in regulating immigrant populations and U.S. borders also further solidified. Some of the most high-profile applications of biometrics in the United States are those used to identify terrorist suspects at airports and other travel hubs, or to determine citizenship status at immigration checkpoints.[51] Biometric technologies sort physical characteristics to identify bodies that move across boundaries and into spaces otherwise imagined as secure, promising control over these improper movements.[52] Senator Orrin Hatch (R-UT) argued in 2001 that with the increased use of biometrics as part of border security, "impersonation would be dramatically curtailed, if not eliminated altogether."[53] Likewise, the U.S. Defense Advanced Research Projects Agency, which develops new military technologies, justified its post-9/11 biometric surveillance projects through claims that "terrorists are able to move freely throughout the world, to hide when necessary."[54] These statements fuse terrorism with unregulated immigration by raising the possibility that surveillance systems "cannot clearly differentiate bodies that might bear a close resemblance," a concern fueled by a belief that certain racial groups are not readily distinguishable as individuals.[55] In Lisa Cacho's terms, in the post-9/11 context terror is "grafted" onto illegality, requiring fresh evaluation of those bodies regularly imagined as illegal. "Because Latina/o bodies have rendered the status of illegality recognizable," she writes, "differently racialized unauthorized immigrants unsettle this racial coupling, producing considerable anxiety over not being able to distinguish 'illegal' immigrants from 'fraudulent' foreigners."[56] Biometric surveillance programs respond to this anxiety by emphasizing the body as proof of individual identity, with biometric identification guarding against fraud and securing spaces such as airports and government buildings.

In addition to policing spatial boundaries, biometric surveillance also produces and reinforces the boundaries around categories such as race, gender, sexuality, and citizenship. Notably, it does so by insisting that it operates outside of such categories. Backed by Western science's claim to a neutral gaze and the supposedly unambiguous truth of the physical body, biometric technologies engage bodies as objective data points untouched by social and political influence. But biometric efforts to scientifically distinguish between safe and threatening bodies, or citizen and noncitizen bodies, must account for how these categories are already shaped by gendered and racialized viewing practices. For example, the familiar fingerprinting process can seem utterly disconnected from questions of race or gender because it focuses on unique individual characteristics rather than on groups of people. But Simone Browne shows how "prototypical whiteness" drives fingerprinting: a 2002 fingerprint study determined that people "of Pacific Rim/Asian descent" are likely to have "faint fingerprint ridges—especially female users."[57] In this framework, some types of fingers will produce prints that are less legible than others. Marking bodies belonging to certain races and genders as inherently difficult to assess naturalizes the process by which white and male prints can appear neutral, easily read, and therefore compliant. Similarly, multiple researchers have undertaken studies to categorize fingerprint samples by gender, pointing out patterned differences that might be used to distinguish between male and female prints.[58] Because such investigations presume fixed and universalized definitions of male and female, when bodies do not conform to such definitions, the studies may regard them as fundamentally disruptive or suspicious. In these ways, biometric technologies do not merely record predetermined physical facts but actively generate meanings about the bodies they analyze: certain raced and gendered bodies can serve as normative standards because they are legible and compliant, while others resist the technician's gaze.[59]

Utah's HB 87, proposed in 2014, exemplifies biometric logic in its attempts to regulate gendered bathrooms in the state's public school system. It first revises the Utah Code throughout, replacing the term *sex* with *gender*, yet it relies on sexed terms to explicitly define gender as "the either male or female phenotype designation of an individual."[60] Although the bill cites a birth certificate as acceptable evidence of phenotype designation, it also notes that this document may not exist or may be unreliable. Anticipating the failure of identification documents, HB 87 turns to a rather rudimentary bodily assessment as the final word on gender: without a birth certificate, gender is to be documented by a physician, "based on a physical examination of the individual's genitalia, designat[ing] the individual as either male or female." As part of an effort to maintain strictly segregated bathrooms, this bill ties the space of the bathroom to a dichotomous sex-gender system that relies on legible and stable external bodily characteristics.

But even as the legislation cites a universalized definition of gender in which bodies can be sorted solely by genital appearance, its own labored definitions destabilize that framework. In the section pertaining to public school bathrooms, HB 87 defines gender identity as something separate from gender: it "means an individual's own opinion of whether the individual is male, female, neither male nor female, both male and female, or another designation." By crafting two separate definitions, the legislation can make allowances for public school students whose "consistently asserted gender identity does not strictly correspond to the student's gender." These students may request "alternate bathroom accommodations," even while the bill's purpose is to align bathroom use with genital appearance. Here, then, the bill itself creates space for multiple gender possibilities, yet recognizes only two—male and female—as valid throughout the Utah Code. It conceptualizes gender as "an unchanging biometric characteristic" that depends on physical attributes as its best evidence, but also acknowledges that gender might change both in individual lives (else why specify a "consistently asserted" gender identity?) and in broader social understandings (since the bill's own language imagines ways that gender might be understood outside of male and female).[61] The more the bill attempts to circumscribe gender, the more expansive it becomes.

Arizona's SB 1045 similarly defines "gender identity or expression" as "an individual's self-identification as male, female, or something in between," including "appearance, mannerisms or other characteristics only insofar as they relate to gender with or without regard to the individual's designated sex at birth."[62] The last phrase gestures to the contingent nature of sex (as something that must be designated), but it does so in the context of a legal document intended to further naturalize and enforce dichotomous sex categories. These categories apply not only to physical bodies but to those material spaces that the bill terms "privacy areas," defined as "places of public accommodation where access is restricted based on sex."[63] Even as the bill itself references sex not as simple fact but as something produced through medical and legal discourse, it also refuses this in its claim that privacy occurs not through one's solitude in a space, but through one's sexed sameness with other bodies sharing a space that can be neatly restricted by the very binary sex characteristics that the bill suggests are contingent. The language choices here are curious, since the bill explicitly addresses gender identity and expression in ways that are not necessarily dependent on an assigned sex. This means that although the legislation is presented as a straightforward measure to protect children from being exposed to "naked men in women's locker rooms and showers" (as Kavanagh explains it), its own definitions position these categories as perhaps even more subjective and slippery than would a bill focused solely on the assessment of sexed bodies.[64] In fact, it is difficult to determine what might constitute evidence of improper bathroom use in SB 1045: although the bill specifies that scrutiny of bodies in gendered spaces concerns appearance and mannerisms rather than the (contingently) sexed body itself, its reliance on the dichotomous sex/gender system structuring public bathrooms suggests that transgressions of gendered space are fundamentally based on bodily difference.[65]

These kinds of legislative efforts generate and reproduce gendered meanings about bodies that they insist can be assessed as straightforward biological facts, all while simultaneously undermining the very definitions they themselves construct, thus illustrating some of the contradictions inherent in biometric surveillance. These contradictions do not necessarily undermine the programs' efficacy; in fact, they may even further justify this surveillance by intimating certain bodies' wider threat. For instance, when

Shoshana Magnet explains that "in general people who cannot be easily categorized as either men or women are interpreted as biometric system failures," her claim suggests that bodies perceived as illegible might endanger not only notions of public safety (as in the bathroom scenes that HB 87 conjures) but the reliability of security practices themselves.[66] Notably, the threat that these troublingly out-of-place bodies pose gains traction in part because those purportedly threatened are not neutral or standard bodies either, but rather the bodies of particular women and children positioned as fundamentally in need of protection. Legislative and public discourse on the transgender threat to other gendered bathroom users draws on familiar viewing practices that simultaneously claim bodies as objective, apolitical data points (we can easily know which bodies are women's bodies) and re-iterate a decidedly social and political meaning given to different types of bodies (women's bodies are vulnerable and need special protection). Certain women's and children's bodies will more readily signal vulnerability, a point that public bathrooms themselves underscore, since the history of bathroom segregation rests largely on the protection of white women.[67]

Although they claim objective measurement of physical characteristics, biometrics programs cannot simply be extracted from the sociopolitical meanings attached to the bodies they assess, nor from the ways that those meanings shape biometrics research and development, data collection and interpretation, and screening procedures. Like many surveillance practices, biometric techniques have often initially focused on identifying those specifically classified as risks, such as the noncitizen and the criminal, and gradually expanded to track entire populations. As with national ID cards and airport X-ray screenings, biometric data collection of noncriminalized bodies is often initially met with opposition because it is perceived as "a practice associating 'good citizens' with 'offenders.'"[68] The normalization of fingerprinting and related archives in the late nineteenth-century United States helped shift biometrics away from something targeting individual transgressors, moving instead toward a broader amassing of data that suggested any citizen is potentially criminal. These blurred lines between the categories of citizen and criminal—of safe and risky body—work in tandem with constantly shifting definitions of crime and criminality themselves.[69] In this context, the concept of a dangerous individual must be understood as always in flux: citizenship does not necessarily guard against the potential for criminality to be read onto bodies. Instead, biometric surveillance of all bodies becomes normalized through risk management frameworks under which "all citizens are being reclassified as potential threats to state security."[70] The use of biometric data to track and sort can reshape the category of citizenship that such surveillance purports to merely identify; as Giorgio Agamben notes, "the citizen is thus rendered a suspect all along."[71]

Even while biometric surveillance programs illustrate the instability of divisions between citizen and criminal bodies, they are most popularly employed as a way to reinscribe those divisions by promising to identify certain persons as threats in disguise. Following Senator Feinstein's lament that "we could not identify" those who carried out the attacks on 9/11, government support for increased biometric data collection pointed to bodily truths as safeguards against both terrorism and unregulated immigration. Disavowing sociopolitical influence, biometric surveillance claims to objectively sort individuals along lines of safety and citizenship, reading those qualities through the body itself. The bathroom bills follow this logic, using presumably immutable physical characteristics to determine which bodies are deceptive interlopers. But this relationship goes beyond a shared logical framework: criminalizing bathroom surveillance measures gain traction precisely through their relationship to anxieties about terrorism and immigration. From their initial institutionalization forward, public bathrooms have been a mechanism for assigning citizenship and national belonging through bodily assessment.

Commonsense Citizenship

In her blog post critiquing Arizona's SB 1432, Abigail Jensen points out that regardless of transgender status, under this legislation all people who "violate societal gender norms in some way can be harassed to prove their right to do what every other citizen takes as a given—the right to use a restroom for its intended purpose without harassment."[72] In one sense, this argument highlights how far the bathroom bills' impact might stretch: in addition to legislating punitive measures for those specifically perceived as noncompliant, the bills' threat of punishment also helps enforce normative gender for everyone who participates in public space. But Jensen's claim also suggests that gender-normative citizenship automatically includes unconstrained access to public space, an assumption that overlooks Arizona's newly intensified laws regarding racialized citizenship, even though Jensen herself connects those laws to SB 1432 in the same post. Regulations governing use of public space have long limited participation in public life for many who would fall into Jensen's category of "every other citizen."[73] Regarding bathrooms in particular, the creation of only men's bathrooms in public spaces and workplaces, the absence or disrepair of accessible bathrooms, and the barring of homeless populations from public restrooms all illustrate how bathrooms concretize "architectural and political assumption[s]" of certain bodies as ideal citizen bodies.[74]

Asking how SB 1432 might be enforced, Jensen notes that "every overzealous restroom patron, security guard, business owner or mere passerby" may participate in that enforcement when confronted with a body that seems out of place in the bathroom.[75] The bill illustrates how enforcement operates not simply through legal code or official state actors, but also through the general public. Even clear compliance with the bathroom bills' gendered requirements cannot ensure access to these spaces, because social or informal surveillance of bathrooms has long been in place for people considered public safety threats or undesirable in public spaces. Those with limited or no access to private space—homeless populations, those living in various forms of public housing, those who spend considerable time in welfare offices and courthouses, and those who rely on public transportation—face the brunt of surveillance of public spaces.[76] Meanwhile, privatization practices increasingly shrink the public sphere, funneling these same populations out of public space into spaces of containment such as the prison and the detention center.[77] Against this backdrop, bathroom bills support a commonsense understanding of belonging in public space that affirms the citizenship of some bathroom users not only through their own bodies but through their ability to assess the bodily attributes said to transparently mark impostors who have improperly entered that space.

Like all boundaries, those related to public bathrooms are porous and contested rather than fixed or self-evident. Functioning as an "object of paradoxical (im)mobility," a spatial boundary (the door to a bathroom, the checkpoint at a border) both allows and limits movement.[78] Efforts to quell the anxieties provoked by this intermingling often focus on the bodies moving through a space, rather than on the structure of the space itself. The logic of biometrics is instructive here: just as biometric surveillance approaches the physical body as a fixed and objective entity, it also assumes an inherent stability of geographical and categorical borders.[79] Biometric surveillance focuses attention on identification of individual bodies, deflecting critical assessment of the spaces in which those bodies are situated. So the language of state-funded biometric surveillance projects highlights the concern that certain bodies might move freely within and across U.S. borders, into government buildings, and so on, without questioning the formation and naturalization of those borders and spaces themselves.[80] Nevertheless, state actors themselves rely on movement that disrupts the borders imagined to protect U.S. citizenship and safety. For instance, a 2008 Fox News report considers how state security practices should respond to what the report's title names as the "Changing Face of Terror," or the potential shift from a large centralized organization led by a single individual to smaller global terrorist cells. The article quotes New York City police commissioner Raymond Kelly as saying, "We have vulnerabilities, absolutely. In an open society, you're going to have vulnerabilities."[81] He continues, "In an effort to close every gap, federal, state and local law enforcement agencies across the country are increasingly sharing their intelligence data." Here, simplified ideals of Western democracy suggest not an alternative to increased policing and border fortification, but rather justification for that policing. The space opened by democratic ideals becomes the primary reason to "close every gap," a closing that itself requires another kind of opening, to more freely distribute information and technologies between state agencies. The relationship here between open and closed geographic borders, sociopolitical structures, and information archives is not one of binary opposition and fixed boundaries, but of connection and interdependence.

Public bathrooms are porous spaces formed not through permanent divisions, but through interactions and movement.[82] Discourses of bathroom contagion merge fears of "real germs" with "the fear of the other"; hence, public toilets provoke more anxiety than other germ-riddled public objects like computer terminals and doorknobs.[83] Concerns about bathroom cleanliness are as much about bodily interactions and the difficulty of regulating public space as they are about actual dirt or waste. The racial integration of some U.S. workplaces during World War II, for example, prompted tremendous white anxiety about shared bathrooms, even as Black people had long cleaned toilets and beds, prepared food, and cared for children as part of their domestic work in white households. But this "private service work reinforced racialized gender hierarchies in ways that public intimacy undermined them."[84] Despite their imagined reputation as cleanly demarcated spaces that provide individual privacy, public bathrooms actually facilitate the intermingling of bodies.

To manage the tenuous boundaries of the restroom, arguments against public accommodations nondiscrimination orders imagine an audience that takes as given the right to unconstrained and safe bathroom use: the general public. When opponents put the broadly conceived Houston Equal Rights Ordinance to a popular vote in 2015, their bathroom-focused campaigns constructed certain public bathrooms (and citizen users) as especially threatened. A video produced by Campaign for Houston, a group formed in August 2015 specifically to counter the ordinance, depicts a multistall public restroom with a door sign using the standardized symbol for women and the international symbol of access. As a white man enters this door and uses the sink and towel dispenser, a voice-over intones, "Houston's Proposition 1 bathroom ordinance: what does it mean to you? Any man at any time can enter a woman's bathroom simply by claiming to be a woman that day. No one is exempt. Even registered sex offenders could follow women or young girls into the bathroom, and if a business tried to stop them, they'd be fined." At this point, a young white girl wearing a skirt and carrying a backpack enters the frame, walking into one of the bathroom stalls. The voice-over continues, "Protect women's privacy. Prevent danger. Vote no on the Proposition 1 bathroom ordinance. It goes too far." On this last sentence, the man opens the stall door, and the girl turns around and looks up at him with an expression of surprise and apprehension.[85] A similar video opposing Delaware's Senate Bill 97 in 2013 begins with mostly white children at a public park and depicts a young blonde girl entering a park bathroom marked "women." The footage shifts from color to black and white as a white man wearing sunglasses looks around furtively before following her in. A title card is then displayed: "Is this what you want for Delaware?" The video's only audio is children's laughter as they play in the park.

Both of these videos speak to a particular kind of public bathroom, one that is understood to be private and safe unless the new law passes. By taking bathrooms frequented by white children and families as representative, the campaigns rely on a universalized notion of the sex-segregated public bathroom as safe, even naming that space as a "sanctuary."[86] Absent from these videos are the violence and harassment—often at the hands of law enforcement—common at public bathrooms in areas with high rates of homelessness, poverty, drug use, public sex, or sex work. Because such spaces are already coded as unsafe, their depiction would disrupt the sanitized vision of bathroom as sanctuary. Yet these less ideal bathrooms and their users shadow the videos, which reenact the quotidian surveillance practices that hinder marginalized people's use of public spaces. Like much of the public and state discourse demanding sex-segregated bathrooms, the videos implicitly encourage viewers to be suspicious of other bathroom users. The racist history of both public bathrooms (including early bathrooms' gender divisions only for white people) and sexual violence (including sexual violence committed by white men against women of color, alongside the persistent myth of the Black male rapist) continues to shape dominant understandings of which bodies pose threats in the bathroom.[87] The videos' narrative draws on long-standing anxieties about public sex and sexual purity, invoking the specter of the sex offender that endangers the childhood innocence regularly assigned to white girlhood.[88] Against the reality of sexual assault and child abuse, this narrative displaces the statistical likelihood of domestic and intimate partner violence onto "stranger danger" in public spaces. And while state governments insist their primary goal is safety for women and girls, many have simultaneously defunded the social services and political organizations working to dismantle rape culture and directly address sexual violence.[89]

The common rhetorical turn to privacy and security for some citizens belies the ongoing erosion of those protections for other groups.[90] North Carolina's notorious HB 2, enacted in March 2016, repeals a citywide nondiscrimination ordinance in Charlotte and is titled the Public Facilities Privacy and Security Act. This law is especially noteworthy because it is the first criminalizing bathroom bill to be enacted on the state level, because it nullifies previously existing local ordinances protecting LGBT people and sets standards for specific groups protected under any future ordinances, because it limits how North Carolina residents can legally pursue claims of discrimination, and because it bars local jurisdictions from raising the minimum wage or changing certain other work and wage laws. The bill's purported concern for women and children is limited at best. Although HB 2 is titled in terms of security, its prohibition against raising the minimum wage strikes directly at the security of the working class, within which women of color are often the most economically vulnerable. Governor Pat McCrory explained that had he not signed the bill into law, "the expectation of privacy of North Carolina citizens could be violated."[91] Of course, taken to its logical end, HB 2 would require bodily exposure of all bathroom users to ensure the kind of sexed sameness that defines privacy here. McCrory's claim is further undercut by the fact that many North Carolinians already have little expectation of bodily privacy. For instance, beginning January 2016, the state required abortion providers to send ultrasound images and fetal measurements to the Department of Health and Human Services when performing abortions after the sixteenth week of a pregnancy.[92] North Carolina is also among many states that mandate drug testing or screening for public assistance recipients.[93]

Claims of protecting privacy through requirements of public exposure can produce complicated rhetorical maneuvers, as when Virginia state delegate Mark Cole introduced HB 663 in early 2016. The bill requires gender-designated public facilities to "solely be used by individuals whose anatomic sex matches" that designation, and it explicitly defines anatomical sex as "the physical condition of being male or female, which is determined by a person's anatomy."[94] In response to media reports that this bill would therefore require public school employees to check students' genitals before allowing entrance into bathrooms, Cole released a statement of clarification on his professional website. His statement first emphasizes that HB 663 is "common sense legislation designed to protect the privacy of children and adults," but insists, "it does NOT require genital checks." Instead, "the legislation would be enforced on a complaint basis."[95] This last clarification is important, because much of the rationale for criminalizing bathroom bills rests on the "common sense" nature of sex-segregated bathrooms and of distinguishing between male and female bodies, between those who belong in the women's bathroom and those who do not. Illinois state representative Tom Morrison, who introduced that state's bathroom bill for public schools, repeatedly emphasizes in interviews and on his professional website that this type of policy is "reasonable, its [sic] rational, its [sic] common sense."[96]

This universal frame of recognition is central to biometric surveillance programs, which rely on the notion of objective bodily differences to help distinguish good citizens from dangerous threats. At the 2001 congressional hearings on biometrics, Joseph J. Atick testified as an industry expert on behalf of Visionics Corporation, a major developer of facial recognition technology. His statement carefully delineates between surveillance of terrorist or criminal bodies and maintenance of privacy for citizen bodies: "The concern for privacy has to do with the misconception that this is an ID system that is identifying every one of us. This is not a national ID system. It does not identify you or me. It is simply a criminal and terrorist alarm. If your face does not match one on the database, on the watchlist, there will be no alarm."[97] This reassurance assumes an easily recognizable difference between the criminal and "you or me." It invokes a solid boundary between citizenship and criminality, yet it simultaneously demonstrates how that boundary shifts, for the facial images captured by Visionics are legible only through a particular frame of reference. Atick's statement implies that this frame is neutral, but his own face helps illustrate its subjectivity: a 2002 *New York Times* profile featured his work and photo as "The Face of Security Technology," a phrase referencing his facial recognition software and positioning Atick—and his face—as exemplary of security and good citizen status.[98] At the same time, U.S. media and government discourse repeatedly employ the phrase "faces of terror" to describe images of those involved in the attacks on 9/11, bodies marked as utterly outside of whiteness and Americanness.[99] The repetition of paired visual and linguistic references to these opposing faces—one connoting security, the other threat—helps create the commonsense frame through which other faces can become legible in terms of risk.

Likewise, the shared commonsense perception of transgender women as deceptive men makes possible a continuity between the "man in a dress" rhetoric justifying bathroom bills as safeguards against deception, and the video campaigns that depict men sneaking into bathrooms wearing trousers (and, in the Delaware video, a beard). Yet retorts to this logic have likewise relied on commonsense recognition of gender difference and good citizenship. In 2015, a social media campaign against bathroom bills featured primarily white, gender-passing transgender people's self-portraits in the public bathrooms that new laws would require them to use. A bearded transgender man, for instance, took a photo of himself in a restroom designated for women, adding the caption "Do I look like I belong in women's facilities?"[100] A transgender woman in Texas posted a photo of herself in a low-cut dress next to urinals, surrounded by men, with the caption "Houston, do you *really* want me in the same restroom as your husband or boyfriend?"[101] Though intended to undermine the logic of the bathroom bill, these images also make claims that gender difference should be obvious and universally recognized, even if based here on facial features and body shape rather than on genitals or chromosomes. Both of these images defend transgender people by arguing for the protection of (non-transgender) women—one implies women's discomfort in sharing a bathroom with someone who does not look like he belongs there, and one implies the threat to heterosexual women's monogamous relationships when some women interact with men in the restroom—and they help construct the category of the general public as one invested in that protectionism and made up of rational citizens who deserve bathroom safety and comfort.

As the captions for these images suggest, gender-passing white transgender people are far more likely to be interpreted as members of the general public than as the deceptive criminals that bathroom bills conjure. Representative Cole's reassurance that enforcement is based on individual complaints is an important reminder that bathroom bills function only through an everyday social surveillance that far exceeds the law itself. These surveillance practices rely on a belief that we know who does and does not belong, knowledge that is in turn based on bodily characteristics presented as both transparent and commonsense. Recall that the Delaware video includes no spoken audio and only a single written question ("Is this what you want for Delaware?"), confident that its visual content will be instantly familiar to viewers like "you or me."

The general public—that group of citizens under the bathroom bills' protection—develops through this everyday surveillance, which the legislation codifies and encourages. As anti-immigrant and antiterrorism programs take up biometric surveillance tactics with renewed fervor, criminalizing bathroom bills carry those ideological and material practices into the quotidian space of the public restroom, relying on objective physical characteristics to define spatial belonging. Investment in and defense of the bathroom's boundaries help constitute citizenship itself: claims to good citizenship entail not only evidence of bodily stability and legibility—and therefore somatic difference from the bathroom interloper—but also active scrutiny of other bodies' potential trespasses. The legislative positioning of transgender bodies as threats demands complicity in bathroom surveillance as part of non-transgender status, naturalizing the process that constructs some bodies as standard, easily interpreted, and inherently compliant. One's identification of bodily difference and illegibility in others can thus confirm one's own belonging. And because the space of the bathroom is central to the development and maintenance of U.S. national identity, this belonging applies not only to the bathroom itself, but also to the category of citizenship that the public bathroom helps construct and maintain.

CHAPTER FOUR

SENSITIVE INFORMATION
IN THE MANNING CASE

IN MAY 2016, attorney general Loretta Lynch announced that the U.S. Department of Justice would file a federal civil rights lawsuit against the state of North Carolina, based on the discriminatory nature of HB 2. Like much of the news media coverage of bathroom bills, Lynch framed HB 2 as a backlash against liberal inclusion. "This is not the first time that we have seen discriminatory responses to historic moments of progress for our nation," she stated, citing as examples Jim Crow laws, resistance to racial desegregation, and state bans on same-sex marriage.[1] She continued, "Let us not act out of fear and misunderstanding, but out of the values of inclusion, diversity, and regard for all that make our country great." In the final lines of her statement, Lynch spoke "directly to the transgender community itself.... No matter how isolated or scared you may feel today, the Department of Justice and the entire Obama Administration wants you to know that we see you; we stand with you; and we will do everything we can to protect you going forward."

For many, Lynch's statement marked a historic moment of recognition for transgender people in the United States.[2] But others were skeptical of her promise, pointing out that the Department of Justice incarcerates over two million people in the United States and asking how Lynch's statement relates to the transgender people who are part of that population. "Even as Lynch and the rest of the Obama administration say that they 'see' trans people," two activists wrote, "they are also responsible for the vast criminal legal system that invisibilizes and victimizes so many trans people. And when compared to the realities of detention and incarceration for trans people, Lynch's historic words have a double meaning: Once locked up, trans people are no longer worth protecting."[3] Their argument about this invisibility considers both Lynch's failure to mention incarcerated transgender people and "the inconsistency between her words and the treatment of incarcerated trans people during her tenure."[4] On this last point, they cite in particular the case of Chelsea Manning. At the time of Lynch's statement, Manning was incarcerated in Fort Leavenworth penitentiary, a men's facility, where administrators repeatedly refused her the right to grow her hair longer than male military standards. For these authors, Manning's case illustrates the Department of Justice's failure to "see" transgender women as women, as well as the ways that incarcerated transgender people remain largely hidden to—and by—the very state agencies that promise protection.

Yet Manning's case speaks to an even more complicated relationship between transgender politics and questions of visibility. An army intelligence analyst, Manning became a whistle-blower who leaked hundreds of thousands of classified military documents as well as diplomatic cables. She was convicted in 2013 on multiple counts, including violations of the Espionage Act. In order to speak to her state of mind at the time of the leaks, during pretrial hearings Manning's defense team introduced the argument that she struggled with her gender identity. For instance, the defense asked a witness if he recalled an email Manning had sent "with a picture of [her]self dressed as a woman . . . and how [her] gender identity affects [her]," as well as "how it impacts [her] ability to think."[5] As media coverage amplified this legal strategy, Manning's transgender identity—which she claimed explicitly in statements immediately following her sentencing—became a key factor in an already highly publicized (if not altogether public) military trial.

The gender-nonconforming figure that Manning represents, or is made to represent, shifts away from those figures that the U.S. government has most often positioned as threats to national safety, particularly in the context of anti-immigrant and antiterrorism programs. As a white U.S. citizen who not only served in the military but had been granted security clearance to top secret materials, Manning departs significantly from the racialized, covert figures of the terrorist agent and the undocumented immigrant that U.S. state policy and practices most commonly cite as threatening. At the same time, as a member of the military, she was subject to the routine forms of surveillance overseeing all enlisted people, and particularly those working as intelligence analysts. Because she was positioned in these two ways at once—already under greater oversight by nature of her military service and not legible as one of the major types most commonly named as hidden dangers—Manning was far less visible to military surveillance technologies as a potential threat.

Focusing on the testimony, evidence, and social context of Manning's trial, this chapter considers how explicitly marking Manning as a transgender figure assists both the defense and prosecution, and ultimately helps normalize the very forms of militarized harm that Manning sought to publicize. I show how the trial links the secrecy of her gender with the secrecy of her whistle-blower actions, a process that guides public attention away from the U.S. government and toward an individual who must be exposed. Although this chapter draws heavily on Manning's own written words and spoken testimony, I make no claims as to the truth of her legal case or her identity. Rather, I wish to show how an implicit and explicit narrative of transgender deception supports the trial's own focus on finding the truth—of Manning's gender, emotional life, intentions, and actions—in order to direct scrutiny toward a specific individual and away from harms committed by U.S. military forces and foreign policy.

Seeking Evidence

Manning entered the army in 2008, and one year later was deployed to Iraq, where she worked as an analyst. According to various testimony and material evidence, Manning began collecting information to leak just a month or two after she arrived in Iraq. Beginning in January 2010, she provided to the whistle-blower website WikiLeaks first a set of hundreds of thousands of SigAct logs—"significant activities," or logs of incident reports—from the wars in Afghanistan and Iraq, and then the video that came to be known as "Collateral Murder," showing a 2007 army helicopter attack that resulted in multiple civilian injuries (including two children) and deaths (including two Reuters journalists). She also leaked over 250,000 U.S. diplomatic cables and other classified or sensitive materials, most of which WikiLeaks subsequently released in the latter half of 2010. Many other materials Manning provided, including over seven hundred classified and internal files about detainees held at Guantánamo Bay, were not made publicly available until 2011. In May 2010, Manning contacted former hacker Adrian Lamo over instant messaging chat, reaching out to him because he had been publicly supportive of WikiLeaks and because she believed he was "someone who would possibly understand."[6] Over the course of these chats, Manning discussed her family and childhood, her feelings of fear and isolation in the military, and her convictions about leaking important information she had access to as an analyst. For instance, she asked Lamo, perhaps rhetorically, "If you had free reign over classified networks for long periods of time . . . and you saw incredible things, awful things . . . things that belonged in the public domain, and not on some server stored in a dark room in Washington DC . . . what would you do? [. . . materials] explaining how the first world exploits the third, in detail, from an internal perspective?"[7]

In her first exchanges with Lamo, Manning identified herself not by name but as "an army intelligence analyst, deployed to eastern baghdad, pending discharge for 'adjustment disorder' in lieu of 'gender identity disorder.'"[8] Within the first ten minutes or so of their chat, Lamo reassured her, "I'm a journalist and a minister. You can pick either, and treat this as a confession or an interview (never to be published) & enjoy a modicum of legal protection."[9] Yet a few days later, Lamo arranged a meeting with the FBI and provided a copy of the chat logs to *Wired* magazine editor and former hacker Kevin Poulson. By the end of May 2010, Manning was arrested, held at Camp Liberty in Iraq for a pretrial confinement hearing, and later transferred to Camp Arifjan in Kuwait.[10] Approximately one month later, she was transferred to Quantico, Virginia, where she was designated a "maximum custody" prisoner on "Prevention of Injury" and "Suicide Risk" statuses.[11] By the time of her arraignment in late February 2012, Manning had been in pretrial confinement for over six hundred days.

Manning's case both aligns with and breaks from the common relationship between state surveillance practices and gender nonconformity. Consider, for example, the case of Duanna Johnson, who in February 2008 was arrested in Memphis, Tennessee, on charges of prostitution that were later dropped. A Black transgender-identified woman, Johnson was held in a county jail where, according to her statements, white booking officer Bridges McRae called her a faggot and a he-she, using both masculine pronouns and Johnson's masculine birth name. When she refused to respond to these names, McRae beat and maced her; another officer held Johnson in her seat during part of this assault, and an attending nurse later examined McRae rather than Johnson. Johnson's case is not particularly unusual among the high rates of violence against and incarceration of transgender women of color, but it is fairly unique in that a surveillance camera installed by the correctional facility captured these events.[12] Johnson's attorney leaked the surveillance footage to a local news station, and the video quickly went viral on the internet. Both officers involved were fired, and Johnson filed a lawsuit against the city. In November of that year, she was found murdered on the streets of Memphis, with police claiming they had no suspects. After a mistrial, McRae pled guilty to the beating and was sentenced to two years in prison.[13]

The surveillance camera in Johnson's case, constructed to visually track the criminalized bodies being processed at the jail, also created a record of physical state violence against one of those bodies, and so it potentially undermines its own intended purpose by turning on the state actors it was meant to support.[14] But the video footage cannot be understood in isolation from the power dynamics at work in this specific interaction or from the social and political context in which these images circulate. As Judith Butler cautioned in the aftermath of the Rodney King verdict, "to the extent that there is a racist organization and disposition of the visible, it will work to circumscribe what qualifies as visual evidence, such that it is in some cases impossible to establish the 'truth' of racist brutality through recourse to visual evidence."[15] Butler's analysis has renewed salience in the context of national calls to mandate body cameras for police officers as preventative measures against police killings of Black people. Critics of this proposed solution observe that cameras worn by law enforcement "are oriented not toward police officers, but rather toward the public" and that the resulting footage, which must be interpreted by law enforcement and court systems, often works against defendants and victims of police violence rather than ensuring police transparency or accountability.[16] Though the surveillance footage from body cameras and county jails may help make visible the inner workings of the U.S. policing system, that visibility is partial at best, filtered through structural racism, sexism, and transmisogyny that shape the visible and the very act of seeing.[17] This constellation of factors made it possible for McRae to file an assault charge against Duanna Johnson, using the surveillance camera footage as visual evidence to argue that she swung at and verbally threatened him. While these images might illuminate state violence, they also reenact violence against Johnson, both in their visual repetition of assault and in their provision of repeated opportunities for viewers to carefully examine Johnson's body and behaviors for evidence of deviance or noncompliance.[18] Johnson's case is a stark reminder that for many people, neither surveillance practices nor explicit visibility as transgender provide protection. Instead, surveillance measures rely on and reinforce the purportedly commonsense sorting between those people in need of protection and those they must be protected from. So even visual evidence that ought to clearly mark law enforcement as acting improperly can serve to reconsolidate police power as that which always acts with necessary force: interpreted in a field of vision wherein Johnson's body already represents criminality and resistance to authority, these surveillance images operate as punitive rather than protective for her.

Complicating this framework, Chelsea Manning's case makes state violence visible not simply through routine surveillance footage but through Manning's deliberate and sustained efforts to publicize classified government materials (and later, the conditions of her own incarceration). Although she navigated military service during the period of Don't Ask, Don't Tell, until she was identified as the source of the leaks her subject position as a white U.S. citizen and service member helped mitigate the possibility of being unduly scrutinized.[19] Because as a military intelligence analyst she was herself a state actor, Manning can be understood as the surveillance mechanism itself, performing that role first on behalf of the U.S. military and later on behalf of the U.S. public by deliberately turning the government's own surveillance practices back onto itself. The publicity surrounding her trial necessarily increased public awareness of the leaked information, further amplifying the material evidence of harmful military actions. But in concert with news media reports, the trial frames Manning's case as one primarily concerned with individual transparency. The defense's introduction of Manning's gender identity suggests a belief that it would benefit her case, but throughout the trial gender secrets join with state secrets such that a visible transgender identity not only helps position Manning as a deceptive individual who is not what she seems, but also justifies intensified surveillance over that individual.

A Very Private Struggle

In June 2010, when *Wired* magazine initially published the Manning-Lamo chat logs—in which Manning claimed responsibility for the leaks—those transcripts consisted only of heavily edited excerpts. *Wired* writers explained that the magazine had not published a complete transcript because the logs "included sensitive personal information" about Manning and also because the editors wanted to "avoid inadvertently revealing sensitive military information."[20] By June, WikiLeaks had already released some of the materials Manning leaked, including the "Collateral Murder" video, so the *Wired* writers' concerns about sensitive military information were unsurprising. It was less clear at that time how Manning's personal information might also be sensitive. This information only emerged for a wider audience in December 2011, when Manning's defense attorneys introduced her gender and sexuality as topics during pretrial hearings, suggesting that the related emotional difficulties influenced her decision to leak classified documents.[21] The implied relationship between these two sets of sensitive information—the classified military documents and the news of Manning's gender identity— helps connect Manning's transgender status to actions that the U.S. government defines as treasonous. At times used as evidence of Manning's emotional distress and isolation under Don't Ask, Don't Tell, this defense strategy necessarily tapped into protracted debates about whether the very presence of LGBT people in the U.S. military compromises national security.[22] In Manning's case, these debates further dovetail with the cultural positioning of transgender people as inherently deceptive.[23] So although her attorneys raised the issue of gender identity to make an argument about her state of mind and not necessarily to suggest causality, it proved difficult to leverage this argument without giving some credence to the theories that transgender people—and perhaps LGB people by association—erode national security and are unfit to serve.[24]

From the first day of the trial, June 3, 2013, Manning's defense team set her leaks of classified information in the context of her inner emotional life. Lead defense attorney David Coombs noted in his opening statement that "Manning is not a typical soldier," and explained that her humanist belief in the value of all human life led her to struggle with her work as an analyst.[25] He elaborated, "The reason why [she] started to struggle was no longer could [she] read SigActs or human reports and just see a name or number. . . . And [her] struggles were public. [She] was struggling not only with the feeling of obligation and duty to people, but also with the struggle and internal struggle, a very private struggle with [her] gender. And this was public for [her] unit to see."[26] This opening statement—a narrative setting the stage for the trial to come—merges Manning's concerns about U.S. military actions with her struggle to come to terms with transgender identity. Notably, it is Manning's commitment to humanism that Coombs cites as the reason she is not a typical soldier, suggesting that her investment in protecting human life is atypical for the U.S. military, even though that body formally rationalizes many of its actions as forms of protection and humanitarianism.[27]

Coombs's brief mention of Manning's gender struggles stands on its own in the opening statement, requiring no further explanation. This is because his statement draws on a familiar understanding of transgender identity formed through Western medicolegal discourse, in which legibility as transgender entails the eventual disclosure of an emotionally burdensome secret and the desire to move linearly to the opposite binary gender category. Coombs relies on this standardized narrative of transgender identity steeped in inner turmoil and private struggle in order to show "what was going on in [his] client's mind."[28] This was not the only defense strategy that Manning's legal team employed; in fact, the trial itself focused more often on Manning's feelings of moral responsibility, and on the particulars of the materials she leaked, than on her gender identity. But by introducing gender as an integral component of the emotional stress Manning suffered, the onerous secret of gender becomes inseparable from the secrecy of her work as an analyst, a combination of stressors prompting what the defense framed as well-intentioned actions to leak classified material.

On the second day of the trial, Coombs questioned Adrian Lamo, the former hacker to whom Manning had confessed the leaks over instant messenging chats. Attempting to clarify the extent of their relationship during that time, Coombs inquires:

Q: During this initial chat conversation [she] told you about [her] life and [her] upbringing?

A: In some amount of detail, yes.

Q: [She] told you that [she] was being challenged due to a gender identity issue?

A: Yes.

Q: [She] also told you that [she] had been questioning [her] gender for years, but started to come to terms with that with [her] gender during the deployment?

A: Yes.

Q: [She] told you [she] believed [she] had made a huge mess?

A: Yes, [she] did.

Q: And [she] confessed [she] was emotionally fractured?

A: Yes.

Q: [She] said [she] was talking to you as somebody that needed moral and emotional support?

A: Yes.[29]

After several more questions regarding the sense of desperation and isolation that Manning expressed, which Lamo likewise confirms, Coombs moves directly into a set of questions about the leaks.

Q: [She] ended up apologizing to you on several occasions for pouring out [her] heart to you since you were total strangers?

A: Correct.

Q: Now at one point [she] asked you if you had access to classified networks and so on, incredible things, awful things, things that belonged to the public domain, not on some servers dark room in Washington, D.C. What would you do? Do you recall [her] asking you that question?

A: Yes, I did.

Q: [She] told you [she] thought that the information that [she] had would have impact on the entire world?

A: That is also correct.[30]

Through this line of questioning, Coombs's approach frames Manning's hidden gender identity as the groundwork that sets the stage for other, larger secrets. By shifting seamlessly between gender concerns and concerns about classified materials, Coombs collapses these two secrets, creating ambiguity about what precisely Manning meant when referring to the "huge mess" or emotional distress. The stress of concealing her gender identity is inextricable here from the stress of concealing vast amounts of state secrets, for Coombs's questions suggest that they are utterly entwined as private emotional struggles. Much media and political discourse followed this model in discussing Manning's case; even commentary that refuted the causality implied by linking transgender identity with national betrayal still tended to accept the premise that Manning was hiding personal struggles with gender identity.[31] During sentencing, the defense called two military psychologists to testify to this end. Both spoke of how the stress of transgender identity combined with and exacerbated other stressors in Manning's everyday life. Captain Dr. Michael Worsley, who treated Manning prior to her arrest, testified that Manning experienced isolation beyond the levels typically created by deployment and by working under top-secret clearance: "being in the military and having a gender identity issue do not exactly go hand-in-hand—it further serves to isolate. [She] finally felt much more comfortable just having it out."[32]

Worsley's testimony may have been a strategy to elicit the court's sympathy, but it also supported the prosecution's narrative of Manning as traitor. Lead prosecutor Major Ashden Fein's closing argument specifically emphasizes that Manning deceived the military, the U.S. public, and the court: "Manning was not a humanist. [She] was a hacker. [She] was not a troubled young soul. [She] was a determined soldier with the knowledge, ability, and desire to harm the United States. [She] was not a whistleblower. [She] was a traitor."[33] Fein's repetitive sentence structure underscores the argument that both during her service and over the course of the trial, Manning was not what she purported to be. Fein does not have to explicitly reference Manning's gender here in order for the notion of transgender deception to support the fundamental argument he makes. In this way, both the defense and prosecution make use of the narrative that Manning's gender deception lay the groundwork for her national deception.

Importantly, however, the chat logs and court testimonies sometimes contradict this framework. In several instances, they illuminate not Manning's psyche or identity—as Coombs's questions attempt to do—so much as the ways that state actors read gender transgression into security discourse. In the chat logs, Manning writes to Lamo that "uncertainty" about gender identity and emotional isolation had made a mess of things, "and little does anyone know, but among this 'visible' mess, theres the mess i created that no-one knows about yet."[34] In light of the fact that *Wired*, military personnel, and Manning's own defense team intentionally delayed making public the gendered aspects of her case, it is noteworthy that Manning herself positions gender questions as visible long before the classified military documents were made public. This timeline is somewhat at odds with the narrative that stressful gender secrets led her to publicize national secrets. In fact, Manning had deliberately provided information about her gender identity to multiple people, both in and outside the military, months before the leaked information surfaced through WikiLeaks.

For instance, in April 2010, Manning sent Master Sgt. Paul Adkins an email titled "My Problem," in which she wrote that the question of gender identity was "not going away, its haunting me more and more as I get older," and attached a photo of herself wearing a blonde wig and lipstick.[35] In mid-2009, before being deployed to Iraq, Manning contacted Lauren McNamara, a transgender activist and blogger, and held extensive discussions with her over instant messenging for several months. McNamara, who testified for the defense, later wrote of that experience, "What I didn't reveal at the trial was that Manning opened up to me in part because we were both gay men. That's not who I am anymore, and by the time Manning contacted Lamo, there were clear signs that [she] too was considering transitioning—signs that any other trans person would see as indicative of someone who was so far into this, they weren't likely to turn back."[36] Indeed, Manning told Lamo, "I already got myself into minor trouble, revealing my uncertainty over my gender identity . . . which is causing me to lose this job," a statement indicating that she had made her gender identity public at least to the extent that she was now being dismissed under Don't Ask, Don't Tell.[37] Although many of these communications clearly indicate that Manning felt some distress related to gender identity and the U.S. military's response to it, the familiar story of transgender identity as inherently characterized by fraught concealment does not fully align with Manning's own narration or actions. Yet by withholding this personal sensitive information—and explicitly marking it as sensitive—the U.S. military and news media reinforce the narrative of secrecy in ways that connect Manning's gender identity to her decision to leak military documents. In this way, they help manufacture a link between gender nonconformity and national security threat.

Manning's own testimony during her trial speaks less to the emotional difficulty of transgender identity than to that of having witnessed U.S. military personnel killing civilians without remorse. Reading from a lengthy prepared statement during her arraignment, Manning explained that the first set of SigActs she released to WikiLeaks constituted what she believed to be "one of the more significant documents of our time, removing the fog of war and revealing the true nature of 21st-century asymmetric warfare."[38] She noted that even before WikiLeaks published the material, "I felt a sense of relief by them having it. I felt I had accomplished something that allowed me to have a clear conscience based upon what I had seen and read about and knew were happening in both Iraq and Afghanistan every day."[39] Regarding the "Collateral Murder" video showing a U.S. aerial weapons team repeatedly firing on children, Reuters journalists, and other civilians with what she described as "seemingly delightful bloodlust," Manning commented, "It's all a big mess and I'm left wondering what these things mean and how it all fits together it burdens me emotionally."[40] She continued, "I hoped that the public would be as alarmed as me about the conduct of the aerial weapons team members. I wanted the American public to know that not everyone in Iraq and Afghanistan were targets that needed to be neutralized, but rather people who were struggling to live in the pressure cooker environment of what we call asymmetric warfare."[41] Manning continually emphasized her belief in the importance of public access to these materials. On the first day of the trial, Coombs's statements framed that commitment to public knowledge as a key aspect of Manning's emotional landscape: her "struggles led [her] to feel that [she] needed to do something, that [she] needed to do something to make a difference in this world. [She] needed to do something to help improve what [she] was seeing. And so from that moment forward, and that was January of 2010, [she] started selecting information that [she] believed the public should hear and should see. Information that [she] believed that if the public saw would make the world a better place."[42] Manning responded to this emotional burden, then, by making public what the U.S. military had categorized as secret, information that Manning believed ought not be concealed from public view.

By folding her "gender identity issue" into her distress about witnessing the effects of asymmetrical warfare, the trial narrates Manning as someone other than she had first appeared: a woman where the army saw a man, a traitor where the government had seen a loyal soldier. The defense seeks to strengthen its case by introducing Manning's transgender status as evidence of the stress and isolation contributing to her "naïve, but good-intentioned" actions.[43] But this strategy also risks strengthening cultural and court beliefs that Manning had merely posed as a patriot—before ultimately betraying her country—just as she masqueraded in terms of gender. Although significant portions of her defense stress the moral and ethical dimensions of her whistle-blowing, the very structure of the trial shifts culpability away from the U.S. government and military: the trial is designed to excavate the truths of Manning's actions. That process is intensified by the prosecution's characterization of her as a duplicitous individual who jeopardized national security, a framing bolstered by dominant narratives of transgender identity.

For the U.S. government, the trial's exposure of Manning makes possible her continued punishment, which in turn helps guard against future leaks. During sentencing, the prosecution asked for sixty years—nearly twice the actual sentence—in order to "send a message to any soldier contemplating stealing classified information," indicating the extent to which the prosecution understood the trial as central to protecting government privacy.[44] Yet achieving this renewed protection by exposing Manning entails publicizing her actions and delving into the specifics of the leaked materials, paradoxically exposing government and military secrets in order to maintain them *as* secret. Throughout the trial process, then, the U.S. government must negotiate a delicate balance between public and private information, visible and invisible actions.

Living an Opaque Life

In her examination of post-9/11 travel regulations, Rachel Hall argues that the framework of the war on terror posits an ever-greater visibility of individuals as the solution to national security concerns: "the aesthetics of transparency belongs to a rationality of government that understands security in terms of visibility."[45] Accordingly, the screening procedures required to grant security clearance to Chelsea Manning in her role as an intelligence analyst make her highly visible to state actors and should, in the framework Hall describes, ensure increased security. Yet the very fact that the U.S. military held Manning so close—that the army had screened, trained, and officially approved this individual service member, who then went on to publicize materials meant to be kept secret—indicates that increased visibility is not the panacea that state policies so often claim it to be. Because those extensive screening processes did not protect the army from information leaks, Manning's case disrupts the notion that greater visibility creates greater security.

To a significant extent, however, visibility remained the standard treatment for the security risk that Manning represented. The conditions under which Manning was held at Quantico while awaiting her trial heavily emphasize detainee visibility. Coombs found these conditions so severe that in December 2010 he published a blog post making them public. He noted that since arriving at Quantico in July that year, Manning had not only been held in "maximum custody," but had been held under Protection of Injury (POI) watch, a status purportedly assigned to ensure that prisoners do not harm themselves. In a six-by-twelve-foot cell by herself, Manning received daytime checks by guards every five minutes. Coombs elaborated, "At night, if the guards cannot see PFC Manning clearly, because [she] has a blanket over [her] head or is curled up towards the wall, they will wake [her] in order to ensure [she] is okay.... When PFC Manning goes to sleep, [she] is required to strip down to [her] boxer shorts and surrender [her] clothing to the guards. [Her] clothing is returned to [her] the next morning."[46] By March 2011, U.S. news media reported even harsher restrictions: Manning was stripped of all clothing at night "as a 'precautionary measure'" to prevent self-injury, according to Quantico officials.[47] Each morning, guards required Manning to stand nude outside her cell for morning inspection. In a subsequent blog post, Coombs noted that a Quantico spokesperson said the forced nudity was "not punitive," but Coombs disputed this claim: "There can be no conceivable justification for requiring a soldier to surrender all [her] clothing, remain naked in [her] cell for seven hours, and then stand at attention the subsequent morning. This treatment is even more degrading considering that PFC Manning is being monitored—both by direct observation and by video—at all times."[48]

For the most part, details of Manning's incarceration at Quantico were shrouded in secrecy and withheld from the public. The spokesperson at Quantico told journalists that he was "not allowed to explain what prompted [the new rule on clothing] 'because to discuss the details would be a violation of Manning's privacy.'"[49] This statement suggests that Manning's privacy had not already been violated through forced nudity, video monitoring, and other regulations. Assigning her to POI status provides justification for her treatment, explaining overt surveillance as an effort to safeguard her health. When Quantico staff claim to protect Manning's privacy and well-being, these statements transfer the burden of transparency onto Manning and away from the U.S. government. Surveillance over Manning in the brig is meant to restore a belief in security through visibility, and the concealment of Quantico's own policies and practices is reassurance that U.S. security and screening systems can still prevent information from circulating in the public realm.

In a manner consistent with many reports about practices in U.S. military and immigration detention facilities, Quantico worked to lay bare the individual detainee while simultaneously concealing that process from public view, with both practices rationalized as part of national security.

Remarkably, the conditions of her own incarceration are precisely the type of information Manning sought to expose through releasing information about other, more sweeping forms of detention. For example, Manning's release of hundreds of files about Guantánamo prisoners—which exposed names and torturous detention conditions as well as the fact that "many innocents or marginal figures [had been] swept up by the Guantánamo dragnet"—was a significant factor in the charges against her.[50] The Guantánamo camps, some of which had previously served as temporary refugee camps for Haitian and Cuban migrants during the mid-1990s, were repurposed after 9/11 as indefinite spaces of detention for people suspected of affiliations with anti-U.S. terrorist groups. The U.S. government readily circulated "depersonalized" images of prisoners in the camps yet also held those individuals in a legally ambiguous space that, in Naomi Paik's terms, rendered them rightless and removed them from the public sphere: "The prisoners have thus been both highly visible and yet shrouded in direct and indirect forms of censorship. Just as the physical bodies of these men have been persistently obscured by the actions of the U.S. government, so too is our understanding of many aspects of life at Guantánamo obscured."[51] For reasons that I clarify in the final section of this chapter, Manning's case is not equivalent to those of the hundreds of people imprisoned at Guantánamo. But these camps inform Manning's own sustained pretrial imprisonment under what the military termed temporary conditions of isolation and POI status. During her arraignment, a Quantico official testified, "Quantico is not about long term—it's about individual short term, but not long term, confinement."[52] The recommended short-term confinement at Quantico is ninety days; Manning was held there for 258 days, spending the majority of those on POI status.[53] Two military psychiatrists who treated Manning testified that these detention conditions were "unprecedented" and "more severe than [those] of death row inmates."[54] Manning's own testimony during her arraignment points to one of these psychiatrists' complicity in extending her temporary status indefinitely: "I started asking [psychiatrist] Captain Hocter why he wasn't recommending me to come off of Prevention of Injury status. He kept saying that he was, but then Gunnery Sergeant Blenis, my counselor, kept on saying it was the docs that were recommending that status. . . . I wasn't sure who was telling the truth."[55]

These types of practices—isolation, high levels of bodily visibility and constant surveillance, and contradictory or undisclosed institutional policies—

mirror many of the aspects of Guantánamo that Manning's leaks made public, and they are not unusual in the context of the U.S. prison system in general, particularly for incarcerated transgender and gender-nonconforming people.[56] In Manning's case, these practices are part of an effort to recuperate national security (and public faith in national security) after her actions had allegedly endangered it. Manning and her defense team repeatedly outlined the care she took to release materials that, even if technically classified, would not actually threaten national security.[57] If the leaks did undermine either national security or the U.S. government's validity, it is not because the leaked materials created new weaknesses, but because the U.S. government and military's own harmful actions—in Iraq, Afghanistan, Guantánamo, and other spaces—became newly visible to the U.S. public through Manning's leaks and the publicity of her trial.[58] Courts-martial have long functioned to secure the respected status of the U.S. military when internal dissent threatens to undermine it. Yet the "legalized spectacle of criminal prosecution" for service members can also erode that legitimacy, since the trial process might reveal internal contradictions, systemic problems, and other damaging information about the U.S. military itself.[59] For this reason, acts of service member misconduct are often addressed in other ways; but if those actions have "undermined faith in American military strength or in the moral and political authority of military institutions," the court-martial can work as a tool to restore faith in that authority both internally and for the U.S. public.[60] The material Manning leaked threatened the military's moral and political authority in just this way, and to mitigate that threat, her trial had to expose Manning as a discrete danger while retroactively safeguarding military secrets that included treatment of Manning during pretrial confinement as well as the hundreds of thousands of documents circulating in the public sphere.

Pretrial motions illustrate the lengths to which the U.S. government would go in order to protect damning information that was in fact already freely available. In an effort to "render the government's case against Manning less secretive," the defense requested access to evidence that the prosecution had not yet provided, including evaluations of how damaging the leaked material had actually been, claiming that without this evidence Manning could not receive a fair trial.[61] The judge ruled that only unclassified material could be disclosed; remarkably, this meant that even the leaked materials—which remained classified despite now being fully accessible to the public—could not be formally disclosed as part of the trial. Likewise, the court limited and strictly regulated press access to the trial. In early 2013, the Center for Constitutional Rights filed a First Amendment lawsuit on behalf of several journalists, requesting media and public access to court materials and challenging secret pretrial proceedings; their suit was denied in a military appeals court.[62] In response, the Freedom of the Press Foundation successfully crowd-funded court stenographers who—after convincing the court to grant them entrance to the courtroom—transcribed the proceedings by hand, since computers and other electronic devices were prohibited.[63] The sections of the pretrial and trial proceedings that I cite in this chapter are drawn from these transcripts as well as documents obtained through Freedom of Information Act (FOIA) requests made by journalists and other media organizations. The transcripts contain some gaps and inaccuracies because they were taken by hand, but except in the case of pronouns used for Manning, I cite them here without corrections or changes, in part to illustrate the obfuscation lingering even after the U.S. government grants a certain form of public access.

Moreover, Manning's testimony demonstrates the U.S. government's failure to adhere to its own policies regarding disclosure and transparency. For example, Manning testified that one of her initial motivations for leaking the "Collateral Murder" video was her discovery that Reuters—whose journalists had been killed in that incident—had filed a FOIA request for it and had not received a proper response for more than a year. Manning explained that she labeled her copy of that video "Reuters FOIA Req." and intended to send it directly to Reuters as well as to WikiLeaks. This testimony suggests that Manning understood her actions as ultimately compliant with U.S. federal policy even if they violated regulations governing her role as an analyst. In making these materials available to the public, she completed the FOIA request that other state actors had not.[64]

The Reuters FOIA request is one of many examples in the trial during which testimony about Manning's ethical framework implicitly calls into question the ethics of government and military actions, including the secrecy surrounding the trial itself. For instance, when the defense team challenged the vague language of the Espionage Act (of which Manning had been charged with eight counts of violation), they pointed out that "national security is not a phrase that is meant to protect the government from things that are embarrassing."[65] And on the first day of pretrial hearings, Coombs stated, "This is a public trial. The hallmark of our democracy is the ability of our government to be open with its public."[66] These statements position Manning's actions as rational, even patriotic efforts to align her work with the national character of the United States, imagined here as one of transparency and commitment to the public good. In the context of antiterrorism rhetoric, such statements can even attempt to characterize Manning as a model citizen who had so internalized the instructions of the If You See Something, Say Something campaign and related government initiatives that she felt compelled as a patriot and citizen to report misconduct she had witnessed. But this role of vigilant citizen relies on lateral surveillance, in which citizens monitor their friends, neighbors, and other members of the public; such surveillance is done in service to the government and cannot register as civic duty when turned against state agencies.[67] Accordingly, while these moments in the trial attempt to shift the burden of deception onto the U.S. government, within the structure of the court-martial Manning's case cannot indict the government for its own harmful acts of deception and obfuscation. Instead, examples like the Reuters FOIA request come to primarily support a narrative about Manning's personal emotional struggle, wherein she grappled with distressing information categorized as private but that she believed was rightly public knowledge.

In many ways, that narrative aligns with Manning's own statements. Her comments in the chat logs and her legal testimony repeatedly suggest that she felt burdened by her access to this material. And she does draw some connections between her life under Don't Ask, Don't Tell and her decision to leak information: early in her chats with Lamo, Manning writes, "Living such an opaque life, has forced me never to take transparency, openness, and honesty for granted."[68] My point is not to propose that discussions of her emotional burden constitute a false narrative, but rather to highlight how that narrative—perhaps inadvertently—complies with the government's demand that Manning be put under greater scrutiny and helps justify increased surveillance over her. Investigations into her emotional life work with the visual surveillance of her incarceration and with the trial's meticulous charting of her military service, personal history, and whistle-blowing actions. These forms of visibility are inextricable from the media and legal discussions of her gender identity throughout the trial, which helps explain the slippage between public and private in Coombs's opening argument noted above: "[Manning] was struggling not only with a feeling of obligation and duty to people, but also with . . . a very private struggle with [her] gender. And this was public for [her] unit to see." Although these sentences read as contradictory (how could a private struggle be public for all to see?), they indicate the complicated relationship between the two types of sensitive information in Manning's case: one that threatens national security if it is exposed, and one that must be exposed to remove its threatening potential.

Even this neat pairing is too simplistic, for although the classified materials are presumably the sensitive information that must be protected from exposure, Manning's gender and sexuality also posed a threat in the context of Don't Ask, Don't Tell and related legacies of sexual anxiety in the U.S. military. Similarly, the trial positions Manning as that which must be exposed to scrutiny in order to (re)secure the nation, even as her defense team's strategy suggests that disclosure of certain military secrets was key to resisting the threat of U.S. military violence both within and outside of U.S. borders. Courtroom and related media discussions of Manning's transgender identity, even when they define that identity as private and individual, are inevitably linked to examination of the leaks. In fact, as I show in the next section, efforts to separate these two aspects of Manning's case result in strengthening the relationship between them.

The Transgender Person of the Moment

It is not difficult to understand why the prosecution narrates Manning as a special case. If the U.S. government can characterize her as a singularly egregious example of national betrayal, it can deflect scrutiny away from its own policies and practices. Her security clearance notwithstanding, Manning's relative anonymity as a low-level analyst provided a kind of invisibility within the Department of Defense that enabled her to access, download, and distribute vast amounts of classified material.[69] The trial confronts this problem not as one that is a function of military and security bureaucracy but as intrinsic to Manning as a duplicitous transgender person. Further, if antiterrorism surveillance programs understand terrorism as fundamentally incoherent, unpredictable, and difficult to identify, then Manning's gender status can implicitly support the expansion of those programs as a response to her leaks, with transgender narratives of deception and ambiguity folded into these broader antiterrorism discourses. Positioning her as a tangible threat in disguise leaves intact state institutions' authority and even paves the way for more intensive government surveillance, with Manning's case as high-profile justification.[70] This rendering of Manning separates her from the actual content of the leaked materials in order to shift focus away from damning evidence of systemic government and military harm, locating harm instead in an individual's exceptional crimes.

The defense team also works to frame Manning as a unique individual (recall Coombs's description of her as "not a typical soldier"), a strategy taken up by other supporters who elevate Manning's individual gendered experience while moving the effects of U.S. military intervention into the background. In the left socialist magazine *Jacobin*, for instance, reporter Samantha Allen writes directly to Manning, analogizing her exposure of war crimes to exposure of transgender status. "You're making a habit out of revealing dangerous pieces of information," she notes. "I don't know which revelation was riskier for you: leaking the war documents or coming out as transgender."[71] Both pieces of information might well be dangerous, but Allen's framing suggests an either/or approach that is undone by the ways that the trial and media coverage merge these two forms of public disclosure. Allen continues, "You are in the unfortunate position of being a symbol. . . . Your announcement was an unwitting choice to be *the* transgender person of the moment, the center of a debate over the legitimacy of an entire group of people." Allen refers here to debates about transgender people's legitimacy, and she writes in explicit support of Manning, that larger group of transgender people, and the act of whistle-blowing. Yet while this supportive position is distinct from the court-martial's skepticism and condemnation, in both cases the attention to Manning's individual circumstances allows the legitimacy of another "entire group of people"—those targeted by U.S. military expansion and related antiterrorism measures—to go largely unnamed.

Even as Manning's actions and testimony focus on those harmed by U.S. military and government practices, a persistent exceptionalism—assisted by the continual return to her personal narrative and individual experiences—mutes their potential to erode public trust in state institutions. When Manning's navy psychiatrist testified about her pretrial confinement at Quantico, his claim that the isolation conditions "were more severe than [those] of death row inmates" conveys the severity of Manning's treatment by distinguishing her from those implicitly understood to deserve that treatment.[72] Captain Dr. Hocter, the psychiatrist who had treated Manning at Quantico, testified about the extended time that Manning spent under POI status: "Even at Guantánamo Bay my recommendations were implemented much faster than at Quantico. [Manning] spent an unprecedented amount of time under precautions."[73] And Manning's father, in a television interview, likewise used Guantánamo as a reference point for her pretrial treatment: "They worry about people down in a base in Cuba, but here they are, have someone on our own soil, under their own control, and they're treating [her] this way. . . . It's shocking enough that I would come out of our silence as a family and say . . . you've crossed a line. This is wrong."[74] These claims suggest that Manning ought not be treated as prisoners on death row or at Guantánamo are, not because this treatment is unacceptable on its face, but because Manning is a well-meaning individual rather than a nameless criminal. Contrary to Manning's own narration of her actions—her concerns about "people down in a base in Cuba" prompted her to leak the Guantánamo files, after all—these arguments further normalize ongoing incarceration practices in order to depict Manning's treatment as a contrasting singular wrong.

Such statements work alongside the defense team's portrayal of Manning as a patriot whose humanist ethics and national loyalty moved her to expose confidential materials. Together, these accounts craft a narrative that individualizes Manning. As Dean Spade and Craig Willse point out, although supporters "leaned on this gay heroism story as one of the only available scripts in the absence of broad public opposition to imperialism and war," that script nonetheless promotes an exceptionalism in which Manning's individual case supersedes the very forms of entrenched violence that Manning herself sought to center.[75] The viability of this script depends at least in part on recourse to whiteness and U.S. citizenship. Manning can be depicted as a singular case not solely because her whistle-blowing or transgender identity make her different, but also because whiteness offers a claim on individuality not readily available to people of color.[76] In this way, whiteness is "atomized into invisibility through the individualization of white subjects" and, accordingly, Manning's whiteness goes unmarked in the trial and media coverage.[77] Moreover, these narrations of Manning as individual follow what C. Riley Snorton and Jin Haritaworn describe as a form of value extraction in which violence against and deaths of people of color serve as "raw material for the generation of respectable trans subjects."[78] Their argument helps illuminate the ways that the Manning trial and related media discourse use Guantánamo detainees, prisoners on death row in the United States, and those enduring armed conflict with the U.S. military in Iraq and Afghanistan—

whether transgender-identified or not—as broad, nameless groups that make Manning's individuality possible. The production of Manning as an exceptional transgender individual occurs through the disposability of other lives, which "act as resources" for the "articulation and visibility of a more privileged transgender subject."[79]

Questions like Samantha Allen's above, which ask whether leaking classified information is riskier than publicly identifying as transgender, suggest that Manning's individual identity as transgender can be distinguished from her actions as a whistle-blower and from the content of the leaked materials. But the use of transgender identity in her trial intertwines that public identification with the government and military actions that she exposed. Manning's case is clearly connected to the secretive conditions of Guantánamo camps, for instance, because her own pretrial detention entailed similar conditions and because her release of the Guantánamo files forms part of the government's justification for her incarceration. Yet her case also differs significantly from those of the Guantánamo detainees, because court and media narratives construct Manning as a singular figure to such a degree that the hundreds of detainees—whose information Manning initially made public—recede further into the background, a group indistinguishable as individuals. But it is in this way that Manning's gender should be understood as utterly inseparable from the content of the materials she leaked: both supporters and detractors engage her as an explicitly transgender figure in order to buttress claims that she is an exceptional case, thereby transferring scrutiny onto her (whether as treasonous criminal or mistreated citizen) and away from the government policies and practices that Manning made public. The standardized narrative of transgender identity, an individual's story of secret emotional distress, works with unmarked whiteness to position Manning as a special case whose secrets about both gender and treason—here discursively folded into one another—must be exposed. Dominant cultural rhetoric linking transgender identity to concealment supports the trial's mandate of exposure, even when that rhetoric is not explicitly cited; it assists the trial's work of making Manning visible as either patriotic or traitorous. The individuality that the court and news media attribute to Manning—narrated as her isolation under Don't Ask, Don't Tell, her secret gender struggles, her atypical humanist beliefs, and her single-handed ability to undermine national security—merges gender secrets with national secrets while simultaneously distinguishing her from those most directly harmed by U.S. military actions, detention and incarceration practices, and foreign policy.

Because it focuses on one explicitly transgender individual, the Manning case operates in ways that are different from yet continuous with the sites I consider in previous chapters of this book. Surveillance practices working through identification documents, air travel, and public bathrooms help construct an understanding of gender noncompliance that then directly and indirectly rationalizes surveillance targeting many different groups, including but not limited to the transgender-identified. These are all practices that state agencies themselves actively publicize through laws and policies, public statements, media interviews, and government hearings. In contrast, the Manning trial draws on a narrative of transgender deception—both in the prosecution's argument of traitorous duplicity and the defense's argument of emotional turmoil amplified by gender secrets—and applies it to a single person. While this characterization of deception rationalizes the heightened surveillance over Manning's body and behaviors (invoking the truth-seeking practices already routinely employed against gender nonconformity), the U.S. government works hard to limit public knowledge of that surveillance, of the trial itself, and of the materials Manning leaked.

In closely reading the Manning trial, this chapter also risks enacting one of the problems it identifies, foregrounding Manning as an exceptional figure through and against others, whose lives and deaths are relegated to a homogenized anonymity that makes it possible to study Manning's case in detail. Yet it is precisely because her trial and incarceration garnered such extensive attention that we should examine how that attention functions, how it is developed and sustained. When we approach Manning's case with this in mind, it can illustrate not merely the hazards of visibility for a specific individual, but also what that visibility then enables in the background, including the routinized surveillance and harming of millions through U.S. military intervention, carceral institutions, and foreign policy decisions. Amplified attention to cases treated as spectacularly unique helps create that background, a space of naturalized disposability in which surveillance practices can run continuously, even mundanely. Just as the characterization of Manning as an exceptional individual helps shift scrutiny away from the specific U.S. military actions she described as awful and alarming, so too does the acute focus on her case facilitate and normalize the less spectacular surveillance practices of the everyday.

ON ENDURANCE

I BEGAN THE RESEARCH for this book during the last years of the George W. Bush administration, and completed the bulk of the writing and revisions under the Barack Obama administration. As I write this conclusion in late 2017, nearly one year into the Donald Trump administration, the political context is shifting rapidly around us, and changes to governing practices and to the fundamental structure of U.S. state agencies continue to unfold. It is difficult to know how to conclude a book about U.S. state surveillance under these uncertain political conditions. Trump's campaign pledges to expand power and protection for law enforcement at all levels, to build a wall along the U.S.-Mexico border and dramatically increase deportations, and to outright ban Muslims and refugees from entering the United States were all codified by executive orders in the weeks after his inauguration. Overt scrutiny of and violence and harassment against multiple marginalized groups intensified noticeably following the 2016 election, demonstrating how surveillance enacted by formal government agents works hand in hand with the everyday informal surveillance practices operating at the local level.

Meanwhile, activist organizations, advocates, and community members persistently contest these programs, not only supporting legal challenges and legislative battles but actively creating innovative support structures that operate beyond courts and formal policy. Community-led rapid response teams in cities across the United States defend against Immigration and Customs Enforcement (ICE) raids and acute instances of police violence, turning surveillance back onto law enforcement. Black Lives Matter chapters fight anti-Black racism and state-sanctioned violence, building a decentralized, transnational resistance movement with Black liberation at its core. Revitalizing the sanctuary practices developed to protect Central

American refugees during the 1980s and building on new local policies enacted by many cities and schools, progressive religious institutions provide
material sanctuary for undocumented immigrants. Native American tribes
organize long-term spiritual and political protests against the Dakota Access and Keystone XL oil pipelines, naming the pipelines' environmental destruction as a mechanism of settler colonialism and genocide. Mass airport
demonstrations mobilize spontaneously to defend refugees, immigrants, and
Muslims against federal bans on travelers from majority-Muslim countries.
Community networks pool financial support to fund abortion access, pay
bail and court fees, and sustain queer and transgender elders. These and
many other forms of organizing endure and expand even as they face intensified, explicit government repression.[1]

One broad task of this book has been to reframe a common approach
to transgender studies and transgender people: it moves away from a search
for truth and legibility to consider instead how surveillance practices make
gender nonconformity visible, constructing it as inherently deceptive in
ways that justify continued surveillance to locate its truth. Sometimes this
scrutiny operates without formally naming the category of transgender, yet
still ensnares many different bodies and identities that transgress normative
gender; in other cases, surveillance measures overtly cite the transgender-
identified while manipulating that focus to also strengthen scrutiny of other
population categories. Yet I have also shown how gender nonconformity
disrupts or confounds surveillance programs by exploiting their internal
inconsistencies and their reliance on normative modes of identification. In
turn, state agencies constantly recalibrate surveillance technologies, and
informal surveillance practices continually adjust to more effectively track
those bodies and identities that evade their grasp. In the volatile—yet often
remarkably generative—political context in which I write now, how might
we navigate the deception attached to gender nonconformity?

This question is complicated by the rise of transgender visibility over the
course of this book's development. This growing visibility—leading to U.S.
news media declarations of a "transgender tipping point" and a still widen-
ing recognition of transgender people across all manner of industries, governmental entities, and public discourse—roughly parallels the progression
of the book's chapters. Greater recognition has not staunched continuing
surveillance practices that take new shapes under the war on terror and the
rapidly ascending authoritarian movements in the United States and else-

where. New surveillance technologies and data-sharing networks—like the linked databases required by the Real ID Act—feed on visibility, which can also refine conceptions of what transgender means and to whom it properly applies, so that the expansion of transgender visibility paradoxically narrows the purview of transgender politics.

This paradox is evident, for example, in the September 2017 news that the New York voter registration form for Jared Kushner—senior White House advisor and Trump's son-in-law—listed his gender as female. This information broke as Kushner faced increased scrutiny about his relationship to Russian interference in the 2016 U.S. election and about his repeated failures to disclose required information about foreign contacts and financial interests on security clearance forms. The news also came some four months into the work of the new Presidential Advisory Commission on Election Integrity, a voter fraud commission that Trump established by executive order following his false postelection claim that millions of people voting illegally had thrown the popular vote to Hillary Clinton. In news headlines about Kushner's voter registration, some outlets reported that he "voted as a woman," while others stated directly, "Jared Kushner is a woman."[2] Both speech acts reflect the ways that, as the early chapters of this book show, government documentation and administrative practices actively produce gender; Kushner becomes a woman through the voter registration records that classify him as such. Yet with few exceptions, the news stories themselves treated Kushner's voter documents as another paperwork failure rather than a serious indication of his gender.[3] The New York State Board of Elections announced that the gender classification was their error, not Kushner's, and had been corrected; the board's executive director, Michael Ryan, insisted that such an "accidental sex swap . . . would have no chance of changing someone's ability to vote," and that "it's not something that would disenfranchise a voter."[4] This is a remarkable statement in the context of systemic voter suppression efforts (including Trump's voter fraud commission). These programs seek to identify fraudulent voting practices in part by flagging inconsistencies in individuals' identification documents and other records, following policies like the Real ID Act and Social Security no-match letters I examined in chapter 1. As with government reassurances about those policies, Ryan's statement speaks to those for whom such inconsistencies would represent obvious clerical errors. It cannot support those whose inconsistent documents result from inability to access ID or from conflicting administrative regulations, nor those whose gendered documents become questionable through racism and xenophobia.

Kushner's story aptly illustrates how identification documents produce the gendered problems (and subject positions) they purport to merely reflect, yet the considerable visibility of transgender people at the time of this story did not help frame it in those terms. Transgender recognition continues to be structured largely through specific medical, legal, and/or self-narration practices, ranging from the claims of medically necessary health care I consider in chapter 2 to the legislation defining transgender status to regulate public bathrooms, as I show in chapter 3. Within these modes of legibility, *transgender* could not really apply to Kushner, and so public discourse on this case could not engage transgender politics in any meaningful way. Instead, Kushner becomes a woman only to the extent that this temporary status highlights either his own incompetence or that of the voter registration process.

Yet in its very absence of a transgender-identified subject, this case can be important to a transgender critique of surveillance. The revelation and casual dismissal of the database error ("It does happen from time to time," Ryan remarked) reaffirms Kushner's gender as normative while pointing out flaws inherent to the data collection process. To be sure, some critics of Trump's voter fraud commission pointed to Kushner's story as one that invalidates the commission's work, because it shows that such data errors do not actually constitute improper voting practices.[5] But inasmuch as the case highlights those errors, it can also justify the refinement and expansion of surveillance over voter databases and voters themselves, to ensure apprehension of "real" criminals who might slip through in similar clerical errors. In this way, the specter of gendered fraud propels broader surveillance practices already underway. Notably, Trump's claim that millions voted illegally relies on data provided by True the Vote, the organization that produced the man-in-a-dress voter fraud image I discussed in chapter 1 and that primarily targets immigrants and people of color, just as do voter ID policies and the longer history of state-regulated identification documents.[6]

While many of Trump's policies and promises do entail important changes in governing practices, then, they are neither exceptional nor unprecedented. Just as we ought not imagine post-9/11 programs as spontaneous, brand-new responses to crisis, the Trump administration's work is likewise made possible by foundations laid long before the 2016 election. To take just one widely discussed example, consider those undocumented immigrants who complied with Obama-era policies requiring them to register with ICE, undergoing regular ICE check-ins and sometimes wearing GPS-enabled ankle monitors. Under the Obama administration, this surveillance of undocumented people could be promoted in part as a benevolent regulation enabling hundreds of thousands of people to remain in the United States. At the same time, undocumented people outside of this surveillance mechanism are assigned greater criminality simply for not being part of a system of compliance and visibility. Meanwhile, because Trump's policies explicitly call for swifter deportations and expand the deportation priorities to those who have committed any act that could be a chargeable criminal offense (which might include anyone who entered the United States without required legal documentation), already ICE agents have begun using the required check-ins to facilitate deportations. This process is helped along by the Obama administration's own record of deporting millions of immigrants and the xenophobia through which U.S. borders have always been constructed, such that the new policies should be understood as a continuation of, rather than a departure from, earlier periods.

Relatedly, we might consider the Deferred Action for Childhood Arrivals (DACA) program, developed by the Obama administration in 2012 to allow eligible undocumented people who entered the United States as minors to register for a renewable two-year deferment from deportation proceedings. The program has allowed tens of thousands of undocumented students to continue high school and college in the United States and to obtain work permits, yet because it requires a formal admission of undocumented status, it also operates as surveillance over this group of people who can now be more effectively monitored. Applications to DACA were always a risk, since being found ineligible during the application process could lead to deportation and since it was always possible that the policy could be revoked. The DACA program provides protection only for those who can withstand rigorous government scrutiny and emerge as compliant, productive individuals. Under the Trump administration, increasing numbers of DACA recipients have had their protected status canceled, a trend reflecting more expansive definitions of criminality that can make one a priority for deportation. Under these conditions, a registry previously promoted as benevolent government protection—but which always invested in criminalization by distinguishing good DACA recipients from other immigrants—becomes an accessible list of undocumented people who can be better tracked and targeted for deportation.

Trump's July 2017 announcement prohibiting transgender people from serving in the U.S. military demonstrates how readily transgender visibility can be incorporated into broader, morphing surveillance projects. The ban responded to U.S. House of Representatives debates over a large defense and security spending bill: a proposed amendment to bar the Pentagon from funding medical care related to gender transition imperiled the bill's passage. Most notably, this spending bill included $1.6 billion for Trump's promised U.S.-Mexico border wall. Trump's pronouncement, claiming that transgender people's "tremendous medical costs and disruption" burden the military, exploits ongoing scrutiny of gender nonconformity in order to further fund border control efforts targeting Mexican immigrants.[7] By discursively tying transgender people to medicalization and suggesting that this link weakens the nation's defense against immigrants, the policy draws on a broader discourse of harmful versus healthful bodies that I consider in chapter 2. Patriotic responses from transgender advocates invest in that discourse toward different ends, arguing that banning transgender service members "will be detrimental to readiness and morale at every level of the armed forces."[8] In a repudiation of Trump's portrayal of transgender service members as burdensome liabilities that undermine U.S. military power, these advocates depict transgender fitness and patriotism as vital to national defense.[9] Such strategies echo the frameworks of national belonging that I discuss in chapter 3, particularly against the backdrop of federal spending on increasingly militarized border control that emphasizes surveillance of physical bodies to fortify spatial boundaries for national security. Moreover, transgender visibility in the form of explicit military inclusion places transgender service members under formal surveillance through the military's standardized screening, documenting, and monitoring of enlistees as well as the informal scrutiny of hostile or skeptical peers, senior officers, and legislators. Like Chelsea Manning, these service members are both objects and agents of surveillance as they carry out tasks from data collection to drone imaging. The transgender military ban therefore entails a more complicated web of surveillance than its most explicit objective suggests. That facet of the policy—the location and removal of transgender-identified people from military service—reminds us that military recognition and inclusion of transgender people facilitates more effective monitoring of them *as* transgender. But the policy also demonstrates how U.S. state agencies incorporate newly recognized transgender people into the formal workings of surveillance, whether by literally putting them to work on military surveillance projects or by using them as incendiary and polarizing figures to fund militarized surveillance against immigrants in the U.S.-Mexico border region and beyond.

Further illustrative of the complex relationship between visibility, protection, and surveillance in this shifting political context are two major policy changes made during the early months of the Trump administration that specifically address transgender people. First, in February 2017, the administration rescinded federal guidelines addressing transgender students in schools that receive federal funding. These guidelines, released in 2016 by Obama's departments of education and justice, draw on Title IX and related case law to inform school officials of their legal requirements for the treatment of transgender students, including use of names and pronouns, restroom policies, and dress codes. The removal of these federal guidelines was one of the first major actions undertaken by Trump's new attorney general (Jeff Sessions) and education secretary (Betsy DeVos) after their confirmations. Second, in March 2017, the U.S. Census Bureau published a list of topics about which the 2020 census would include questions. The list included sexual orientation and gender identity as a proposed topic, but several hours later a revised list eliminated this topic altogether, with a Census Bureau spokesperson stating that its initial inclusion was made inadvertently. The agency's director later released a statement explaining that "there must be a clear statutory or regulatory need for data collection" for a topic to be included in the census, and that in response to a formal request for its inclusion made by seventy-five members of Congress, the bureau had determined that no change in this area was needed.[10]

In the wake of these changes, multiple LGBT advocates and organizations explained how important the school guidelines are, how federal data collection on sexual orientation and gender identity would be beneficial, and the possible harm that could result from the absence of these policies.[11] Certainly both of these policies have the potential to offer support and protection for vulnerable people. The rollback of guidelines for transgender students, in particular, can be interpreted as an act designed to mark the Trump administration's explicit withdrawal of support for transgender people, since the guidelines provided no new protection and carried no legal force in themselves; they merely clarified federal regulations already in place under Title IX, and so primarily served to signal the Obama administration's care for transgender youth. Meanwhile, in an October 2017 amicus brief in the lawsuit against Trump's ban on transgender service members, eight transgender advocacy organizations (including NCTE) cite removal of the school guidelines and census questions as evidence of the Trump administration's pattern of discrimination against transgender people. Regarding the census questions and similar elimination of LGBT-related questions in other government surveys, the brief argues, "there has been a coordinated effort within the Executive Branch to *avoid* collecting data about LGBT Americans," thereby "ensuring that there is no data to study."[12] Without such data, the brief suggests, the White House can (and does) abandon federal efforts to protect transgender people: professing the need for further study while declining to collect new data for that research allows protective measures to atrophy through calculated delay and disuse.

Yet both the school guidelines and the now-withdrawn census questions are also state surveillance practices that help construct the category of transgender through identifying and counting particular people. Census questions make this clear, since the particular types of questions and identity categories provided change from one census period to the next, structuring participants' responses accordingly. Reading the U.S. census's shifting racial categories as a way of managing blackness, for instance, Simone Browne shows how "census enumeration is a means through which a state manages its residents by way of formalized categories that fix individuals within a certain time and a particular space, making the census a technology that renders a population legible in racializing as well as gendering ways."[13] What would it mean to include the term *transgender* on the U.S. census at this particular moment in time? According to what standards will that identity be defined and determined? To what uses might this new data be put, especially against a cultural backdrop that links deception with gender nonconformity, and which self-identified transgender citizens would benefit? Likewise, in the case of school guidelines, how will a student's transgender identity be recognized as such, and how might legibility as transgender depend upon race or class status, or be determined differently in different types of schools or geographical regions? Could not some schools use legible, recorded transgender status as a tool to reinforce gender segregation (and related surveillance) of bathrooms and locker rooms by extending use of these spaces only to students whom such policies designate as male or female, whether transgender or not? Might formal records of transgender identity facilitate school officials' ability or desire to monitor certain students' behaviors and bodies? State projects like these offer protection and recognition that necessarily entail forms of identification and monitoring and, as the Obama-era policies managing undocumented immigrants demonstrate, may shift into more harmful—or differently harmful—forms.

Going Stealth has tried to show that while surveillance practices may well take new shapes or gain new significance in moments of crisis, they are rooted in—and routed through—longer histories of classification and biopolitical management. Already the crisis of the Trump era has reinvigorated a desire to protect the forms of state recognition that themselves claim to protect transgender people, as advocacy organizations' defense of the census questions and school guidelines illustrate. Following the longer trajectories of surveillance practices through their production—and, importantly, their use—of gender nonconformity helps demonstrate both the surveillance intrinsic to these protective gestures and the limitations of calls for visibility. More accurate state recognition may increase protection for the recognized while simultaneously optimizing state agencies' ability to monitor them (as in TSA's continually revised categories of care, or the tracking of transgender identity across ID documents). Meanwhile, those agencies can employ new categories as justification for expanding surveillance in other ways, for instance through claims of protecting now-legible groups from those who remain outside the newly drawn lines of recognition.[14]

Part of this book's project has been to show how the category of transgender is produced through surveillance practices that both draw and dissolve its parameters, not only through spectacular or formal actions undertaken by state actors but also in the most mundane conditions of our gendered lives. In refusing to take for granted the boundaries of that category, we can begin to understand both how aspects of surveillance that never explicitly use the term *transgender*—from the official policy of the Real ID Act to the casual humor surrounding Kushner's voter registration—play a significant role in transgender politics and how surveillance efforts specifically targeting transgender people reverberate far beyond those directly named in such practices. With this in mind, we might pursue new avenues of political solidarity that address the ways that legibility facilitates surveillance programs' efficacy and demands differentiation from illegible others.

Yet neither does this book call for an easy, uncritical turn to illegibility that would actively take up deception as a political tool to render targeted populations ungovernable. Those new lines of solidarity should remind us of the uneven possibilities offered by any embrace of deception, a tactic that may open new space for some but reignite the truth-seeking mission against others. In many cases, surveillance practices thrive on the illegibility that they themselves assign to certain populations. That assignation then rationalizes the proliferation of surveillance through state agencies, formal policies, and interpersonal engagements, modifying internal logics and frames of reference to track us more effectively. In itself, gender nonconformity cannot be an inherently resistant foil to the workings of surveillance. This book shows how surveillance continually exploits and incorporates projects of transgender visibility, even while those projects—along with endeavors less legible—gum up the works by exposing normative assumptions and slipping through the cracks of classificatory systems, both intentionally and inadvertently. Any promise of lasting evasion is tenuous in this context. Yet tracing the continuities of surveillance practices across fluctuating population categories, political moments, and technological developments shows how their endurance depends on a dynamic relationship with us. As we look to the political landscape ahead, we might attune to the possibilities in the spaces that open, however briefly, through that interplay.

NOTES

Introduction: Suspicious Visibility

1 Emilia Askari, "Brief Cranbrook Lockdown Over after Report of Man Wearing Women's Clothing," *Detroit Free Press*, April 17, 2007.

2 Askari, "Brief Cranbrook Lockdown."

3 "The danger, deception, and dishonesty allegedly embedded in sexual and gender nonconformity" is a key theme in the historical criminalization of queer, transgender, and gender-nonconforming people [Mogul, Ritchie, and Whitlock, *Queer (In)Justice*, 43].

4 Cranbrook Lockdown, April 30, 2007, accessed October 31, 2009, http://www.cranbrooklockdown.com/index.html.

5 Askari, "Brief Cranbrook Lockdown."

6 Monahan, "Questioning Surveillance."

7 See, for example, Bridges, *Poverty of Privacy Rights*; Roberts, *Killing the Black Body*; Clare, "Body Shame"; and Siebers, "Sexual Culture."

8 Desai and Brandzel, "Race, Violence, and Terror," 72.

9 Desai and Brandzel, "Race, Violence, and Terror," 74.

10 Valentine, *Imagining Transgender*, 166.

11 In her introduction to the first volume of *The Transgender Studies Reader*, Susan Stryker notes that while selecting the book's fifty essays, she and her coeditor "were struck by the overwhelming (and generally) unmarked whiteness of practitioners in the academic field of transgender studies" [Stryker, "(De)Subjugated Knowledges," 15]. In their introduction to the reader's second volume, Stryker and Aren Aizura write that recent work in transgender studies "often directs its critical gaze at the inadequacies of the field's first iteration, . . . taking aim at its implicit whiteness, U.S.-centricity, Anglophone bias, and the sometimes suspect ways in which the category *transgender* has been circulated transnationally" (Stryker and Aizura, "Introduction," 4).

12 Valentine, *Imagining Transgender*, 169. In particular, Valentine cautions against uses of transgender as a modern or progressive category that classifies gender systems in a variety of cultural and temporal contexts according to a dominant

Western framework. For analysis of the ways such framings play out, see Towle and Morgan, "Romancing the Transgender Native."

13 Spade, "Resisting Medicine."

14 Butler, *Undoing Gender*, 52.

15 I draw on Valentine's use of this term as one that works in two related ways: "On the one hand, it validates those who adopt transgender as a meaningful category of self-identity; but it also draws attention to how people are identified by others as being transgender even though they may not necessarily use this term in talking about themselves. This phrasing thus highlights how self-identity and one's identification by others are complexly intertwined and shaped by relationships of social power" (Valentine, *Imagining Transgender*, 26).

16 I am grateful to Benjamin D'Harlingue for many conversations and collaborations that helped me work through these complicated, ever-shifting terms.

17 Enke, "Education of Little Cis."

18 Enke, "Education of Little Cis," 74.

19 Gossett, "Queerstions: What Does Cisgender Mean?"

20 Stryker, "(De)Subjugated Knowledges," 8–9.

21 Stryker and Aizura, "Introduction," 9.

22 Cohen, "Punks, Bulldaggers," 45; emphasis in original.

23 Eng, Halberstam, and Muñoz, "What's Queer," 3.

24 Ferguson, *Aberrations in Black*, 4.

25 I note here also Simone Browne's important work putting surveillance studies "into conversation with the enduring archive of transatlantic slavery and its afterlife, . . . making visible the many ways that race continues to structure surveillance practices" (Browne, *Dark Matters*, 11).

26 Minich, *Accessible Citizenships*, 17. For further discussion of these varied understandings of citizenship, see for example Lowe, *Immigrant Acts*; Ong, *Flexible Citizenship*; Ngai, *Impossible Subjects*; and Rosaldo, "Cultural Citizenship."

27 Gopinath, "Bollywood Spectacles," 159.

28 Foucault, *Discipline and Punish*, 187.

29 Hammonds, "Black (W)holes," 141.

30 Foucault, *Discipline and Punish*, 200.

31 Lyon, *Surveillance after September 11*, 150.

32 Brown, *States of Injury*, 174.

33 Canaday, *Straight State*, 6.

34 Foucault, "Risks of Security," 372.

35 Foucault, *History of Sexuality*, 94.

36 Foucault, *History of Sexuality*, 93.

37 Puar, *Terrorist Assemblages*.

38 For further explanation of the "trickle-up" model as Spade understands it, see Laura Flanders, "Dangerous Rush to Legislate on Surveillance and Mental Health?," *The Nation*, December 28, 2012.

39 "Responding to Hate Crimes: A Community Resource Manual," National Center

for Transgender Equality, July 1, 2009, accessed August 15, 2009, http://www
.transequality.org/issues/resources/responding-hate-crimes-community-resource
-manual.

40 "SRLP on Hate Crime Laws," Sylvia Rivera Law Project, 2009, accessed April 2,
2010, https://srlp.org/action/hate-crimes/. Multiple other queer and transgender
organizations forwarded a similar analysis of hate crimes legislation and incorporated it into their work. For example, the New York–based Audre Lorde Project
developed and continues to support the Safe OUTside the System Collective,
an antiviolence project "devoted to challenging hate and police violence by using community based strategies rather than relying on the police" ["Safe Outside the System (SOS)," Audre Lorde Project, 2017, accessed November 11, 2017,
https://alp.org/programs/sos]. In the California Bay Area, Community United
Against Violence for two years held Safetyfest, a multiday event that provided
a range of tools and workshops for queer and transgender antiviolence organizing. The festival's offerings ranged from "community accountability skills to
deal with partner abuse and sexual assault . . . without necessarily relying on the
cops" to fund-raisers for incarcerated queer people of color (Mandy Van De-
ven, "The Bay Area's Safetyfest Queers Anti-violence Activism," *Bitch Magazine*, April 5, 2010, accessed June 15, 2011, http://www.bitchmedia.org/post/on
-the-map-the-bay-areas-safetyfest-queers-anti-violence-activism).

41 Hammonds, "Black (W)holes," 141.

Chapter 1: Deceptive Documents

1 "DHS Advisory to Security Personnel; No Change in Threat Level," Department of
Homeland Security, September 4, 2003, accessed September 9, 2003, http://www
.dhs.gov/xnews/releases/press_release_0238.shtm.

2 Parenti, *Soft Cage*, 28.

3 In her analysis of *The Book of Negroes*, an eighteenth-century ledger documenting
thousands of self-emancipating ex-slaves who traveled out of the United States,
Simone Browne argues that "the body made legible with the modern passport system has a history in the technologies of tracking blackness" and that this history is
"an important, but often absented, part of the genealogy of the passport" (Browne,
Dark Matters, 70). For discussion of how legal documentation of mixed-race and
racially passing people under U.S. slavery worked to maintain racial purity, see,
for example, Zackodnik, "Fixing the Color Line."

4 Salter, *Rights of Passage*, 7.

5 U.S. Department of State, *United States Passport*, 73.

6 Mongia, "Race, Nationality, Mobility," 550.

7 Mongia, "Race, Nationality, Mobility," 528; emphases in original.

8 Torpey, *Invention of the Passport*, 97.

9 Pegler-Gordon, "Chinese Exclusion," 69.

10 For the Supreme Court decision, see *Shelby County, Alabama v. Holder, Attorney*

General, et al., 570 U.S. (2013). Analyses of the decision include Chris Brook, "In North Carolina and across the Nation, the Voting Rights Act Is Still Necessary," *ACLU Blog of Rights*, June 27, 2013, accessed July 29, 2013, http://www.aclu.org /blog/voting-rights/north-carolina-and-across-nation-voting-rights-act-still -necessary; Andrew Cohen, "On Voting Rights, a Decision as Lamentable as Plessy or Dred Scott," *The Atlantic*, June 25, 2013, accessed June 26, 2013, http://www .theatlantic.com/national/archive/2013/06/on-voting-rights-a-decision-as -lamentable-as-plessy-or-dred-scott/276455/; and Tim Murphy, "Supreme Court: The Voting Rights Act Worked—So Now It's Unconstitutional," *Mother Jones*, June 25, 2013, accessed June 26, 2013, http://www.motherjones.com/politics/2013 /06/supreme-court-voting-rights-act-decision.

11 For summaries of these six states' proposals, see Joseph Diebold, "Six States Already Moving Forward with Voting Restrictions after Supreme Court Decision," *ThinkProgress*, June 27, 2013, accessed June 28, 2013, http://thinkprogress.org /justice/2013/06/27/2223471/six-states-already-moving-forward-with-voting -restrictions-after-supreme-court-decision/.

12 Brentin Mock, "I Have Photo ID, Therefore I Am," *ColorLines*, August 2, 2012, accessed August 15, 2012, http://colorlines.com/archives/2012/08/pennsylvania _voter_id_court_hearing.html.

13 Brentin Mock, "Pa. Supreme Court Doubts State Can Comply with Its Own Voter ID Law," *ColorLines*, September 19, 2012, accessed November 11, 2012, http:// colorlines.com/archives/2012/09/pa_supreme_court_doubts_state_can_comply _with_its_own_voter_id_law.html.

14 "History of True the Vote," True the Vote, June 21, 2013, accessed July 29, 2013, http://www.truethevote.org/about/history/.

15 "About Us," National Center for Transgender Equality, 2016, accessed July 12, 2016, http://www.transequality.org/about.

16 "Tea Party Group Targets Trans Voters," *Advancing Transgender Equality* (blog), November 4, 2012, accessed November 11, 2012, http://transgenderequality.word press.com/2012/11/04/tea-party-group-targets-trans-voters.

17 It also illustrates the false reliance on identification documents as either protective of transgender people or as evidence of compliance, since even if officials deem the photo ID to properly match the body in front of them, deviation from racialized gender expectations can still be cause for suspicion.

18 WPATH was formerly the Harry Benjamin International Gender Dysphoria Association. The current and previous versions of the *Standards* can be found at http://www.wpath.org.

19 Sandy Stone, among others, discusses this process more extensively in "The *Empire* Strikes Back." She argues that as medical science made available more information about the standards for determining the category of transsexual, individuals were more able to deliberately perform to these standards, thus convincing doctors of transsexual identities and personal histories in order to gain access to medical transition. In *Sex Changes*, Patrick Califia discusses similar tactics taken

up by transgender-identified people in postoperative interviews and medical surveys (269–70).

20 See, for example, Somerville, *Queering the Color Line*, chap. 1; Terry, *American Obsession*.

21 Spade, "Resisting Medicine," 26.

22 Birth certificates are increasingly contentious documents, in part because of their role in the bathroom bills that I discuss in chapter 3. For instance, Arkansas currently allows a change of gender marker on birth certificates, but state legislators introduced a 2017 bill stipulating that "the biological sex listed on a birth certificate shall not be amended"; the bill did not pass the Arkansas House (H.B. 1894, 91st General Assembly, State of Arkansas, 2017).

23 Nolan Clay, "Oklahoma Judge Refuses to Let Men Planning Sex-Change Operations Have Feminine Names," *The Oklahoman*, September 16, 2012. A similar case emerged in Atlanta, Georgia, in 2016, when a superior court judge denied a legal name change for a transgender man, writing in his decision that "name changes which allow a person to assume the role of a person of the opposite sex are, in effect, a type of fraud on the general public" (Kate Brumback, "Transgender Man's Name Change Rejected by Georgia Judge as 'Fraud,'" *Mercury News*, June 9, 2016).

24 For further analysis of the Araujo case, see Bettcher, "Evil Deceivers." Bettcher importantly outlines how misogyny and racism work with transphobia both in the Araujo case and more broadly in the construction of so-called authentic gender, such that transgender women of color experience disproportionate violence.

25 For further discussion, see Spade, "Documenting Gender"; Currah and Moore, "Legally Sexed."

26 For in-depth discussion of these administrative conflicts and their effects, see Spade, *Normal Life*, chap. 4.

27 This language is typical of most U.S. news reports on Nepal's policy. See, for example, Associated Press, "Nepal to Issue 'Third Gender' IDs," *Salon*, January 22, 2013, accessed December 6, 2017, https://www.salon.com/2013/01/22/nepal_to_issue _third_gender_ids/.

28 The terms *hijra, transvestite, eunuch,* and *hermaphrodite* are each subject to ongoing and nuanced discussions about their limits and connotations in various contexts. I reference them here to show that these are the terms commonly used by U.S. media reporting the Pakistan policy. See, for example, Zeeshan Haider, "Pakistan's Transvestites to Get Distinct Gender," Reuters, December 23, 2009.

29 For extensive analysis of the use of third gender categories, particularly in anthropological work, see Towle and Morgan, "Romancing the Transgender Native." We might also ask how third gender categories construct new boundaries around gender definitions and thus bolster policing and classification processes. What criteria must one meet in order to be classified as third gender? Does matching those criteria then foreclose the possibility of being assigned a male or female marker? How might a third gender marker create new forms of stigma? For instance, for more than thirty years, New York City maintained a policy wherein individuals

who provided evidence of particular medical procedures could receive an amended birth certificate that simply left the gender marker blank; this practice may have solved some problems, but it also created others and enabled new forms of scrutiny and stigmatization. See Currah and Moore, "Legally Sexed."

30 "Fact Sheet: Vital Statistics Modernization Act AB 433," Equality California, October 15, 2011, accessed November 22, 2011, http://www.eqca.org/atf/cf/%7B34 f258b3-8482-4943-91cb-08c4b0246a88%7D/AB%20433%20vital%20statistics% 20modernization%20act%20eqca%20tlc%20fact%20sheet.pdf.

31 In 2017, California passed the Gender Recognition Act to become the first U.S. state to provide a third gender option on all state identification documents. The law also removes the requirement to provide a physician's letter for any legal gender marker change. One obstacle to the law's passage was the significant expense required for the California Department of Motor Vehicles to update its systems with a new gender category; thus while the new law dispenses with some medicalized forms of tracking, it also further refines data collection practices and classification schemas.

32 Mark Dreyfus, "New Guidelines on the Recognition of Gender," Attorney-General for Australia Minister for Emergency Management, June 13, 2013, accessed July 29, 2013, http://www.attorneygeneral.gov.au/Mediareleases/Pages/2013 /Second%20quarter/13June2013-Newguidelinesontherecognitionofgender.aspx.

33 In "Electronic Identity Cards," Felix Stalder and David Lyon explain that this type of surveillance "seeks techniques for identifying, classifying, and managing groups sorted by levels of dangerousness" (89). They note that the shift to anticipatory surveillance and away from identification of individual criminals to impose punishment directly is conducted in part through the advent of searchable databases, in which identification documents and their supporting data are stored and made available to state agencies.

34 Mary Poole outlines how the Social Security program was created as a method for reconsolidating racial segregation that sorted workers into those receiving Social Security benefits for their labor and those relegated to public assistance via welfare. Despite the fact that the Social Security Act did not specify race and was widely considered "colorblind," Poole explains how the language of the legislation helped create "work" and "dependence" as opposing categories, such that Black workers carried the stigma of dependency on the state while white workers earned benefits through legitimate labor (Poole, *Segregated Origins*). For further analysis of the racial classifications enacted—if not overtly stated—by the Social Security Act and other U.S. legislation, see Lipsitz, *Possessive Investment*.

35 Bergeron, Terrazas, and Meissner, "Social Security," 6.

36 "Social Security Gender No-Match Letters and Transgender Employees," National Center for Transgender Equality, January 15, 2008, accessed January 22, 2008, http://transequality.org/Issues/nomatch.html.

37 Michael T. Kaufman, "What Does the Pentagon See in 'Battle of Algiers'?" *New York Times*, September 7, 2003.

38 Somerville, *Queering the Color Line*, 26.

39 James, *Resisting State Violence*, 26.

40 National Commission, "9/11 Commission Report," 384.

41 The process for implementing the Real ID Act has undergone several deferrals alongside multiple legislative efforts to reform or repeal the act. At the time of this writing, the Real ID Act is set to be implemented in four phases, each requiring compliant ID documents for a different area, including restricted areas of federal facilities and federally regulated commercial aircraft. The latter is the final phase, which began January 22, 2018.

42 Torpey, *Invention of the Passport*, 163–66.

43 U.S. Congress, "Will Real ID," 4.

44 U.S. Congress, "Vulnerabilities," 9.

45 National Commission, "9/11 Commission Report," 389.

46 Agar, "Modern Horrors," 116.

47 Caplan and Torpey, "Introduction," 7.

48 Spade, "Methodologies," 249.

49 Mara Keisling, "NCTE No-Match Comment," National Center for Transgender Equality, August 15, 2006, accessed September 11, 2007, http://nctequality.org/Issues/I-9-nomatch-comment.pdf2.

50 Keisling, "NCTE No-Match Comment," 1.

51 National Transgender Advocacy Coalition, "Security Alert: 'Males Dressed as Females' to Be Scrutinized When Traveling," *Transgender Crossroads*, September 14, 2003, accessed March 20, 2004, http://www.tgcrossroads.org/news/archive.asp?aid=767.

52 National Transgender Advocacy Coalition, "Security Alert."

53 To some degree, NTAC's suggestion of strategic visibility resonates with Sandy Stone's call in "The *Empire* Strikes Back" for transgender people to resist the medical impetus to erase or hide their gendered pasts. Urging transgender people to remain visible as transgender regardless of their medical transition status, Stone writes, "in the transsexual's erased history we can find a story disruptive to the accepted discourses of gender" (295). Stone argues for a transformation of dominant understandings of transgender identity, asserting, "it is difficult to generate a counterdiscourse if one is programmed to disappear" (295). Because it is partly a response to the suppression of transgender identities in mainstream gay, lesbian, and feminist movements, Stone's essay was viewed both as controversial and as crucial to the galvanization of transgender scholars, activists, and communities in the United States. To be sure, there are significant differences between Stone's call and NTAC's. But the connections nevertheless indicate how visibility has long been a key point of contention in transgender studies and politics.

54 In making this argument, I am indebted to Jasbir Puar's analysis of homonationalist and sexual exception discourses leveraged against the perverse terrorist other (*Terrorist Assemblages*, chap. 1).

55 Torpey, *Invention of the Passport*, 166.

56 Foucault, *History of Sexuality*, 60.

57 Foucault, *History of Sexuality*, 61.

58 Discussing "mandatory volunteerism" in response to "soft surveillance" measures grounded in persuasion rather than punishment, Gary Marx also points to the pleasure produced through compliance with state requests. Because one aspect of soft surveillance involves appeals to good citizenship and patriotic duty, he argues, "there can be psychological gratifications from the revelation for both the voluntary revealer and the recipient of the information" ("Soft Surveillance," 45).

59 Foucault, *History of Sexuality*, 45.

60 "Statement: Open Letter to LGBTST Communities Opposing War," Audre Lorde Project, January 27, 2003, accessed March 15, 2017, https://alp.org/open-letter-lgbtst-communities-opposing-war. For further information about ALP's community meetings and other antiviolence work, see "Safe Outside the System: The SOS Collective," Audre Lorde Project, accessed March 20, 2017, https://alp.org/safe-outside-system-sos-collective. The ALP uses "LGBTST" for lesbian, gay, bisexual, Two Spirit, and transgender.

61 "Action Alert: A Decade of Resistance; Trans Day of Action 2014 Political Points of Unity," Audre Lorde Project, June 27, 2014, accessed March 20, 2017, https://alp.org/decade-resistance-trans-day-action-2014-political-points-unity.

62 The ALP is also a member of the ROOTS Coalition, a network of fourteen queer and trans people of color organizations in the United States working together since 2007, which took the Real ID Act as a "naturally intersectional" activist issue. For further discussion, see Steele, "Queering Intersectionality," 58–59.

63 "The Real ID Act: Bad Law for Our Community," National Center for Transgender Equality and Transgender Law Center, June 21, 2005, accessed July 29, 2009, http://www.realnightmare.org/images/File/NCTE%20realid.pdf.

64 "Our Approach and Principles," Sylvia Rivera Law Project, 2017, accessed June 15, 2017, https://srlp.org/about/principles/.

65 "The Impact of the War on Terror on LGBTSTQ Communities," Sylvia Rivera Law Project, July 15, 2008, accessed January 10, 2010, http://archive.srlp.org/impact-war-terror-lgbtstq-communities. Among other ways that SRLP put this framework into practice, it joined a coalition of immigrant rights organizations in New York to resist that state's new no-match program targeting driver's licenses for undocumented immigrants. Sylvia Rivera Law Project thus worked in solidarity with non-transgender immigrants while contributing its own analysis of how the no-match program and related policies like the Real ID Act affect both immigrant and nonimmigrant transgender people (Spade, *Normal Life*, 90–91).

66 In "Monster, Terrorist, Fag," Jasbir Puar and Amit Rai examine the production of "docile patriots" in the demand for hegemonic nationalist loyalty as a response to past and future terrorist attacks, arguing that these patriots' ability to become good citizens is directly dependent on their ability to clearly distinguish themselves from the figure of the terrorist.

67 Volpp, "Citizen and the Terrorist."

Chapter 2: Flying under the Radar

1   TSA's Frequently Asked Questions webpage explains, in response to the question "What are the screening procedures for transgender persons?" that AIT "has software that looks at the anatomy of men and women differently" ("Frequently Asked Questions," Transportation Security Administration, 2017, accessed June 11, 2017, https://www.tsa.gov/travel/frequently-asked-questions).

2   In late 2015, TSA replaced the term *anomaly* with *alarm*, after a transgender-identified woman posted on social media about being held by TSA "because of an 'anomaly' (my penis)" (Dawn Ennis, "Goodbye, 'Anomaly'—TSA's New Word for Trans Bodies Is 'Alarm,'" *The Advocate*, December 24, 2015).

3   For example, the Transgender Law Center released a 2011 statement noting, "While we understand the need for heightened airport security . . . we are fearful that transgender air travelers will be subjected to discriminatory or degrading conduct by TSA staff" ("Airport Screening and Travel Concerns for Transgender Passengers," Transgender Law Center, January 13, 2011, accessed March 15, 2011, https://transgenderlawcenter.org/archives/363). The National Center for Lesbian Rights released a similar statement: "New TSA Security Procedures Violate Privacy of Transgender Travelers," National Center for Lesbian Rights, November 23, 2010, accessed March 15, 2011, http://www.nclrights.org/press-room/press-release/new-tsa-security-procedures-violate-privacy-of-transgender-travelers/. The NCTE produced a resource guide for transgender travelers explaining which carry-on items are considered medically necessary and encouraging travelers to "be prepared to briefly explain the purpose of the item if asked": "Know Your Rights: Airport Security," National Center for Transgender Equality, 2017, accessed June 11, 2017, https://www.transequality.org/know-your-rights/airport-security. The NCTE also filed comments with TSA in 2013, urging it to "shift away from the current model to one that is more tailored, effective, and privacy-protective" ("Despite Some Progress in Airport Security, Bigger Changes Needed," National Center for Transgender Equality, October 23, 2014, accessed November 9, 2014, http://www.transequality.org/blog/despite-some-progress-airport-security-bigger-changes-needed).

4   See, for example, Hausman, *Changing Sex*. Other scholarship argues that transgender people are detrimental to feminism and women's rights in part because transgender bodies are crafted through the sexist medical establishment (see, for example, Raymond, *Transsexual Empire*). More recent work situates transgender identities within shifting social, cultural, political, and legal understandings of sex and gender, and continues to foreground medical and scientific authority as playing key roles in the production of such identities (see, for example, Meyerowitz, *How Sex Changed*). Likewise, the structure of *The Transgender Studies Reader* (ed. Stryker and Whittle) illustrates the centrality of medicine not only to basic understandings of transgender identity but to the formation of transgender studies as a field: the anthology's first section, titled "Sex, Gender, and Science," primarily

deals with sexology and other medical studies of nonnormative sex and gender. I cite these various texts here not to suggest that they are equivalent or even representative, but rather to gesture at the extent to which medicine and medical developments shape conceptions of transgender identities and bodies across a variety of sites.

5 Nick Gorton summarizes these debates from a physician's perspective in "Transgender as Mental Illness," proposing a middle ground in which transgender identity is still considered a medical condition but not stigmatized as a disorder. In *Undoing Gender*, chap. 4, Judith Butler addresses the social and political contexts in which diagnosis functions.

6 Much of the groundwork for this type of claim has been laid by disability rights organizations, which have used medical necessity frameworks to challenge health insurance companies' refusal to cover care. In addition to some of the complications outlined in this chapter, one drawback of the "medically necessary" approach is that it is frequently determined on an individual, case-by-case basis. Nevertheless, this work signals some of the ways that transgender theory and activism are indebted and connected to disability studies and disability political organizing. For further discussion of this relationship, see, for example, Clare, "Body Shame"; Levi and Klein, "Pursuing Protection"; Mog, "Threads of Commonality."

7 It is important not to confuse the recognition of care as medically necessary with the actual provision of that care. Particular forms of medical care may still be withheld for many reasons, including denial of claims on a case-by-case basis and lack of providers for a specific type of care within a reasonable geographic distance. This echoes broader frameworks of health care in the U.S., from abortion services to the distribution of health insurance more generally, wherein formal access to care alone cannot ensure its meaningful provision.

8 "Professional Organization Statements Supporting Transgender People in Health Care," Lambda Legal, June 8, 2012, accessed November 11, 2012, https://www.lambdalegal.org/publications/fs_professional-org-statements-supporting-trans-health. The World Professional Association for Transgender Health released its own formal statement supporting the classification of transgender-specific care, as well as ongoing routine care of transgender patients, as medically necessary. "Medical Necessity Statement," WPATH, June 17, 2008, accessed November 11, 2012, http://www.wpath.org/medical_necessity_statement.cfm.

9 Shakespeare, "Social Model," 216.

10 "Whole Body Imaging FAQ," National Center for Transgender Equality, June 2009, accessed July 29, 2009, http://transequality.org/Resources/NCTE_Body_Scan.pdf, 2.

11 "Whole Body Imaging FAQ," 3.

12 "Whole Body Imaging FAQ," 3.

13 "Air Travel Tips for Transgender People," National Center for Transgender Equality, accessed December 16, 2011, http://transequality.org/Issues/travel.html.

14 "Airport Security and Transgender People," National Center for Transgender

Equality, accessed November 30, 2012, http://transequality.org/Resources/Airport Security_November2012.pdf.

15 "What to Expect at the TSA Checkpoint if You Are a Breast Cancer Survivor," Transportation Security Administration, accessed September 15, 2012, http://www.tsa.gov/travelers/airtravel/breast_prosthetic.shtm.

16 "Transgender Travelers: Special Considerations," Transportation Security Administration, accessed December 6, 2012, http://www.tsa.gov/traveler-information/transgender-travelers.

17 Davis, "End of Identity Politics," 273.

18 Kevles, *Naked to the Bone*, 74.

19 Eugene Greneker, "Development of Inexpensive RADAR Flashlight for Law Enforcement and Corrections Applications," report submitted to the U.S. Department of Justice, Georgia Institute of Technology, April 30, 2000, https://www.ncjrs.gov/pdffiles1/nij/grants/185251.pdf, 1–2.

20 Jane M. Sanders, "New Flashlight Sees Through Doors as Well as Windows," *UniSci: Daily University Science News*, April 16, 2001, accessed June 9, 2009, http://www.unisci.com/stories/20012/0416015.htm.

21 Carissa Caramanis, "Backscatter Imaging Technology Reveals the Suspicious," *Corrections Connection Network News*, July 26, 2000; de Moulpied, Rothschild, and Smith, "X-Ray BodySearch Eliminates Strip Search."

22 See for example U.S. Food and Drug Administration, Technical Electronic Product Radiation Safety Standards Committee, meeting transcript, October 1, 2003, accessed March 15, 2004, http://www.fda.gov/ohrms/dockets/ac/03/transcripts/3987T1.htm.

23 Assmus, "Early History," 11.

24 Cartwright, *Screening the Body*, 152–53.

25 "Age Determination Procedures for Custody Decisions," Immigration and Customs Enforcement, August 20, 2004, accessed March 15, 2010, https://www.ice.gov/doclib/foia/dro_policy_memos/agedeterminationproceduresforcustodydecisionsaug202004.pdf; Chris Hedges, "Crucial I.N.S. Gatekeeper: The Airport Dentist," *New York Times*, July 22, 2000.

26 Hedges, "Crucial I.N.S. Gatekeeper."

27 "Ethics Abandoned: Medical Professionalism and Detainee Abuse in the 'War on Terror,'" Institute on Medicine as a Profession, 2013, accessed January 10, 2016, http://imapny.org/wp-content/themes/imapny/File%20Library/Documents/IMAP-EthicsTextFina12.pdf.

28 For example, in *Dark Matters*, Simone Browne outlines various studies and legal cases naming the extent to which Black women were disproportionately singled out for detention and strip searches in airport screenings prior to 9/11 (132–34). Likewise, in "The Case against Race Profiling," Kevin Johnson cites multiple instances of detention and harassment targeting people of color and immigrants in airports prior to 9/11, including anti-immigrant actions undertaken by groups of private citizens.

29 Paul Giblin and Eric Lipton, "New Airport X-Rays Scan Bodies, Not Just Bags," *New York Times*, February 24, 2007.

30 Dana Bash, "TSA Turns Away Sen. Rand Paul at Airport Checkpoint," CNN, January 23, 2012.

31 David G. Savage, "The Fight against Full-Body Scanners at Airports," *Los Angeles Times*, January 13, 2010. These comments also imply a special, commonsense kind of protection needed for certain girls and women, a framework that I consider in greater depth in chapter 3.

32 Bash, "TSA Turns Away."

33 A 2005 DHS report reviewing the TSA pat-down procedures notes that as part of their training, screeners are "provided with a script to follow regarding what information to tell the passengers" ("Review of the Transportation Security Administration's Use of Pat-Downs in Screening Procedures," Office of Inspector General, Department of Homeland Security, November 2005, accessed March 20, 2010, https://www.oig.dhs.gov/assets/Mgmt/OIGr_06-10_Nov05.pdf). In early 2017, TSA instituted a new "universal pat-down" procedure, "standardizing its physical search procedure rather than allow[ing] screeners to choose among types of searches to reduce the chance of poor decisions at crucial security checkpoints" (Hugo Martin, "TSA Quietly Launches New 'Enhanced' Pat-Down Procedure," *Los Angeles Times*, March 6, 2017). The rationale for this change in procedure makes clear the variability intrinsic to the pat-down, even as it is continually standardized.

34 "Letters Received by the Transportation Security Administration (TSA) Complaining about Revised Pat-Down Airline Security Procedures, 2010," Transportation Security Administration, 2012, accessed July 12, 2013, http://www.tsa .gov/sites/default/files/publications/pdf/f-4_statement_of_s_gentry_to_asac_18 sep12.pdf.

35 See Somerville, *Queering the Color Line*, chap. 1; Terry, *An American Obsession*; Fausto-Sterling, "Gender, Race, and Nation."

36 Elizabeth Fernandez, "State Prisons Scanning Visitors with X-Rays," *San Francisco Chronicle*, November 3, 1997.

37 Formal legal rights to privacy, including bodily privacy, can vary somewhat according to different carceral facilities' policies. In making this argument about the function of privacy in the prison, I am less concerned with the specific legal parameters than with a conception of the prison as an institution that evacuates bodily privacy for incarcerated persons.

38 Fernandez, "State Prisons Scanning."

39 Among many texts discussing these issues, see, for example, Bridges, *Poverty of Privacy Rights*; Roberts, *Killing the Black Body*; and Silliman and Battacharjee, *Policing the National Body*.

40 In general, disability advocacy organizations have not addressed such misinterpretations as explicitly as transgender advocacy groups. The Amputee Coalition of America's magazine published an article on the organization's educational efforts

with TSA that notes this concern: "Screeners are being educated about the different kinds of prosthetic equipment, as well as alterations that could indicate a hidden weapon" (Bill Dupes, "Making the Skies Safe Once Again," *InMotion* 1.4, no. 1 [January–February 2004]: 64). More commonly, disability advocacy groups have focused on the need to familiarize TSA employees with different medical devices, but these discussions can then lead to individuals describing instances in which their medical technologies are misread. For instance, at the end of an online interview with the American Diabetes Association's lead legal advocate, several people commented with anecdotes about how TSA agents demanded special screenings of insulin pumps and syringes, or how TSA machines interpreted insulin as an explosive (Joslin Communications, "Q&A with Katharine Gordon: TSA Diabetes Policy," Joslin Diabetes Center, February 5, 2014, accessed March 15, 2017, http://blog.joslin.org/2016/04/qa-with-katharine-gordon-tsa-diabetes -policy/). Since 2002, TSA has hosted an annual Disability and Multicultural Coalition Conference, at which TSA officials meet with many different advocacy groups, including NCTE as well as the two disability organizations named above.

41 Volpp, "Citizen and the Terrorist," 1576.
42 Asad, *On Suicide Bombing*, 59.
43 Hage, "'Comes a Time,'" 71.
44 Hage, "'Comes a Time,'" 74.
45 Puar, *Terrorist Assemblages*, 218.
46 Asad, *On Suicide Bombing*, 22.
47 Asad, *On Suicide Bombing*, 61.
48 Terry, "Significant Injury," 206.
49 Howell, *Technology in the Hospital*, 118.
50 Cartwright, *Screening the Body*.
51 These assurances connect with those that insist the X-ray scanner is a less intrusive form of surveillance than the pat-down, because it works at a distance. But the machines' use of radiation enables a literal (if less immediately visible) penetration of the body, the traces of which belie repeated claims of safety and comfort through distance.
52 See, for example, Arneri, "Reconstruction of the Male Genitalia"; Jarvis, *Male Body at War*, 112–18; Serlin, *Replaceable You*.
53 Wettlaufer and Weigel, *Urology in the Vietnam War*, 160.
54 David Brown, "Amputations and Genital Injuries Increase Sharply among Soldiers in Afghanistan," *Washington Post*, March 4, 2011.
55 Asad, *On Suicide Bombing*, 61.
56 Clancy Sigal, "The US Isn't Facing Up to the Literal Emasculation of Its Soldiers," *UK Guardian*, April 19, 2001. For further discussion of the concept of "signature wounds," see Terry, "Significant Injury."
57 Mercer, *Welcome to the Jungle*, 185.
58 Eng, *Racial Castration*, 3.
59 Among the news articles appearing on the rise in wartime genital trauma among

U.S. soldiers, several describe these injuries as emasculating (see, for example, Sigal, "The US Isn't"). Following from the focus on testicles in describing the war's signature wound of genital injuries, this focus on emasculation presumes a particular type of body upon which rests a particular gendered status (or loss thereof) in U.S. military combat.

60 As of 2013, although TSA had ended its contract with Rapiscan, the manufacturer of most of the airport backscatter scanners (and of the early Secure 1000 used in prisons), it was still contracted with at least one backscatter manufacturer. The TSA's removal of Rapiscan machines from airports appears to be in part because the company failed to comply in a timely manner to a congressional request for increased privacy measures in the machinery, and in part because the company was accused of falsifying data. Jeff Plungis, "Naked-Image Scanners to Be Removed from US Airports," *Bloomberg*, January 18, 2013.

61 Hugo Martin, "Full-Body Scanners Pulled from Airports Get Use in Prisons," *Los Angeles Times*, May 25, 2014.

62 See, for example, "Traveling While Trans: Questions Remain with TSA's New Software," *Advancing Transgender Equality* (blog), July 25, 2011, accessed July 29, 2011, https://transgenderequality.wordpress.com/2011/07/25/traveling-while -trans-questions-remain-with-tsa's-new-software/; and "New TSA Policy Codifies Discrimination against Transgender People," National LGBTQ Task Force, March 4, 2016, accessed July 9, 2016, http://www.thetaskforce.org/new-tsa-policy -codifies-discrimination-against-transgender-people/.

63 Carter, *Heart of Whiteness*, 1–2. In *Building Access*, Aimi Hamraie shows how these two sculptures, along with other images of the standard or ideal human figure, served as a "normate template" that shaped architecture and design as well as citizenship in the early twentieth century. Like Carter, Hamraie contends that this work is accomplished through the purported neutrality and universality of the figures, adding that "the standardization of normate world-building often hid them in plain view" (*Building Access*, 29).

64 Jos Truitt, "The TSA Makes It Dangerous to Fly While Trans," Feministing, August 18, 2011, accessed August 18, 2011, http://feministing.com/2011/08/18/the -tsa-makes-it-dangerous-to-fly-while-trans/.

65 "TSA PreCheck Reaches Milestone with More Than 5 Million Travelers Enrolled," Transportation Security Administration, July 5, 2017, accessed July 9, 2017, https://www.tsa.gov/news/releases/2017/07/05/tsa-precheck-reaches-milestone -more-5-million-travelers-enrolled.

66 While avoiding AIT scans is commonly understood as a perk of Precheck, the TSA website does not officially list it alongside the program's other benefits, and multiple news articles demonstrate that, like all airport security practices, this expected protocol varies widely in practice. Christopher Elliot, "Travelers Are Less Certain about the Airport Screening Experience Than They've Been in Years," *Washington Post*, January 28, 2016.

67 The video is available at "Enroll in TSA Pre✓ for a Smarter Security Checkpoint Ex-

perience," Transportation Security Administration, https://www.tsa.gov/videos
/enroll-tsa-precheck-smarter-security-checkpoint-experience-0.

Chapter 3: Bathrooms, Borders, and Biometrics

1 "Bad for Business: What the Phoenix City 'Bathroom Bill' Means for Your Business," Center for Arizona Policy, February 2013, accessed April 24, 2014, http://
www.azpolicy.org/media-uploads/pdfs/Bathroom%20Bill/Bathroom%20
Bill%20Bad%20for%20Business.pdf.

2 Mike Morris, "Equal Rights Law Opponents Deliver Signatures Seeking Repeal,"
Houston Chronicle, July 3, 2014.

3 HB 87, Utah State Legislature, 2014 General Session. This bill failed to pass the
Utah House in March 2014.

4 Currah and Minter, *Transgender Equality*, 21.

5 West, *Transforming Citizenships*, 29.

6 In "Colonial Visions," Alison Moore notes that a lack of public toilets for women
"served to encourage the limitation of women to the private sphere, with forays into
the public only as long as the intervals between bladder and bowel movements" (110).
These social norms lingered even when bathrooms were available specifically for
women, creating a dilemma for many white, class-privileged women: "On one hand
was the opportunity to move through the city with a new freedom; on the other
was the necessity to maintain the appearance of respectable female behavior, which
included the denial of the existence of bodily processes and needs. Toilets were especially fraught through being associated, rightly or wrongly, with immoral behavior"
(Brown-May and Fraser, "Gender, Respectability," 85).

7 Kogan, "Sex Separation," 156.

8 Kogan, "Sex Separation," 156, 164.

9 Lauren Quock, *Modified Bathroom Signs*, Laurenquock.com, accessed April 2,
2016, http://laurenquock.com/section/270348-Modified-Bathroom-Signs.html.

10 Among the many examples of policies and practices that criminalize people of
color in U.S. public spaces are the disproportionate suspension, expulsion, and
arrest of students of color, especially Black students, in public schools (see, for
example, 2013 data collected for Chicago public schools by Project NIA at http://
chiyouthjustice.files.wordpress.com/2013/10/chicago-school-to-prison-updated-
9-13-w-lgbt.pdf, accessed July 12, 2016) and the Special Registration program
implemented in 2002, which primarily targeted men from twenty-three Muslim-
majority countries and required them to be registered, fingerprinted, and photographed by U.S. immigration authorities, with this information often used to
arrest, detain, or deport them (see Cainkar and Maira, "Targeting Arab/Muslim/
South Asian Americans"), as well as legislation such as Arizona's SB 1070, discussed later in this chapter.

11 George Lipsitz provides a cogent history of these spatial practices. See Lipsitz,
Possessive Investment; Lipsitz, "Racialization of Space."

12 Quock's piece uses an original sign about racially marked drinking fountains as the base for a commentary on present-day gendered bathrooms, though images of racially segregated bathroom signs are widely available in historical archives. This is a curious substitution that might suggest a basic equivalence of various public spaces that are divided along lines of race and gender. As this chapter shows, however, public bathrooms host a particular set of bodily surveillance practices and related anxieties distinct from (though related to) scrutiny in other public spaces.

13 Wasserstrom, "Racism, Sexism," 109.

14 For instance, Norbert Elias's classic sociological work, *The Civilizing Process*, which traces the methods by which Western cultures imagined themselves to have developed linearly from barbaric to civilized, notes that the earliest such efforts occur particularly through individuals' bodily control and modesty. Notably, he suggests that the Westernized toilet formed a key part of this civilizing process (109–20). For further discussion of the relationship between cleanliness and civilizing processes, see Douglas, *Purity and Danger*; and Ross, *Fast Cars*, chap. 2.

15 Wasserstrom, "Racism, Sexism," 110. Mary Anne Case argues against this distinction, yet still tends to reference race and gender as separate and analogous rather than as mutually informing categories, and relies on the bodily secrecy primarily available to white bodies. Citing interviews with officers at a military institute that had recently begun admitting women for the first time, for instance, Case writes that "women to them, like blacks to their Jim Crow predecessors, were 'dirty and impure' and that, if anything, [gendered] segregation of the toilets, perhaps by preserving precisely that mystery about the bodies of the opposite sex on which Wasserstrom focuses, fosters the conviction that space with women threatens with the possibility of contamination" (Case, "Why Not Abolish," 223).

16 Bederman, *Manliness and Civilization*, 25. Likewise, Alison Moore notes that several ethnographers linked "improper" excretory practices with primitive status in language that supports Bederman's argument about civilizational discourse: "Europeans, while once prone to such behavior, had progressed to another stage of social development, and those who still practiced excretory rituals were embodiments of what Europeans once were in the timeline of progress" (Moore, "Colonial Visions," 111).

17 Segregated public spaces in the U.S., perhaps especially bathrooms, help construct and reinforce racial categories and the meanings assigned to them. For instance, Lisa García Bedolla shows how Latinos "complicated the U.S. racial structure" inasmuch as that structure commonly depends on visual assessment of racial characteristics within a narrow frame of racial categories. In the case of Latino siblings whose different skin colors might position one as white and one as Black, Bedolla notes that "at the height of segregation, this meant that they would go to separate schools, get to use separate bathroom facilities, and in general would have a very different set of opportunities" (Bedolla, *Latino Politics*, 8).

18 Bederman, *Manliness and Civilization*, 25.

19 For further discussion of this labeling of bathroom doors, see Abel, *Signs of the Times*, chap. 4.

20 For examples of this claim, see Annie Knox, "Utah Proposal Dictates Transgender Bathroom Use," Associated Press, February 4, 2014; Nicole Maines, "I Am Proof That Bathrooms Should Be Gender Free," *Time*, November 2, 2015; and Sonali Kolhatkar, "'Bathroom Bills' Are Attacks on the Humanity of Transgender People," *Common Dreams*, April 2, 2016. Kenyon Farrow offers an extended critique of the "second-class citizens" analogy, noting that it emerged in earnest in the early 1990s, pushed forward by mainstream and primarily white gay organizations to support same-sex marriage arguments (Farrow, "Is Gay Marriage Anti-Black???").

21 Ong, *Buddha Is Hiding*, 15.

22 See, for example, "Transgender Law Center Outraged by Discriminatory Arizona Bill," Transgender Law Center, March 28, 2013, accessed April 2, 2013, http://transgenderlawcenter.org/archives/3800; and "NCTE Condemns Committee Action on AZ Anti-trans Bathroom Bill, SB 1045," National Center for Transgender Equality, March 28, 2013, accessed April 2, 2013, http://www.transequality.org/blog/ncte-condemns-committee-action-on-az-anti-trans-bathroom-bill-sb-1045. The revised bill (SB 1045) was also eventually withdrawn.

23 Champaign, IL, Municipal Code, Section 17-3; Urbana, IL, Municipal Code, Section 12-39. Urbana also adds "or the ability to become pregnant."

24 Los Angeles, CA, Municipal Code, Article 12, Section 49.71.

25 St. Paul, MN, Municipal Code, Section 183.02. Champaign, Illinois, includes an exception allowing "differential treatment" when it is "designed to promote the safety, health or welfare of individuals" and includes "single sex bathrooms" as one possible example. It is important not to view these kinds of exceptions as easy precursors to the explicitly criminalizing bathroom legislation beginning with Arizona. The later legislative efforts certainly capitalize on the keyword *safety*, yet they also drastically constrict definitions of sex and gender that many previous ordinances conceptualized so broadly. Because definitions in earlier legislation encompass a variety of sex and gender possibilities, safety cannot be understood as linked to any particular sex or gender. However, more recent bathroom bills implicitly define safety through sexed and gendered sameness, with public discourse positioning transgender people—and transgender women in particular—as threats to that safety.

26 Megan Rolland, "Transgender Ordinance Backlash," *Gainesville Sun*, February 3, 2008.

27 Rolland, "Transgender Ordinance."

28 For discussion of other prominent state-level challenges to transgender use of public bathrooms, see Levi and Redman, "Cross-Dressing Case." Of particular note is the Minnesota case *Goins v. West Publishing*, which denied a transgender person's claim despite the state's transgender-inclusive nondiscrimination ordinance.

29 More than thirty states introduced legislation similar to Arizona's SB 1070 during 2010 and 2011, and these copycat laws passed in Utah, Indiana, Alabama, Georgia, and South Carolina.

30 Among others, see the ACLU's statement on SB 1070 at http://www.aclu.org /arizonas-sb-1070 and Alto Arizona's explanation of how the law allows racial profiling at "About SB 1070," http://www.altoarizona.com/sb1070.html. Sandra Soto and Miranda Joseph argue that laws like SB 1070 also "license bald racism from the public" (Soto and Joseph, "Neoliberalism," 47).

31 For a history of the state regulations and practices that preceded and lay the groundwork for SB 1070, see Campbell, "Road to S.B. 1070."

32 Jan Morris's 1974 memoir, *Conundrum*, is perhaps the most classic example of narrating gender transition through the lens of travel, particularly travel away from and then back to the United States. This metaphor also occurs in academic work: Jay Prosser suggests that "an appropriate analogical frame for the transsexual's writing of transition as a journey may be that of immigration," implicitly casting "the transsexual" as a single universalized figure for whom immigration appears as metaphor rather than political process or legal status (Prosser, "Exceptional Locations," 88). Other scholars critically question the use of such analogies (see Halberstam, *Female Masculinity*, 170). For further discussion and other examples of travel metaphors, see Aizura, "The Persistence."

33 The slide show is linked on the TLC website at Transgender Law Center, http:// transgenderlawcenter.org/archives/3144, accessed July 12, 2016.

34 Among other reasons, widely varying policies governing nationality and sex designation mean that many people do not in fact have a legal nationality or consistent documented sex.

35 Commonly cited problems with analogy include its emphasis on similarity at the expense of complex relationships between different categories, generalization at the expense of historical or political specificity, and reliance on two separate groups that cannot then be understood as interacting or overlapping. See, for example, Grillo and Wildman, "Obscuring the Importance"; and Butler, "Against Proper Objects."

36 Christina Hanhardt traces neighborhood safety campaigns not only against but among LGBT communities in urban U.S. spaces, for instance, in turns to quality-of-life rhetoric targeting LGBTQ youth and transgender women of color. Hanhardt, *Safe Space*.

37 Abby Jensen, "Welcome to Arizona—Papers, Please!," Transgender Law Center, March 20, 2013, accessed April 2, 2013, http://transgenderlawcenter.org/archives /3661.

38 Danielle Dobrusin, "Bathroom Bill Could Affect Transgender Students, Sending AZ Politics Down Toilet Again," *Daily Wildcat*, October 23, 2014.

39 Jorge Rivas, "Arizona Doesn't Want Transgender Folks to Use Public Restrooms," *ColorLines*, March 28, 2013, accessed April 2, 2013, http://colorlines.com

/archives/2013/03/toilet_papers_please_arizona_doesnt_want_transgender_folks
_to_use_public_restrooms.html.

40 SB 1432, Fifty-First Arizona State Legislature, 2013.

41 Among many texts addressing the relationship between disability and citizenship,
see, for example, Dilts, "Incurable Blackness"; Russell, *Reading Embodied Citizenship*; and Hirschmann and Linker, *Civil Disabilities*.

42 Schweik, *Ugly Laws*.

43 For an overview of the literature addressing the desexualization and related in-
fantilization of disabled people, as well as analysis of how this work can erase and
stigmatize asexual people with disabilities, see Kim, "Asexuality in Disability
Narratives."

44 Levi and Klein, "Pursuing Protection"; Spade, "Resisting Medicine."

45 Arizona's Proposition 200, passed by a narrow majority in 2004, required proof of
U.S. citizenship when registering to vote or accessing public benefits in the state.
The legislation sparked a lengthy legal battle and was ultimately overturned by the
U.S. Supreme Court in 2013. See Ross D. Franklin, "Supreme Court Strikes Down
Arizona Voting Law," CBS News, June 17, 2013.

46 As of April 2017, four U.S. states—Idaho, Kansas, Ohio, and Tennessee—and
Puerto Rico either explicitly prohibit or refuse to allow the amendment of sex designation on birth certificates. "State-by-State Overview: Changing Gender Markers
on Birth Certificates," Transgender Law Center, April 2017, accessed April 24, 2017,
https://transgenderlawcenter.org/resources/id/state-by-state-overview-changing
-gender-markers-on-birth-certificates.

47 In *When Biometrics Fail*, Shoshana Magnet notes that "analog forms of biometric
science date back to the nineteenth century," linking current digital biometric
surveillance to early anthropometry and fingerprinting (8). Keith Breckenridge
traces the development of biometric data collection through Francis Galton's work
on statistics and early eugenics programs in the late 1800s, particularly as part
of British imperialism in South Africa (Breckenridge, *Biometric State*, chap. 1).
In *Dark Matters*, Simone Browne points out that anthropometry "is still being
invoked in biometric information technology R&D" (111).

48 U.S. Congress, "Biometric Identifiers," 36.

49 In 1993, the Immigration and Naturalization Services implemented the Passenger
Accelerated Service System, which used hand geometry as biometric identification
to streamline entry into the U.S. for certain prescreened frequent travelers. And
by the late 1990s, U.S. border control agents were using fingerprinting to identify
and track undocumented immigrants crossing the U.S.-Mexico border (Verne G.
Kopytoff, "A Silicon Wall Rises on the Border," *New York Times*, January 14, 1999).

50 U.S. Congress, "Biometric Identifiers," 72.

51 For further discussion of these applications, see Gates, *Our Biometric Future*;
Magnet, *When Biometrics Fail*; and Hall, "Of Ziploc Bags." The Information
Awareness Office, established by the U.S. Department of Defense in 2002 and

charged with designing new technologies to track and identify human bodies, explained its objectives as providing "critical early warning support for force protection and homeland defense against terrorist, criminal, and other human-based threats" through biometric data collection. Although these overarching goals clearly centralize anti-terrorism efforts, the Information Awareness Office also notes that results from its facial recognition research will "provide input to the design of the United States Border Entry/Exit System," illustrating how intertwined antiterrorism and anti-immigration practices can be, particularly in the context of biometric surveillance ("Human ID at a Distance," Defense Advanced Research Projects Agency, 2002, accessed April 16, 2003, http://www.darpa.mil/iao/HID .htm).

52 Irma van der Ploeg argues in "Borderline Identities" that such technologies effectively move the border into the body itself, "transform[ing] geographical borders into lived and embodied identities" (179).

53 U.S. Congress, "Biometric Identifiers," 9.

54 "Home," Defense Advanced Research Projects Agency, 2002, accessed April 20, 2003, https://www.darpa.mil/iao/index.htm.

55 Rana, *Terrifying Muslims*, 61.

56 Cacho, *Social Death*, 101.

57 Browne, *Dark Matters*, 113. This 2002 study also noted that elderly people and people who work with their hands are likely to have worn fingerprints that are difficult to read. In addition to positing certain groups as less legible to biometric technologies, these claims illustrate the depth of investment in the body as a site of objective truth: the study itself observes that bodily characteristics including fingerprints may change over time for many reasons, yet fingerprinting remains one of the most well known and routine forms of biometric identification.

58 For discussion of some of these studies, see Beauchamp, "When Things Don't Add Up."

59 In addition to these reading practices, fingerprinting and other biometric data collection practices shape and are shaped by racial and economic disparities. For example, disproportionate arrest rates in communities of color and among poor and immigrant populations mean these groups are overrepresented in biometric databases and more vulnerable to future surveillance and detention (see Levine et al., "Drug Arrests"; and Lynch, "From Fingerprints").

60 HB 87, Utah State Legislature, 2014 General Session. The following four quotations are also drawn from this text.

61 Currah and Mulqueen, "Securitizing Gender," 571. Careful readers of HB 87 may also wonder whether physicians could assess their own gender, and if so, whether this assessment would then constitute gender or gender identity.

62 SB 1045, Fifty-First Arizona State Legislature, 2013.

63 SB 1045, Fifty-First Arizona State Legislature, 2013.

64 Eric Brown, "Everything You Should Know about Arizona's Controversial 'Transgender Bathroom Bill,'" *International Business Times*, March 28, 2013.

65 This professed shift away from bodies to focus on mannerisms was also a contentious point in the debates over Arizona's SB 1070. Although that legislation was amended one week after its passage to specify that officers "may not consider race, color, or national origin" in enforcing the law, such identity categories often come to stand in for citizenship, leaving some bodies disproportionately vulnerable to the new policies. In some cases, state actors' firm denial of racial profiling makes clear that racial classification may be read off the body in a variety of ways, as when representative Brian Bilbray (R-CA) suggested how law enforcement officers could identify undocumented immigrants without relying on race: "They will look at the kind of dress you wear, there is a different type of attire, there is a different type of—right down to the shoes, right down to the clothes." Mimi Nguyen notes that these shifts of legal status from skin to clothing "do not constitute any sort of departure from race discourses that target the body as a continuous surface of legible information about pathology, capacity, and so forth." Because "clothes are often *epidermalized*—that is, they are understood as contiguous with the body that wears them, a sort of second skin," race and color can be persistently read onto bodies by other means, despite the explicit prohibition against their consideration (see Nguyen, "Clothes Epidermalized").

66 Magnet, *When Biometrics Fail*, 48.

67 See, for example, Boris, "You Wouldn't Want"; Godfrey, "Bayonets, Brainwashing."

68 Ceyhan, "Technologization of Security," 111.

69 Finn, *Capturing the Criminal Image*, 82.

70 Lyon, *Surveillance after Snowden*, 113.

71 Agamben, "Bodies without Words," 169.

72 Jensen, "Welcome to Arizona."

73 Among many important works concerning regulation and foreclosure of public space for marginalized populations, see, for example, Hanhardt, *Safe Space*; Lipsitz, "Racialization of Space"; Mananzala, "FIERCE Fight for Power"; Schweik, *Ugly Laws*; Sears, *Arresting Dress*.

74 Kafer, *Feminist, Queer, Crip*, 154.

75 Jensen, "Welcome to Arizona."

76 As I revised this chapter amid the flood of news about North Carolina's HB 2 in mid-2016, two other news stories filtered through my social media feeds. One exposed the demeaning and injurious labor practices for line workers in U.S. poultry-processing plants, including routine denial of bathroom breaks, forcing many workers to limit their fluid intake and wear diapers on the job (Tom Philpott, "Oxfam: Poultry Industry Routinely Denies Workers Bathroom Breaks," *Mother Jones*, May 16, 2016). The other reported that a white police officer at a public high school in Philadelphia wrestled a Black student to the ground for attempting to use the school restroom without a pass (Daniel Denvir, "'I Felt Like I Was Going to Die': Philly Student Alleges Police Assault over Bathroom Visit," *Salon*, May 12, 2016, http://www.salon.com/2016/05/12/i_felt_like_i_was_going_to_die_philly _students_allege_police_assault_over_bathroom_visit/). These stories, among

others, suggest the limitations of framing criminalizing bathroom bills as either new developments or as simply transphobic or homophobic in intent or effect. Surveillance of public facilities can be understood through these stories as part of a larger process of control mobilized against those who depend upon public accommodations or have limited access to private space.

77 Billies, "Low Income LGBTGNC."

78 Adey, *Mobility*, 109.

79 This is true even when biometric projects specifically consider transgender people. Recent studies attempt to categorize transgender-identified bodies in order to develop biometric technologies to better track and identify them. Thus even bodies that biometric programs themselves acknowledge as changeable are understood as simply needing to be sorted correctly. For further analysis of these projects, see Beauchamp, "When Things Don't Add Up."

80 See, for example, Leti Volpp's assessment of the ways that immigration law naturalizes national borders by imagining the state as "innocent and natural, while the bodies that move inside and outside this space are suspect" ("Imaginings of Space," 464).

81 Shannon Bream, "New Al Qaeda Manual Reflects Changing Face of Terror," *Fox News*, August 14, 2008.

82 I draw loosely here on Doreen Massey's argument about how places should be defined: not through "simple counterposition to the outside," but "through the particularity of linkage *to* that 'outside,' which is therefore itself what constitutes the place. This helps get away from the common association between penetrability and vulnerability. For it is this kind of association which makes invasion by newcomers so threatening" (Massey, *Space, Place, and Gender*, 155).

83 Barcan, "Dirty Spaces," 36.

84 Boris, "You Wouldn't Want," 94.

85 I describe the actors' gender and race here not to make my own assumptions about them, but to convey my analysis of how the video intends these bodies to be interpreted.

86 "How Will the November Election in Houston Affect You?," Campaign for Houston, 2015, accessed December 12, 2015, http://www.campaignforhouston.com/news /how-will-the-november-election-in-houston-affect-you.

87 Davis, *Violence against Women*, 6–7. While non-transgender white men play the role of deceptive predator in these videos, as a group they are perhaps least likely to experience the intensified policing and community surveillance that the videos implicitly call for.

88 On the innocence attached to white childhood, see Bernstein, *Racial Innocence*. It is worth noting that the age of childhood is sometimes itself contentious in these debates. North Carolina's HB 2 includes an exception for parents of children aged six or younger. State representative Tricia Cotham, a Democrat, argued for expanding this exception to those aged eleven and younger, but "Republican House leaders would not allow it" (Paul Woolverton, "North Carolina's 'Bathroom' Law

Is about More Than Who's in the Next Stall," *Fayetteville Observer*, April 3, 2016). The arbitrary line drawn here to mark the age of properly innocent childhood recalls Gayle Rubin's prescient 1991 discussion of moral panics regarding cross-generational sex and desire (Rubin, "Thinking Sex").

89 Illinois's HB 4474, for example, would require students in public schools to use bathrooms and changing rooms according to their physical sex (based on chromosomes and anatomy at birth). After the bill's introduction in early 2016, the conservative Christian organization Illinois Family Institute urged their membership to contact state legislators in support, stressing on their website that the bill was necessary to protect students' safety. During the same period, Illinois dramatically reduced and closed public services statewide; owed more than $200,000 from the state government, for instance, Champaign County's rape crisis center was forced to cut staff and operating hours, working under continual threat of closure (Debra Pressey, "Rape Crisis Center Seeks Help," *The News-Gazette*, February 2, 2016).

90 The language of privacy is ubiquitous: South Dakota's HB 1008, which the state's governor vetoed in 2016, applied to public schools and was informally titled the Student Physical Privacy Act. Another Student Physical Privacy Act, HB 2737, introduced in Kansas in 2016, states that "children and young adults have natural and normal concerns about physical privacy when they are in various states of undress" and stipulates that students may sue for $2,500 in statutory damages if they encounter "a person of the opposite sex" in a sex-segregated space on public school grounds.

91 Woolverton, "North Carolina's 'Bathroom' Law."

92 See North Carolina's Women and Children's Protection Act of 2015, which also extends the waiting period for abortion services. For information regarding state-level ultrasound requirements, see the Guttmacher Institute's summary, "Requirement for Ultrasound," http://www.guttmacher.org/state-policy/explore/requirements-ultrasound, accessed May 4, 2016.

93 "Drug Testing for Welfare Recipients and Public Assistance," National Conference of State Legislatures, March 28, 2016, accessed May 4, 2016, http://www.ncsl.org/research/human-services/drug-testing-and-public-assistance.aspx.

94 HB 663, Virginia General Assembly, 2016.

95 "Delegate Cole Files Legislation to Protect the Privacy of Schoolchildren and Adults," Delegate Mark Cole, January 13, 2016, accessed May 10, 2016, http://marklcole.com/MarkColePR12Jan2016.html.

96 "Rep. Morrison Discusses Need for HB 4474," Tom Morrison, February 2, 2016, accessed May 10, 2016, http://www.repmorrison54.com/2016/02/rep-morrison-discusses-need-for-hb-4474.html.

97 U.S. Congress, "Biometric Identifiers," 37.

98 Barnaby Feder, "Private Sector; The Face of Security Technology," *New York Times*, January 20, 2002.

99 Gates, "Identifying the 9/11," 434.

100 Mitch Kellaway, "Trans Folks Respond to 'Bathroom Bills' with #WeJustNeed

toPee Selfies," *The Advocate*, March 14, 2015, accessed June 19, 2016, http://www
.advocate.com/politics/transgender/2015/03/14/trans-folks-respond-bathroom-bills
-wejustneedtopee-selfies.

101 James Michael Nichols, "Trans Woman Asks: 'You Really Want Me in the Same Bathroom as Your Husband?,'" *Huffington Post*, November 5, 2015, accessed June 19, 2016,
http://www.huffingtonpost.com/entry/this-trans-woman-asks-you-really-want
-me-in-the-same-bathroom-as-your-husband_us_563b997fe4b0411d3070003a.

Chapter 4: Sensitive Information in the Manning Case

1 "Attorney General Loretta E. Lynch Delivers Remarks at Press Conference Announcing Complaint against the State of North Carolina to Stop Discrimination
against Transgender Individuals," U.S. Department of Justice, May 9, 2016, accessed July 9, 2016, https://www.justice.gov/opa/speech/attorney-general-loretta-e
-lynch-delivers-remarks-press-conference-announcing-complaint.

2 Amber Phillips, "How Loretta Lynch's Speech Brought Some Transgender Advocates to Tears," *Washington Post*, May 11, 2016.

3 Kapp-Klote and Peoples, "Loretta Lynch." This line of inquiry follows from an
argument made by many scholars and activist organizations, who caution against
reliance on hate crimes legislation in part because it works through a criminal
legal system that prioritizes ideal victims—those deemed most sympathetic and
innocent by juries and prosecutors—and uses the prison system to punish individuals, a process that increases incarceration rates and surveillance of marginalized
populations. See Spade, *Normal Life*, chap. 2; Kandaswamy, "Innocent Victims";
"SRLP Announces Non-support of the Gender Employment Non-discrimination
Act," Sylvia Rivera Law Project, April 6, 2009, accessed June 15, 2012, http://srlp
.org/genda/.

4 Kapp-Klote and Peoples, "Loretta Lynch."

5 Transcript, *U.S. v. Pfc. Manning*, Article 32 Pretrial, December 17, 2011, 14, https://
assets.documentcloud.org/documents/680870/20111217-transcript-of-us-v-pfc
-bradley-manning.pdf. I have left direct quotations from these court transcripts
unchanged except for replacing masculine pronouns with feminine ones; these
pronoun changes are marked by their inclusion in brackets.

6 Evan Hansen, "Manning-Lamo Chat Logs Revealed," *Wired*, July 13, 2011, accessed November 11, 2013, http://www.wired.com/threatlevel/2011/07/manning
-lamo-logs/. Because these are direct transcripts of the chats, they contain multiple
typos and other errors. Throughout, I have preserved these as initially published.

7 Hansen, "Manning-Lamo Chat Logs."

8 Hansen, "Manning-Lamo Chat Logs."

9 Hansen, "Manning-Lamo Chat Logs."

10 Kevin Gosztola, "Bradley Manning Takes the Stand: Being Detained in Kuwait,"
ShadowProof, November 29, 2012, https://shadowproof.com/2012/11/29/bradley
-manning-takes-the-stand-being-detained-in-kuwait/.

11 Stoeckley, *United States vs. Private Chelsea Manning*, 27. The summaries and direct quotations in Stoeckley's book are taken from journalist and stenographer transcriptions of the pretrial and trial proceedings.

12 For data on incarceration and violence rates for transgender people, see Mogul, Ritchie, and Whitlock, *Queer (In)Justice*. Dean Spade names Duanna Johnson as one of many transgender women of color "whose murders have been mourned by local communities but mostly ignored by media, large nonprofits, and lawmakers," even though "people of color lose their lives at higher rates" than do white transgender people (Spade, *Normal Life*, 181n18).

13 For a more detailed narrative of the Duanna Johnson case, drawing on local news sources, see Mogul, Ritchie, and Whitlock, *Queer (In)Justice*, 141–45, 200n5. Matt Richardson assesses Johnson's case as an example of how "the recognition of anti-Black violence disappears when it comes to Black queers" (Richardson, *Queer Limit*, 164).

14 This is not to say that such surveillance measures are not used to scrutinize law enforcement employees. U.S. state agencies regularly perform surveillance on their own security staff; for instance, other state employees go undercover to test TSA screeners on their ability to properly locate prohibited objects. See, for example, Justin Fishel et al., "Exclusive: Undercover DHS Tests Find Security Failures at US Airports," *ABC News*, June 1, 2015. Nevertheless, the routine surveillance recordings in correctional facilities focus on criminalized persons and, as the remainder of this paragraph explains, are often used against those persons even when the footage could support them.

15 Butler, "Endangered/Endangering," 17.

16 Shahid Buttar, "Police Violence? Body Cams Are No Solution," Truthout, January 6, 2015, http://www.truth-out.org/opinion/item/28357-police-violence-body-cams-are-no-solution. Drawing on Mariame Kaba's work, Jacqui Shine notes that less spectacular forms of police violence—stop-and-frisks, harassment—may be captured by body cameras but not register as actions requiring accountability, while the camera footage simultaneously shifts "greater responsibility to civilians for police use of force": in the 2015 Sandra Bland case, for instance, dashboard camera footage of her initial arrest was used to support the arresting officer's statement that Bland was combative. Jacqui Shine, "Inside the Police-Industrial Complex," *Pacific Standard*, January 12, 2016. See also "Considering Police Body Cameras."

17 Butler, "Endangered/Endangering," 16.

18 A report produced by the National Association of Criminal Defense Lawyers outlines several concerns about these technologies, including the possibility that police may review video footage "with enhanced lighting and the ability to slow and replay segments" to seek out visual evidence that can be used against defendants. Joel Schumm, "Policing Body Cameras: Policies and Procedures to Safeguard the Rights of the Accused," National Association of Criminal Defense Lawyers, 2017, accessed March 20, 2017, https://www.nacdl.org/policingbodycameras/report/.

Likewise, Joshua Reeves's analysis of lateral surveillance, which I discuss later in this chapter, can extend to assessment of video footage, such that viewers are inclined to scrutinize the defendant's actions rather than those of state agents (Reeves, *Citizen Spies*).

19 Discharges under Don't Ask, Don't Tell disproportionately affected women of color, with Black women in particular discharged "at almost three times their presence in the military" according to 2001 data (Servicemembers Legal Defense Network, "Conduct Unbecoming: The Ninth Annual Report on 'Don't Ask, Don't Tell, Don't Pursue, Don't Harass" [Washington, DC: Author, 2003], 44).

20 Hansen, "Manning-Lamo Chat Logs."

21 In the chat logs, Manning tells Lamo that she had a boyfriend and had sexual relationships with other military personnel but was aware that these relationships made her vulnerable in the context of Don't Ask, Don't Tell, which would not be repealed for another year. There is some conflation of sexual orientation and gender identity in the ways that various commentators—in both court and media accounts—discuss the factors contributing to Manning's feelings of isolation in the army.

22 The many arguments over installing and then ending the Don't Ask, Don't Tell policy, themselves often drawing on a longer history of queer figures as traitors to the nation and as communist spies vulnerable to blackmail, help contextualize the Manning case. For discussion of this longer history, see Johnson, *Lavender Scare*.

23 When news of this defense strategy initially broke, many feminist, queer, and transgender activists and media outlets critiqued its use of gender identity disorder and related stress as possible explanations for Manning's alleged actions. See, for example, Emily McAvan, "Why Does the Media Still Refer to 'Bradley' Manning? The Curious Silence around a Transgender Hero," Global Comment, December 22, 2011, accessed January 10, 2014, http://globalcomment.com/why-does-the-media-still-refer-to-bradley-manning-the-curious-silence-around-a-transgender-hero/.

24 The strategic use of Manning's transgender identity as one aspect of her legal defense met with complicated reactions from LGBT communities. Within the mainstream rights discourse that had long advocated for LGBT inclusion in military service, Manning might have been an important symbolic figure, but her sustained criticism of U.S. military actions also made her a liability for homonationalist campaigns that sought approval from state agencies (see Cloud, "Private Manning"; Goldsmith, "Rich Man's War"). Other would-be supporters strategically edited Manning's narrative to construct her as a sympathetic figure aligned with military inclusion rhetoric, with some disregarding her transgender identity "in order to depict her within a friendly white gay pro-military masculinity," a strategy that nonetheless often failed to garner broader support (Spade and Willse, "Sex, Gender, and War," 17). Others distanced themselves from her in ways that emphasized their own national loyalty. For instance, the Human Rights Campaign released a statement affirming their support for transgender service mem-

bers and for Manning's right to protection and medical care while incarcerated, but also implicitly differentiating her from other patriotic service members; relatedly, several transgender-identified veterans criticized Manning as a traitor to the United States. For further discussion of these responses, see Fischer, "Contingent Belonging."

25 Coombs's opening statement referenced Manning's specially made dog tags, which featured the word *human*, as an indication of her humanist values (*United States vs. PFC Bradley E. Manning*, June 3, 2013, Morning Session, 75, https://www.documentcloud.org/documents/711351-06-03-13-am-session.html).

26 *United States vs. PFC Bradley E. Manning*, June 3, 2013, Morning Session, 77.

27 Among the many important texts addressing this, see Abu-Lughod, "Do Muslim Women"; Bacchetta et al., "Transnational Feminist Practices," both of which particularly elucidate the racial and gendered dimensions of this rationale.

28 Kirit Radja and Luis Martinez, "Bradley Manning Defense Reveals Alter Ego Named 'Breanna Manning,'" *ABC News*, December 17, 2011.

29 *United States vs. PFC Bradley E. Manning*, June 4, 2012, Morning Session, 62–63, https://www.documentcloud.org/documents/711353-06-04-13-am-session.html.

30 *United States vs. PFC Bradley E. Manning*, June 4, 2012, Morning Session, 64.

31 See, for example, Emily Manuel, "Are Rumors Accused WikiLeaks Source Bradley Manning Is Transgender behind Harsh Treatment?," AlterNet, July 6, 2011, http://www.alternet.org/story/151541/are_rumors_accused_wikileaks_source_bradley_manning_is_transgender_behind_harsh_treatment/?page=1.

32 Stoeckley, *United States vs. Private Chelsea Manning*, 181.

33 Stoeckley, *United States vs. Private Chelsea Manning*, 158.

34 Hansen, "Manning-Lamo Chat Logs."

35 Julie Tate, "The History of Bradley Manning's 'My Problem' E-mail," *Washington Post*, August 22, 2013.

36 Lauren McNamara, "The Humanity of Private Manning," Zinnia Jones, July 30, 2013, accessed October 31, 2015, https://the-orbit.net/zinniajones/2013/07/the-humanity-of-private-manning-by-lauren-mcnamara/.

37 Hansen, "Manning-Lamo Chat Logs."

38 Record of Trial of Bradley E. Manning, February 28, 2013, 6760, https://assets.documentcloud.org/documents/1102833/volume-foia-034.pdf.

39 Record of Trial of Bradley E. Manning, February 28, 2013, 6761.

40 Record of Trial of Bradley E. Manning, February 28, 2013, 6765, 6768.

41 Record of Trial of Bradley E. Manning, February 28, 2013, 6769.

42 Both Coombs and Manning, at different points during the trial, emphasized that Manning carefully assessed the national security risks posed by the various materials she eventually leaked, working to ensure that—though many were formally classified—they were not materials that would actually undermine U.S. security (*United States vs. PFC Bradley E. Manning*, June 3, 2013, Morning Session, 77).

43 Stoeckley, *United States vs. Private Chelsea Manning*, 87.

44 Amy Davidson Sorkin, "Manning's Sentence, Miranda's Detention," *New Yorker*, August 21, 2013.

45 Hall, "Of Ziploc Bags," 42.

46 David Coombs, "Typical Day for PFC Bradley Manning," *An Army Defense Firm*, December 18, 2010, accessed January 10, 2015, https://www.armycourtmartial defense.com/2010/12/a-typical-day-for-pfc-bradley-manning.html.

47 Charlie Savage, "Soldier in Leaks Case Will Be Made to Sleep Naked Nightly," *New York Times*, March 4, 2011.

48 David Coombs, "PFC Manning Stripped Naked Again," *An Army Defense Firm*, March 4, 2011, accessed January 10, 2015, https://www.armycourtmartialdefense .com/2011/03/pfc-manning-stripped-naked-again.html.

49 Savage, "Soldier in Leaks Case."

50 David Leigh et al., "Guantánamo Leaks Lift Lid on World's Most Controversial Prison," *The Guardian*, April 24, 2011.

51 Paik, *Rightlessness*, 155.

52 Stoeckley, *United States vs. Private Chelsea Manning*, 27. This appeared to be a way to argue that Manning was not held in solitary confinement or punitive segregation.

53 Stoeckley, *United States vs. Private Chelsea Manning*, 27.

54 Stoeckley, *United States vs. Private Chelsea Manning*, 28, 29.

55 Stoeckley, *United States vs. Private Chelsea Manning*, 35. The defense used this testimony to seek significant credit for the time Manning had been "unlawfully punished . . . in confinement, for over two hundred days." The judge granted only 112 days of sentence credit (53).

56 See, for example, Stanley and Smith, *Captive Genders*.

57 For example, Manning testified that she understood the SigActs as historical data that were "not very sensitive" (Record of Trial of Bradley E. Manning, February 28, 2013, 6742). Coombs reiterated Manning's belief that the SigActs, diplomatic cables, and other materials "could not be used against the United States" (Stoeckley, *United States vs. Private Chelsea Manning*, 84).

58 Mark Fenster explains in *The Transparency Fix* that while Manning's leaks most notably prompted new government efforts to control classified information, it is difficult to identify any other substantive and lasting effects stemming from the leaked materials, whether in terms of military practices, intelligence agencies, U.S. diplomatic relations, or U.S. public opinion (176–85).

59 Hillman, *Defending America*, 46. Hillman notes, for instance, that courts-martial often backfired in cases of U.S. military dissent against the war in Vietnam, because they "provided the very vehicles for publicity that antiwar activists sought" (67).

60 Hillman, *Defending America*, 46.

61 Stoeckley, *United States vs. Private Chelsea Manning*, 14.

62 "Press and Public Denied Access to Documents in Bradley Manning Case,"

Center for Constitutional Rights, April 17, 2013, accessed March 15, 2016, http://ccrjustice.org/home/press-center/press-releases/press-and-public-denied-access-documents-bradley-manning-case.

63 Rainey Reitman and Trevor Timm, "Freedom of the Press Foundation Crowd-Funding a Court Reporter to Transcribe Bradley Manning's Trial," Freedom of the Press Foundation, May 9, 2013, accessed March 20, 2016, https://freedom.press/news-advocacy/freedom-of-the-press-foundation-crowd-funding-a-court-reporter-to-transcribe-bradley-manningas-trial/.

64 We might also interpret Manning's actions here as compliant with social norms even if not with the letter of the law; as legal scholar David Pozen argues in "The Leaky Leviathan," the U.S. government tacitly condones a steady stream of leaks that are never prosecuted but instead are regulated through "a nuanced set of informal social controls" so that "much of what we call leaking occurs in a gray area between full authorization and no authorization" (155). Against this backdrop, Manning's leaks are prosecuted not merely because they violated the formal law itself, but because they also destabilized that tenuous set of social controls.

65 Stoeckley, United States vs. Private Chelsea Manning, 20.

66 Stoeckley, United States vs. Private Chelsea Manning, 7.

67 For further discussion of these concepts, in the context of antiterrorism programs and otherwise, see Reeves, Citizen Spies.

68 Hansen, "Manning-Lamo Chat Logs."

69 Fenster, Transparency Fix, 81.

70 Government agencies did indeed install new security measures in response to Manning's leaks. See Fenster, Transparency Fix, 181; Reeves, Citizen Spies, 163.

71 Samantha Allen, "A Letter to Chelsea Manning," Jacobin, August 27, 2013, accessed March 15, 2014, http://www.jacobinmag.com/2013/08/a-letter-to-chelsea-manning/.

72 Stoeckley, United States vs. Private Chelsea Manning, 29. Queer and transgender organizations using an abolition framework refused this separation of Manning's case from the systematic incarceration of millions of people in the United States. For instance, the prisoner support organization Black and Pink insisted that "the fight for Chelsea Manning is part of the fight for abolition, the fight for a day where we live free from police, militaries, judges, and the cages that steal millions from our communities" (Spade and Willse, "Sex, Gender, and War," 19).

73 Stoeckley, United States vs. Private Chelsea Manning, 28.

74 Mitchell and Gosztola, Truth and Consequences, 77.

75 Spade and Willse, "Sex, Gender, and War," 19. Spade and Willse note that Manning's postsentencing statement speaks to her understanding of "her current role of prosecuted enemy" as an "extension" of imperialist war.

76 For discussions of this racist refusal of individuality specifically relating to surveillance practices, see, for example, Pugliese, "In Silico Race"; Kamaloni, "What Are You Doing Here?"

77 Chambers, "The Unexamined," 145.
78 Snorton and Haritaworn, "Trans Necropolitics," 74.
79 Snorton and Haritaworn, "Trans Necropolitics," 71.

Conclusion: On Endurance

1 An August 2017 FBI report assessing domestic terrorism warns against "Black Identity Extremist" groups, a category that multiple commentators understand as targeting Black Lives Matter without explicitly naming it as such (FBI Counterterrorism Division, "Black Identity Extremists Likely Motivated to Target Law Enforcement Officers," Federal Bureau of Investigation, August 3, 2017, accessed September 9, 2017, https://assets.documentcloud.org/documents/4067711/BIE-Redacted.pdf; Khaled A. Beydoun and Justin Hansford, "The F.B.I.'s Dangerous Crackdown on 'Black Identity Extremists,'" *New York Times*, November 15, 2017). In May 2017, leaked documents showed that a private security firm previously contracted with the U.S. military worked with local law enforcement in at least five states to infiltrate and conduct extensive surveillance on protests against the Dakota Access Pipeline (Alleen Brown, Will Parrish, and Alice Speri, "Leaked Documents Reveal Counterterrorism Tactics Used at Standing Rock to 'Defeat Pipeline Insurgencies,'" The Intercept, May 27, 2017, accessed September 11, 2017, https://theintercept.com/2017/05/27/leaked-documents-reveal-security-firms-counterterrorism-tactics-at-standing-rock-to-defeat-pipeline-insurgencies/). These state actions echo COINTELPRO tactics and work alongside the everyday racist scrutiny enacted by individuals. We might also consider here multiple levels of surveillance over abortion services, including legislation demanding that clinics withstand ever greater levels of scrutiny and compliance with new regulations, surveillance performed by antiabortion organizations in attempts to discredit providers (then sometimes used as evidence in crafting new restrictive laws), and surveillance conducted by individuals over abortion providers and clinic staff, in addition to the abortion data collected by the Centers for Disease Control and Prevention.

2 Ashley Feinberg, "Jared Kushner Voted as a Woman, According to His Registration," *Wired*, September 27, 2017, https://www.wired.com/story/jared-kushner-voter-registration-woman/; John Haltiwanger, "Jared Kushner Is a Woman, According to Voter Registration Records," *Newsweek*, September 27, 2017.

3 Another article opened with the line, "It was the board of elections that gave Jared Kushner his sex change," a sentence that plays on the spectacle of transgender identity for a story about the board correcting its own error and changing Kushner's gender marker from F to M (Jason Silverstein, "Jared Kushner Actually Is Registered to Vote as a Male, Despite Database Error Saying Otherwise," *New York Daily News*, September 28, 2017). Various transgender-related jokes about this case also circulated through social media, their intended humor reliant on understanding that Kushner could never really be considered transgender.

4 Silverstein, "Jared Kushner Actually."

5 Kushner's story follows several related voter registration problems in the Trump administration and family. See, for example, Erin McCann, "Who Is Registered to Vote in Two States? Some in Trump's Inner Circle," *New York Times*, January 27, 2017.

6 Garance Burke, "Trump's Voter Fraud Expert Registered in 3 States," *AP News*, January 31, 2017.

7 Julie Hirschfeld Davis and Helene Cooper, "Trump Says Transgender People Will Not Be Allowed in the Military," *New York Times*, July 26, 2017.

8 Ray Duval and Harper Jean Tobin, "The Trans Military Ban Is Already Causing Harm—but There's a Way to Stop It," Trans Equality Now!, September 29, 2017, accessed October 31, 2017, https://medium.com/transequalitynow/the-trans-military-ban-is-already-causing-harm-but-theres-a-way-to-stop-it-e19a35455479.

9 On the history of figuring transgender people as socioeconomic burdens, particularly in relation to medical transition and productive citizenship, see Irving, "Normalized Transgressions."

10 John H. Thompson, "Planned Subjects for the 2020 Census and the American Community Survey," United States Census Bureau, March 29, 2017, accessed June 13, 2017, https://www.census.gov/newsroom/blogs/director/2017/03/planned_subjects_2020.html.

11 See, for example, "FAQ on the Withdrawal of Federal Guidance on Transgender Students," National Center for Transgender Equality, February 21, 2017, accessed March 15, 2017, http://www.transequality.org/issues/resources/faq-on-the-withdrawal-of-federal-guidance-on-transgender-students; Ivey DeJesus, "Transgender Advocates Denounce Trump Decision to Roll Back Guidelines for Schools on Bathroom Use," PennLive, February 22, 2017, http://www.pennlive.com/news/2017/02/transgender_lgbt_gay_schools_e.html; Hansi Lo Wang, "U.S. Census to Leave Sexual Orientation, Gender Identity Questions Off New Surveys," National Public Radio, March 29, 2017, http://www.npr.org/sections/thetwo-way/2017/03/29/521921287/u-s-census-to-leave-sexual-orientation-gender-identity-questions-off-new-surveys; and Emily Waters, "We Count: Why Data Matters More Than Ever for LGBTQ People," *Huffington Post*, March 30, 2017.

12 Brief for National Center for Transgender Equality, et al. as Amici Curiae Supporting Plaintiffs, *Doe 1 v. Trump* (2017) (no. 1:17-cv-01597), 19, 20. http://www.transequality.org/sites/default/files/2017.10.16%20Proposed%20Brief%20of%20Amici%20Curiae%20-%20NCTE.pdf.

13 Browne, *Dark Matters*, 56.

14 These concerns, among others, drive important work in transgender scholarship, cultural production, and organizing that suggests the political potential in unrecognizability (Aizura, "Introduction"), in being nobodies who are invaluable and incalculable (Gossett, Dunham, and Zavitsanos, "Commencement Address"), and in the possibility of impossibility (Bassichis, Lee, and Spade, "Building an Abolitionist").

BIBLIOGRAPHY

Abel, Elizabeth. *Signs of the Times: The Visual Politics of Jim Crow*. Berkeley: University of California Press, 2010.

Abu-Lughod, Lila. "Do Muslim Women Really Need Saving? Anthropological Reflections on Cultural Relativism and Its Others." *American Anthropologist* 104, no. 3 (2002): 783–90.

Adey, Peter. *Mobility*. New York: Routledge, 2010.

Agamben, Giorgio. "Bodies without Words: Against the Biopolitical Tatoo." *German Law Journal* 5 (2004): 167–69.

Agar, Jon. "Modern Horrors: British Identity and Identity Cards." In *Documenting Individual Identity: The Development of State Practices in the Modern World*, edited by Jane Caplan and John Torpey, 101–20. Princeton, NJ: Princeton University Press, 2001.

Aizura, Aren Z. "Introduction." *South Atlantic Quarterly* 116, no. 3 (July 2017): 606–11.

Aizura, Aren Z. "The Persistence of Transgender Travel Narratives." In *Transgender Migrations: The Bodies, Borders, and Politics of Transition*, edited by Trystan T. Cotton, 139–56. New York: Routledge, 2012.

Arneri, Vinko. "Reconstruction of the Male Genitalia." In *Reconstructive Plastic Surgery*, vol. 7, edited by John Converse, 3902–21. Philadelphia: W. B. Saunders, 1977.

Asad, Talal. *On Suicide Bombing*. New York: Columbia University Press, 2007.

Assmus, Alexi. "Early History of X Rays." *Beam Line: A Periodical of Particle Physics* 25, no. 2 (summer 1995): 10–24.

Bacchetta, Paola, Tina Campt, Inderpal Grewal, Caren Kaplan, Minoo Moallem, and Jennifer Terry. "Transnational Feminist Practices against War." *Meridians* 2, no. 2 (2002): 302–8.

Barcan, Ruth. "Dirty Spaces: Separation, Concealment, and Shame in the Public Toilet." In *Toilet: Public Restrooms and the Politics of Sharing*, edited by Harvey Molotch and Laura Norén, 25–41. New York: New York University Press, 2010.

Bassichis, Morgan, Alexander Lee, and Dean Spade. "Building an Abolitionist Trans and Queer Movement with Everything We've Got." In *Captive Genders: Trans*

Embodiment and the Prison Industrial Complex, edited by Eric A. Stanley and Nat Smith, 15–40. Oakland, CA: AK Press, 2011.

Beauchamp, Toby. "When Things Don't Add Up: Transgender Bodies and the Mobile Borders of Biometrics." In *Trans Studies: The Challenge to Hetero/ Homo Normativities*, edited by Yolanda Martínez-San Miguel and Sarah Tobias, 103–12. New Brunswick, NJ: Rutgers University Press, 2016.

Bederman, Gail. *Manliness and Civilization: A Cultural History of Gender and Race in the United States, 1880–1917*. Chicago: University of Chicago Press, 1995.

Bedolla, Lisa García. *Latino Politics*. Cambridge, MA: Polity, 2009.

Bergeron, Claire, Aaron Matteo Terrazas, and Doris Meissner. "Social Security 'No Match' Letters: A Primer." *MPI Backgrounder* 5 (2007): 1–11. http://www .migrationpolicy.org/pubs/BR5_SocialSecurityNoMatch_101007.pdf.

Bernstein, Robin. *Racial Innocence: Performing American Childhood from Slavery to Civil Rights*. New York: New York University Press, 2011.

Bettcher, Talia Mae. "Evil Deceivers and Make-Believers: On Transphobic Violence and the Politics of Illusion." *Hypatia* 22, no. 3 (August 2007): 43–65.

Billies, Michelle. "Low Income LGBTGNC (Gender Nonconforming) Struggles over Shelters as Public Space." *ACME: An International E-Journal for Critical Geographies* 14, no. 4 (2015): 989–1007.

Boris, Eileen. "'You Wouldn't Want One of 'Em Dancing with Your Wife': Racialized Bodies on the Job in World War II." *American Quarterly* 50, no. 1 (March 1998): 77–108.

Breckenridge, Keith. *Biometric State: The Global Politics of Identification and Surveillance in South Africa, 1850 to the Present*. Cambridge: Cambridge University Press, 2014.

Bridges, Khiara M. *The Poverty of Privacy Rights*. Stanford, CA: Stanford University Press, 2017.

Brown, Wendy. *States of Injury: Power and Freedom in Late Modernity*. Princeton, NJ: Princeton University Press, 1995.

Brown-May, Andrew, and Peg Fraser. "Gender, Respectability, and Public Convenience in Melbourne, Australia, 1859–1902." In *Ladies and Gents: Public Toilets and Gender*, edited by Olga Gershenson and Barbara Penner, 75–89. Philadelphia: Temple University Press, 2009.

Browne, Simone. *Dark Matters: On the Surveillance of Blackness*. Durham, NC: Duke University Press, 2015.

Butler, Judith. "Against Proper Objects." *Differences* 6, nos. 2–3 (1994): 1–26.

Butler, Judith. "Endangered/Endangering: Schematic Racism and White Paranoia." In *Reading Rodney King, Reading Urban Uprising*, edited by Robert Gooding-Williams, 15–22. New York: Routledge, 1993.

Butler, Judith. *Undoing Gender*. New York: Routledge, 2004.

Cacho, Lisa. *Social Death: Racialized Rightlessness and the Criminalization of the Unprotected*. New York: New York University Press, 2012.

Cainkar, Louise, and Sunaina Maira. "Targeting Arab/Muslim/South Asian Americans: Criminalization and Cultural Citizenship." *Amerasia Journal* 31, no. 3 (2005): 1–28.

Califia, Patrick. *Sex Changes: Transgender Politics*. San Francisco: Cleis, 2003.

Campbell, Kristina M. "The Road to S.B. 1070: How Arizona Became Ground Zero for the Immigrants' Rights Movement and the Continuing Struggle for Latino Civil Rights in America." *Harvard Latino Law Review* 14 (2011): 1–21.

Canaday, Margot. *The Straight State: Sexuality and Citizenship in Twentieth-Century America*. Princeton, NJ: Princeton University Press, 2009.

Caplan, Jane, and John Torpey. "Introduction." In *Documenting Individual Identity: The Development of State Practices in the Modern World*, edited by Jane Caplan and John Torpey, 1–12. Princeton, NJ: Princeton University Press, 2001.

Carter, Julian B. *The Heart of Whiteness: Normal Sexuality and Race in America, 1880–1940*. Durham, NC: Duke University Press, 2007.

Cartwright, Lisa. *Screening the Body: Tracing Medicine's Visual Culture*. Minneapolis: University of Minnesota Press, 1995.

Case, Mary Anne. "Why Not Abolish Laws of Urinary Segregation?" In *Toilet: Public Restrooms and the Politics of Sharing*, ed. Harvey Molotch and Laura Norén, 211–25. New York: New York University Press, 2010.

Ceyhan, Ayse. "Technologization of Security: Management of Uncertainty and Risk in the Age of Biometrics." *Surveillance and Society* 5, no. 2 (2008): 102–23.

Chambers, Ross. "The Unexamined." *Minnesota Review* 47 (fall 1996): 141–56.

Clare, Eli. "Body Shame, Body Pride: Lessons from the Disability Rights Movement." In *The Transgender Studies Reader 2*, edited by Susan Stryker and Aren Z. Aizura, 261–65. New York: Routledge, 2013.

Cloud, Dana L. "Private Manning and the Chamber of Secrets." *QED: A Journal in GLBTQ Worldmaking* 1, no. 1 (spring 2014): 80–104.

Cohen, Cathy J. "Punks, Bulldaggers, and Welfare Queens: The Radical Potential of Queer Politics?" In *Black Queer Studies: A Critical Anthology*, edited by E. Patrick Johnson and Mae G. Henderson, 21–51. Durham, NC: Duke University Press, 2005.

"Considering Police Body Cameras." *Harvard Law Review* 128, no. 6 (April 2015): 1794–1817.

Currah, Paisley, and Shannon Minter. *Transgender Equality: A Handbook for Activists and Policymakers*. New York: Policy Institute of the National Gay and Lesbian Task Force, 2000.

Currah, Paisley, and Lisa Jean Moore. "Legally Sexed: Birth Certificates and Transgender Citizens." In *Feminist Surveillance Studies*, ed. Rachel E. Dubrofsky and Shoshana Amielle Magnet, 58–76. Durham, NC: Duke University Press, 2015.

Currah, Paisley, and Tara Mulqueen. "Securitizing Gender: Identity, Biometrics, and Transgender Bodies at the Airport." *Social Research* 78, no. 2 (summer 2011): 557–82.

Davis, Angela Y. *Violence against Women and the Ongoing Challenge to Racism*. Latham, NY: Kitchen Table: Women of Color Press, 1985.

Davis, Lennard J. "The End of Identity Politics: On Disability as an Unstable Category." In *The Disability Studies Reader*, 4th ed., edited by Lennard J. Davis, 263–77. New York: Routledge, 2013.

de Moulpied, David S., Peter J. Rothschild, and Gerald J. Smith. "X-Ray BodySearch Eliminates Strip Search in Montana Prison." In *SPIE Proceedings*, vol. 3575: *Enforcement and Security Technologies*, edited by A. Trent DePersia and John J. Pennella, 175–81. Bellingham, WA: SPIE, December 1998.

Desai, Jigna, and Amy L. Brandzel. "Race, Violence, and Terror: The Cultural Defensibility of Heteromasculine Citizenship in the Virginia Tech Massacre and the Don Imus Affair." *Journal of Asian American Studies* 11, no. 1 (February 2008): 61–85.

Dilts, Andrew. "Incurable Blackness: Criminal Disenfranchisement, Mental Disability, and the White Citizen." *Disability Studies Quarterly* 32, no. 3 (2012).

Douglas, Mary. *Purity and Danger: An Analysis of the Concepts of Pollution and Taboo*. New York: Routledge, 1966.

Elias, Norbert. *The Civilizing Process: Sociogenetic and Psychogenetic Investigations*. Oxford: Blackwell, 2000.

Eng, David L. *Racial Castration: Managing Masculinity in Asian America*. Durham, NC: Duke University Press, 2001.

Eng, David L., Judith Halberstam, and José Esteban Muñoz. "What's Queer about Queer Studies Now?" *Social Text* 84–85 (fall–winter 2005): 1–17.

Enke, A. Finn. "The Education of Little Cis: Cisgender and the Discipline of Opposing Bodies." In *Transfeminist Perspectives in and beyond Transgender and Gender Studies*, edited by A. Finn Enke, 60–77. Philadelphia: Temple University Press, 2012.

Farrow, Kenyon. "Is Gay Marriage Anti-Black???" In *Against Equality: Queer Critiques of Gay Marriage*, edited by Ryan Conrad, 21–32. Lewiston, ME: Against Equality Publishing Collective, 2010.

Fausto-Sterling, Anne. "Gender, Race, and Nation: The Comparative Anatomy of 'Hottentot' Women in Europe, 1815–1817." In *Deviant Bodies: Critical Perspectives on Difference in Science and Popular Culture*, edited by Jennifer Terry and Jacqueline Urla, 19–48. Bloomington: Indiana University Press, 1995.

Fenster, Mark. *The Transparency Fix: Secrets, Leaks, and Uncontrollable Government Information*. Stanford, CA: Stanford University Press, 2017.

Ferguson, Roderick A. *Aberrations in Black: Toward a Queer of Color Critique*. Minneapolis: University of Minnesota Press, 2004.

Finn, Jonathan. *Capturing the Criminal Image: From the Mug Shot to Surveillance Society*. Minneapolis: University of Minnesota Press, 2009.

Fischer, Mia. "Contingent Belonging: Chelsea Manning, Transpatriotism, and Iterations of Empire." *Sexualities* 19, nos. 5–6 (2016): 567–86.

Foucault, Michel. *Discipline and Punish: The Birth of the Prison*. New York: Vintage, 1995.

Foucault, Michel. *The History of Sexuality*, vol. 1: *An Introduction*. New York: Random House, 1978.

Foucault, Michel. "The Risks of Security." In *Essential Works of Michel Foucault*, vol. 3: *Power*, edited by James D. Faubion, 365–81. New York: New Press, 2001.

Gates, Kelly. "Identifying the 9/11 'Faces of Terror': The Promise and Problem of Facial Recognition Technology." *Cultural Studies* 20, nos. 4–5 (July 2006): 417–40.

Gates, Kelly. *Our Biometric Future: Facial Recognition Technology and the Culture of Surveillance*. New York: New York University Press, 2011.

Godfrey, Phoebe. "Bayonets, Brainwashing, and Bathrooms: The Discourse of Race, Gender, and Sexuality in the Desegregation of Little Rock's Central High." *Arkansas Historical Quarterly* 62, no. 1 (spring 2003): 42–67.

Goldsmith, Larry. "Rich Man's War, Poor (Gay) Man's Fight." In *Why Are Faggots So Afraid of Faggots?*, edited by Mattilda Bernstein Sycamore, 181–84. Oakland, CA: AK Press, 2012.

Gopinath, Gayatri. "Bollywood Spectacles: Queer Diasporic Critique in the Aftermath of 9/11." *Social Text* 84–85 (fall–winter 2005): 157–69.

Gorton, Nick. "Transgender as Mental Illness: Nosology, Social Justice, and the Tarnished Golden Mean." In *The Transgender Studies Reader 2*, edited by Susan Stryker and Aren Z. Aizura, 644–52. New York: Routledge, 2013.

Gossett, Che. "Queerstions: What Does Cisgender Mean?" *Philadelphia Magazine*, July 8, 2014. Accessed June 22, 2017. http://www.phillymag.com/g-philly/2014/07/08/queerstions-cisgender-mean.

Gossett, Reina, Grace Dunham, and Constantina Zavitsanos. "Commencement Address at Hampshire College." *Reina Gossett* (blog), May 17, 2016. http://www.reinagossett.com/commencement-address-hampshire-college/.

Grillo, Trina, and Stephanie M. Wildman. "Obscuring the Importance of Race: The Implication of Making Comparisons between Racism and Sexism (Or Otherisms)." *Duke Law Journal* 40, no. 2 (1991): 397–412.

Hage, Ghassan. "'Comes a Time We Are All Enthusiasm': Understanding Palestinian Suicide Bombers in Times of Exighophobia." *Public Culture* 15, no. 1 (winter 2003): 65–89.

Halberstam, Judith. *Female Masculinity*. Durham, NC: Duke University Press, 1998.

Hall, Rachel. "Of Ziploc Bags and Black Holes: The Aesthetics of Transparency in the War on Terror." In *The New Media of Surveillance*, edited by Shoshana Magnet and Kelly Gates, 41–68. New York: Routledge, 2009.

Hammonds, Evelynn. "Black (W)holes and the Geometry of Black Female Sexuality." *differences: A Journal of Feminist Cultural Studies* 6, nos. 2–3 (summer–fall 1994): 126–45.

Hamraie, Aimi. *Building Access: Universal Design and the Politics of Disability*. Minneapolis: University of Minnesota Press, 2017.

Hanhardt, Christina B. *Safe Space: Gay Neighborhood History and the Politics of Violence*. Durham, NC: Duke University Press, 2013.

Hausman, Bernice. *Changing Sex: Transsexualism, Technology, and the Idea of Gender*. Durham, NC: Duke University Press, 1995.

Hillman, Elizabeth Lutes. *Defending America: Military Culture and the Cold War Court-Martial*. Princeton, NJ: Princeton University Press, 2005.

Hirschmann, Nancy J., and Beth Linker, eds. *Civil Disabilities: Citizenship, Membership, and Belonging*. Philadelphia: University of Pennsylvania Press, 2014.

Howell, Joel D. *Technology in the Hospital: Transforming Patient Care in the Early Twentieth Century*. Baltimore: Johns Hopkins University Press, 1995.

Irving, Dan. "Normalized Transgressions: Legitimizing the Transsexual Body as Productive." *Radical History Review* 100 (winter 2008): 38–59.

James, Joy. *Resisting State Violence: Radicalism, Gender, and Race in U.S. Culture*. Minneapolis: University of Minnesota Press, 1996.

Jarvis, Christina S. *The Male Body at War: American Masculinity during World War II*. DeKalb: Northern Illinois University Press, 2010.

Johnson, David K. *The Lavender Scare: The Cold War Persecution of Gays and Lesbians in the Federal Government*. Chicago: University of Chicago Press, 2006.

Johnson, Kevin R. "The Case against Race Profiling in Immigration Enforcement." *Washington University Law Review* 78, no. 3 (January 2000): 675–736.

Kafer, Alison. *Feminist, Queer, Crip*. Bloomington: Indiana University Press, 2013.

Kamaloni, Sunshine M. "What Are You Doing Here? The Politics of Race and Belonging at the Airport." In *Security, Race, Biopower: Essays on Technology and Corporeality*, edited by Holly Randell-Moon and Ryan Tippet, 61–78. London: Palgrave Macmillan, 2016.

Kandaswamy, Priya. "Innocent Victims and Brave New Laws: State Protection and the Battered Women's Movement." In *Nobody Passes: Rejecting the Rules of Gender and Conformity*, edited by Mattilda a.k.a. Matt Bernstein Sycamore, 83–94. Emeryville, CA: Seal, 2006.

Kapp-Klote, H., and Angela Peoples. "Loretta Lynch and the Criminalization of Trans People." *Truthout*, May 18, 2016. http://www.truth-out.org/opinion/item/36078-loretta-lynch-and-the-criminalization-of-trans-people.

Kevles, Bettyann Holtzmann. *Naked to the Bone: Medical Imaging in the Twentieth Century*. Reading, MA: Addison-Wesley, 1997.

Kim, Eunjung. "Asexuality in Disability Narratives." *Sexualities* 14, no. 4 (2011): 479–93.

Kogan, Terry S. "Sex Separation: The Cure-All for Victorian Social Anxiety." In *Toilet: Public Restrooms and the Politics of Sharing*, edited by Harvey Molotch and Laura Norén, 145–64. New York: New York University Press, 2010.

Levi, Jennifer L., and Bennett H. Klein, "Pursuing Protection for Transgender People through Disability Laws." In *Transgender Rights*, edited by Paisley Currah, Richard M. Juang, and Shannon Price Minter, 74–92. Minneapolis: University of Minnesota Press, 2006.

Levi, Jennifer, and Daniel Redman. "The Cross-Dressing Case for Bathroom Equality." *Seattle University Law Review* 34 (2010): 133–71.

Levine, Harry G., Jon B. Gettman, Craig Reinarman, and Deborah Peterson Small.

"Drug Arrests and DNA: Building Jim Crow's Database." Council for Responsible Genetics Forum on Racial Justice Impacts of Forensic DNA Databanks, June 19, 2008. http://www.councilforresponsiblegenetics.org/pagedocuments/orrxbggaei.pdf.

Lipsitz, George. *The Possessive Investment in Whiteness: How White People Profit from Identity Politics*. Philadelphia: Temple University Press, 2006.

Lipsitz, George. "The Racialization of Space and the Spatialization of Race: Theorizing the Hidden Architecture of Landscape." *Landscape Journal* 26, no. 1 (2007): 10–23.

Lowe, Lisa. *Immigrant Acts: On Asian American Cultural Politics*. Durham, NC: Duke University Press, 1996.

Lynch, Jennifer. "From Fingerprints to DNA: Biometric Data Collection in U.S. Immigrant Communities and Beyond." Electronic Frontier Foundation, May 2012. https://www.eff.org/files/filenode/biometricsimmigration052112.pdf.

Lyon, David. *Surveillance after September 11*. Cambridge: Polity, 2003.

Lyon, David. *Surveillance after Snowden*. Cambridge: Polity, 2015.

Magnet, Shoshana Amielle. *When Biometrics Fail: Gender, Race, and the Technology of Identity*. Durham, NC: Duke University Press, 2011.

Mananzala, Rickke. "The FIERCE Fight for Power and the Preservation of Public Space in the West Village." *Scholar and Feminist Online* 10, nos. 1–2 (fall 2011–spring 2012).

Marx, Gary T. "Soft Surveillance: The Growth of Mandatory Volunteerism in Collecting Personal Information—'Hey Buddy Can You Spare a DNA?'" In *Surveillance and Security: Technological Politics and Power in Everyday Life*, edited by Torin Monahan, 37–56. New York: Routledge, 2006.

Massey, Doreen. *Space, Place, and Gender*. Minneapolis: University of Minnesota Press, 1994.

Mercer, Kobena. *Welcome to the Jungle*. New York: Routledge, 1994.

Meyerowitz, Joanne. *How Sex Changed: A History of Transsexuality in the United States*. Cambridge, MA: Harvard University Press, 2004.

Minich, Julie Avril. *Accessible Citizenships: Disability, Nation, and the Cultural Politics of Greater Mexico*. Philadelphia: Temple University Press, 2014.

Mitchell, Greg, and Kevin Gosztola. *Truth and Consequences: The U.S. vs. Private Manning*. New York: Sinclair, 2013.

Mog, Ashley. "Threads of Commonality in Transgender and Disability Studies." *Disability Studies Quarterly* 28, no. 4 (fall 2008).

Mogul, Joey L., Andrea J. Ritchie, and Kay Whitlock. *Queer (In)Justice: The Criminalization of LGBT People in the United States*. Boston: Beacon, 2011.

Monahan, Torin. "Questioning Surveillance and Security." In *Surveillance and Security: Technological Politics and Power in Everyday Life*, edited by Torin Monahan, 1–25. New York: Routledge, 2006.

Mongia, Radhika Viyas. "Race, Nationality, Mobility: A History of the Passport." *Public Culture* 11, no. 3 (1999): 527–56.

Moore, Alison. "Colonial Visions of 'Third World' Toilets: A Nineteenth-Century Discourse That Haunts Contemporary Tourism." In *Ladies and Gents: Public Toilets and Gender*, edited by Olga Gershenson and Barbara Penner, 105–25. Philadelphia: Temple University Press, 2009.

Morris, Jan. *Conundrum*. London: Faber and Faber, 1974.

National Commission on Terrorist Attacks upon the United States. "The 9/11 Commission Report." U.S. Government Publishing Office, July 22, 2004. Accessed July 29, 2017. https://www.gpo.gov/fdsys/pkg/GPO-911REPORT/pdf/GPO-911REPORT.pdf.

Ngai, Mae M. *Impossible Subjects: Illegal Aliens and the Making of Modern America*. Princeton, NJ: Princeton University Press, 2004.

Nguyen, Mimi Thi. "Clothes Epidermalized, as Republican Representative Targets 'Illegals.'" *Threadbared*, April 24, 2010. Accessed June 22, 2010. http://iheartthreadbared.wordpress.com/2010/04/24/foucault-was-right-gop-rep-targets-illegals-via-dress.

Ong, Aihwa. *Buddha Is Hiding: Refugees, Citizenship, the New America*. Berkeley: University of California Press, 2003.

Ong, Aihwa. *Flexible Citizenship: The Cultural Logics of Transnationality*. Durham, NC: Duke University Press, 1999.

Paik, A. Naomi. *Rightlessness: Testimony and Redress in U.S. Prison Camps since World War II*. Chapel Hill: University of North Carolina Press, 2016.

Parenti, Christian. *The Soft Cage: Surveillance in America from Slave Passes to the War on Terror*. New York: Basic Books, 2003.

Pegler-Gordon, Anna. "Chinese Exclusion, Photography, and the Development of U.S. Immigration Policy." *American Quarterly* 58, no. 1 (2006): 51–77.

Poole, Mary. *The Segregated Origins of Social Security: African Americans and the Welfare State*. Chapel Hill: University of North Carolina Press, 2006.

Pozen, David E. "The Leaky Leviathan: Why the Government Condemns and Condones Unlawful Disclosures of Information." *Harvard Law Review* 127, no. 512 (2013): 512–635.

Prosser, Jay. "Exceptional Locations: Transsexual Travelogues." In *Reclaiming Genders: Transsexual Grammars at the Fin de Siècle*, edited by Kate More and Stephen Whittle, 83–114. New York: Continuum, 1999.

Puar, Jasbir. *Terrorist Assemblages: Homonationalism in Queer Times*. Durham, NC: Duke University Press, 2007.

Puar, Jasbir, and Amit S. Rai. "Monster, Terrorist, Fag: The War on Terror and the Production of Docile Patriots." *Social Text* 20, no. 3 (2002): 117–48.

Pugliese, Joseph. "*In Silico* Race and the Heteronomy of Biometric Proxies: Biometrics in the Context of Civilian Life, Border Security and Counter-terrorism Laws." *Australian Feminist Law Journal* 23, no. 1 (2005): 1–32.

Rana, Junaid. *Terrifying Muslims: Race and Labor in the South Asian Diaspora*. Durham, NC: Duke University Press, 2011.

Raymond, Janice. *The Transsexual Empire: The Making of the She-Male.* London: Women's Press, 1979.

Reeves, Joshua. *Citizen Spies: The Long Rise of America's Surveillance Society.* New York: New York University Press, 2017.

Richardson, Matt. *The Queer Limit of Black Memory: Black Lesbian Literature and Irresolution.* Columbus: Ohio State University Press, 2013.

Roberts, Dorothy. *Killing the Black Body: Race, Reproduction, and the Meaning of Liberty.* New York: Random House, 1997.

Rosaldo, Renato. "Cultural Citizenship, Inequality, and Multiculturalism." In *Latino Cultural Citizenship*, edited by William V. Flores and Rina Benmayor, 27–38. Boston: Beacon, 1997.

Ross, Kristin. *Fast Cars, Clean Bodies: Decolonization and the Reordering of French Culture.* Cambridge, MA: MIT Press, 1995.

Rubin, Gayle. "Thinking Sex: Notes for a Radical Theory of the Politics of Sexuality." In *The Lesbian and Gay Studies Reader*, edited by Henry Abelove, Michéle Aina Barale, and David M. Halperin, 3–44. New York: Routledge, 1993.

Russell, Emily. *Reading Embodied Citizenship: Disability, Narrative, and the Body Politic.* New Brunswick, NJ: Rutgers University Press, 2011.

Salter, Mark B. *Rights of Passage: The Passport in International Relations.* Boulder, CO: Lynne Rienner, 2003.

Schweik, Susan M. *The Ugly Laws: Disability in Public.* New York: New York University Press, 2009.

Sears, Clare. *Arresting Dress: Cross-Dressing, Law, and Fascination in Nineteenth-Century San Francisco.* Durham, NC: Duke University Press, 2014.

Serlin, David. *Replaceable You: Engineering the Body in Postwar America.* Chicago: University of Chicago Press, 2004.

Shakespeare, Tom. "The Social Model of Disability." In *The Disability Studies Reader*, 4th ed., edited by Lennard J. Davis, 214–21. New York: Routledge, 2013.

Siebers, Tobin. "A Sexual Culture for Disabled People." In *Sex and Disability*, edited by Robert McRuer and Anna Mollow, 37–53. Durham, NC: Duke University Press, 2012.

Silliman, Jael, and Annya Battacharjee, eds. *Policing the National Body: Race, Gender, and Criminalization.* Cambridge, MA: South End, 2002.

Snorton, C. Riley, and Jin Haritaworn. "Trans Necropolitics: A Transnational Reflection on Violence, Death, and the Trans of Color Afterlife." In *The Transgender Studies Reader 2*, edited by Susan Stryker and Aren Z. Aizura, 66–76. New York: Routledge, 2013.

Somerville, Siobhan. *Queering the Color Line: Race and the Invention of Homosexuality in American Culture.* Durham, NC: Duke University Press, 2000.

Soto, Sandra K., and Miranda Joseph. "Neoliberalism and the Battle over Ethnic Studies in Arizona." *Thought and Action* (fall 2010): 45–56.

Spade, Dean. "Documenting Gender." *Hastings Law Journal* 59 (2008): 731–842.

Spade, Dean. "Methodologies of Trans Resistance." In *A Companion to Lesbian, Gay, Bisexual, Transgender, and Queer Studies*, edited by George E. Haggerty and Molly McGarry, 237–61. Oxford: Blackwell, 2007.

Spade, Dean. *Normal Life: Administrative Violence, Critical Trans Politics, and the Limits of Law*. Durham, NC: Duke University Press, 2011.

Spade, Dean. "Resisting Medicine, Re/Modeling Gender." *Berkeley Women's Law Journal* 18 (2003): 15–37.

Spade, Dean, and Craig Willse. "Sex, Gender, and War in an Age of Multicultural Imperialism." *QED: A Journal in GLBTQ Worldmaking* 1, no. 1 (spring 2014): 5–29.

Stalder, Felix, and David Lyon. "Electronic Identity Cards and Social Classification." In *Surveillance as Social Sorting: Privacy, Risk and Digital Discrimination*, edited by David Lyon, 77–93. New York: Routledge, 2003.

Stanley, Eric A., and Nat Smith, ed. *Captive Genders: Trans Embodiment and the Prison Industrial Complex*. Oakland, CA: AK Press, 2011.

Steele, Sarah M. "Queering Intersectionality: Practical Politics and Southerners on New Ground." Master's thesis, University of Florida, 2011. http://ufdc.ufl.edu /UFE0043001/00001.

Stoeckley, Clark. *The United States vs. Private Chelsea Manning: A Graphic Account from Inside the Courtroom*. New York: O/R Books, 2015.

Stone, Sandy. "The *Empire* Strikes Back: A Posttranssexual Manifesto." In *Body Guards: The Cultural Politics of Gender Ambiguity*, edited by Julia Epstein and Kristina Straub, 280–304. New York: Routledge, 1991.

Stryker, Susan. "(De)Subjugated Knowledges: An Introduction to Transgender Studies." In *The Transgender Studies Reader*, edited by Susan Stryker and Stephen Whittle, 1–17. New York: Routledge, 2006.

Stryker, Susan, and Aren Z. Aizura. "Introduction: Transgender Studies 2.0." In *The Transgender Studies Reader 2*, edited by Susan Stryker and Aren Z. Aizura, 1–12. New York: Routledge, 2013.

Stryker, Susan, and Stephen Whittle, eds. *The Transgender Studies Reader*. New York: Routledge, 2006.

Terry, Jennifer. *An American Obsession: Science, Medicine, and Homosexuality in Modern Society*. Chicago: University of Chicago Press, 1999.

Terry, Jennifer. "Significant Injury: War, Medicine, and Empire in Claudia's Case." *WSQ: Women's Studies Quarterly* 37, nos. 1–2 (spring–summer 2009): 200–225.

Torpey, John. *The Invention of the Passport: Surveillance, Citizenship and the State*. Cambridge: Cambridge University Press, 2000.

Towle, Evan, and Lynn Morgan. "Romancing the Transgender Native: Rethinking the Use of the 'Third Gender' Concept." *GLQ* 8, no. 4 (2002): 469–97.

U.S. Congress, Senate Committee on Homeland Security and Governmental Affairs. "Vulnerabilities in the U.S. Passport System Can Be Exploited by Criminals and Terrorists." Washington, DC: U.S. Government Printing Office, 2006.

U.S. Congress, Senate Committee on the Judiciary. "Will Real ID Actually Make Us

Safer? An Examination of Privacy and Civil Liberties Concerns." Washington, DC: U.S. Government Printing Office, 2007.

U.S. Congress, Senate Committee on the Judiciary, Subcommittee on Technology, Terrorism, and Government Information. "Biometric Identifiers and the Modern Face of Terror: New Technologies in the Global War on Terrorism." Washington, DC: U.S. Government Printing Office, 2001.

U.S. Department of State, Passport Office. *The United States Passport: Past, Present, Future.* Washington, DC: U.S. Government Printing Office, 1976.

Valentine, David. *Imagining Transgender: An Ethnography of a Category.* Durham, NC: Duke University Press, 2007.

van der Ploeg, Irma. "Borderline Identities: The Enrollment of Bodies in the Technological Reconstruction of Borders." In *Surveillance and Security: Technological Politics and Power in Everyday Life*, edited by Torin Monahan, 177–93. New York: Routledge, 2006.

Volpp, Leti. "The Citizen and the Terrorist." *UCLA Law Review* 49 (2002): 1575–99.

Volpp, Leti. "Imaginings of Space in Immigration Law." *Law, Culture and the Humanities* 9, no. 3 (2012): 456–74.

Wasserstrom, Richard A. "Racism, Sexism and Preferential Treatment: An Approach to the Topics." In *Applied Ethics: Critical Concepts in Philosophy*, vol. 6, edited by Ruth Chadwick and Doris Schroeder, 103–42. New York: Routledge, 2002.

West, Isaac. *Transforming Citizenships: Transgender Articulations of the Law.* New York: New York University Press, 2014.

Wettlaufer, John N., and John W. Weigel. *Urology in the Vietnam War: Casualty Management and Lessons Learned.* Washington, DC: Office of the Surgeon General, U.S. Army, 2005.

Zackodnik, Teresa. "Fixing the Color Line: The Mulatto, Southern Courts, and Racial Identity." *American Quarterly* 53, no. 3 (2001): 420–51.

INDEX

Abdulmutallab, Umar Farouk, 50, 72

abortion services, 104, 132, 150n7, 163n92, 170n1

advanced imaging technologies (AIT): anomalies and, 51, 56–57, 74–78; backscatter scanners, 59, 61–62, 66–68, 74, 153n60; disability and, 51–52, 68; military settings and, 71–73; pat-downs vs., 50–51, 54–57, 65, 153n51; privacy and, 61–68; prosthetics and, 21, 51–52, 54–56; race and, 51–52, 62–63, 69–71; Rapiscan, 154n60; terrorism discourse and, 69–71; transgendered-identified people and, 53–57, 149nn1–2; visibility and, 53–54; X-ray machines, 21, 50–51, 57–62, 66–68, 74, 153n60

advocacy organizations: abolition frameworks and, 169n72; airport security screenings and, 21, 51, 149n3; citizenship discourse and, 18–20, 24–25, 29–31, 43–49, 88; class discourse and, 29–31; disability advocacy groups, 21, 68, 152n40; hate crimes legislation, 18–20, 143n40; identity documents and, 21, 24–25, 36, 43–49, 148n62; immigrant rights and, 89–90, 148n65, 158n33; inclusion campaigns and, 18–20; Manning case and, 127–28, 169n72; medicolegal discourse and, 36, 45–46, 52, 53–55, 73; military service ban and, 138; privacy discourse and, 21, 43–45; race and, 24–25, 29–31, 43–45, 47–49,

68; recognition frameworks, 18–20, 51, 138, 139; rights discourse and, 18; social justice frameworks and, 18–20, 47–49; strategic visibility, 18, 45–49; trickle up model, 18, 142n38

Agamben, Giorgio, 99

airport security screenings: advocacy organizations and, 21, 51, 149n3; citizenship discourse and, 53–54, 64, 68–69; disability and, 21, 55–57, 63–64, 152n40; National Center for Transgender Equality and, 51, 53–56, 62, 68, 76, 149n3; national security and, 21, 50–51; normative bodies and, 77–78; pat-down procedures, 50–51, 54–57, 63–65, 67–68, 152n33, 153n51; Precheck program, 77–78, 154n66; privacy and, 21, 51–52, 64, 153n51; prosthetics and, 21, 51–52, 53–57; race and, 21, 53–54, 63–64, 151n28; recognition and, 54–55; safety discourse and, 21, 50–51, 152n31, 152n33; terrorism discourse and, 51, 68; transgender-identified people and, 51, 52–57; underwear bomber, 50–51, 72–73; violence discourse, 21, 51–52; voluntary surveillance and, 77–78; vulnerability discourse and, 51–52, 53–57, 63–65, 76; whiteness and, 76. *See also* advanced imaging technologies (AIT); biometric surveillance

Aizura, Aren Z., 12, 141n11

Allen, Samantha, 126, 128

American Express commercial (2008), 8–9, 10

anomalies, 51, 56–57, 74–78

anthropometry, 74–76, 93–94, 159n47

Antiterrorism and Effective Death Penalty Act (1996), 45

Araujo, Gwen, 33, 145n24

Asad, Talal, 70–71

Asian Americans, 4, 26–27, 95

assimilation, 48–49. *See also* going stealth

Atick, Joseph J., 104–5

Audre Lorde Project (ALP), 47, 143n40, 148n58, 148n60, 148n62

bathroom bills: biometric surveillance and, 80–81, 93–99; citizenship and, 81, 85–86, 88–93, 99–106, 161n65; criminalization and, 80–81, 88–91, 104, 106, 157n25, 161n76; deception and, 79–80; disability and, 91–92; fraud and, 79; gender identity discourse and, 87–88; genital recognition and, 80–81, 88–89, 96, 104–5; identity documents and, 81, 88–89, 93, 96; immigration policy and, 80, 88–91, 92–93, 99–100, 106, 161n65; National Center for Transgender Equality and, 86–87; nondiscrimination ordinances and, 79–81, 86–90, 102, 103–4, 157n28; privacy and, 103–4, 107, 155n6, 161n76, 162n88, 163n90; public schools and, 80, 96–97, 104, 163nn89–90; public space and, 99–106, 161n76; race and, 88–93, 99–100; safety discourse and, 79–81, 97–98, 102, 103–4, 157n25; sexuality and, 87; terrorism discourse and, 80, 99

Battle of Algiers (1965), 38–39

Bederman, Gail, 85, 156n16

Bedolla, Lisa García, 156n16

Benjamin, Harry, 31

Bettcher, Talia Mae, 145n24

biometric surveillance: anthropometry, 74–76, 93–94, 159n47; bathroom bills and, 80–81, 93–99; citizenship discourse and, 98–99; class and, 160n57,

160n59; contradictions of, 97–98; criminalization and, 81, 98–99, 155n10; deception and, 104–6; eugenics and, 66, 74–76, 93–94, 159n47; facial recognition technology, 93–94, 104–6, 159n51; fingerprinting and, 81, 95–96, 98–99; fraud and, 95; gender identity discourse and, 93–99; immigration policy and, 60, 81, 94–95, 106, 155n10, 159n47, 159n49; Information Awareness Office and, 159n51; legibility of, 95–96, 160n57; national security and, 94–95, 159n51; neutrality of, 95–96; 9/11 and, 81, 94–95; objective identification and, 81, 93–94; public bathrooms and, 21–22, 81, 93–99; public schools and, 96; race and, 95–96, 160n59; recognition and, 104–6; terrorism discourse and, 81, 94–95, 106; transgender-identified bodies and, 162n79; voluntary surveillance and, 78; whiteness and, 95–96

biopolitical management, 19–20, 49, 56–57, 139

biopower, 20, 36–37. *See also* disciplinary power

birth certificates, 25, 28, 32, 34–35, 40, 88, 93, 145n22, 159n46. *See also* identity documents

Black and Pink (prisoner support organization), 169n72

Black Identity Extremists, 170n1

blackness, 8–9, 10, 12, 138–39, 143n3

Bland, Sandra, 165n16

bodily visibility. *See* visibility

Brandzel, Amy, 4–5

Breckenridge, Keith, 159n47

Brown, Wendy, 17

Browne, Simone, 95, 138, 142n25, 143n3, 151n28, 159n47

Bush (George W.) administration, 22

Butler, Judith, 8, 111, 150n5

Cacho, Lisa, 95

Camp X-ray, 60–61

Guantánamo Bay detention facility, 4, 60–61, 109, 121–22, 127–28

individualism, 41–42, 95, 112, 125–29
Information Awareness Office, 159n51

James, Joy, 39–40
Jensen, Abigail, 90, 99–100
Johnson, Duanna, 110–12, 165nn12–13
Johnson, Kevin, 151n28
Johnson, Michael, 41

Kaba, Mariame, 165n16
Kavanagh, John, 86–88, 91, 97
Keisling, Mara, 76
Kennedy, Michael, 80
Kushner, Jared, 133–34, 139, 170n3

Lamo, Adrian, 109–10, 112, 114–17, 124, 166n21
law enforcement officers: body cameras and, 111–12, 165n16, 165n18; National Center for Transgender Equality and, 19; surveillance of police violence, 165n16
legibility: of biometric surveillance, 95–96, 160n57; citizenship discourse and, 49, 85–86, 106; going stealth, 34–35, 45–46, 48–49; vs. illegibility, 98, 139–40; medicolegal discourse and, 31, 52–55, 106, 114, 161n65; production of transgender subject, 1–2, 17–18, 20–21, 31–38, 52–53, 139–40, 149n4; race and, 25–26, 143n3; recognition and, 134, 139–40; of transgender-identified people, 7, 15–16, 23, 39, 49, 52–55, 132–40; visibility and, 7, 15–16, 23
legitimacy: citizenship discourse and, 28–31; identity documents and, 25–26, 89; Manning case and, 48–49, 52–53, 55–57, 122, 126; medical necessity frameworks and, 56–57; medicolegal frameworks and, 25, 48–49, 52–53, 55–57; militarism and, 56–57, 70–71; paternity and, 25–26; violence and, 56–57, 70–71, 73
Lynch, Loretta E., 107–8
Lyon, David, 16, 146n33

Magnet, Shoshana Amielle, 98, 159n47
Manning, Chelsea: abolition framework and, 169n72; advocacy organizations and, 127–28, 169n72; citizenship discourse and, 108–9, 112, 127–28; as deceptive individual, 22, 109, 112–13, 116, 117, 125–26, 128–29; Don't Ask, Don't Tell policy and, 112–13, 117, 124–25, 128, 166n19, 166nn21–22; emotional life of, 109, 113–19, 124–25; exceptional heroic individualism of, 112, 125–29; gender identity and, 22, 108, 114–19, 125, 128–29, 166n21, 166nn23–24; Guantánamo Bay detention facility and, 4, 60–61, 109, 121–22, 127–28; humanist beliefs of, 113–14, 116, 127, 167n25; incarceration of, 108, 119–22, 126–28; isolation and, 110, 113–16, 118, 121–22, 126–27, 128, 166n21; Adrian Lamo and, 109–10, 112, 114–17, 124, 166n21; legal defense strategy, 22, 112–19, 126–29, 166nn23–24; legitimacy and, 48–49, 52–53, 55–57, 122, 126; medicolegal discourse and, 114; national security and, 22, 108–9, 117, 119, 122, 128–29, 167n42, 168n58; pretrial confinement, 22, 110, 121, 122, 126–27, 128, 168n52, 168n55; privacy and, 113–20, 128–29, 156n15; Reuters FOIA requests, 123–24; sentencing, 108, 115–16, 119, 168n55, 168n59, 169n75; sexual orientation conflation, 113, 166n2; surveillance practices of, 22, 108–9, 112; as terrorist agent, 108–9, 125–26; transgender identification and, 112–13, 116–19, 126, 129; visibility and, 108–9, 119–24, 125–26, 129; whistleblower leaks, 108, 109–10, 112, 113, 117–18, 122–23, 127–29, 168n57; whiteness and, 108–9, 112, 127–29
Marx, Gary T., 148n58
Massey, Doreen, 162n82
McNamara, Lauren, 117
McRae, Bridges, 110–11
McRory, Pat, 103–4
medical surveillance: concealment dis-

national security (*continued*)
Manning case and, 22, 108–9, 117, 119, 122, 128–29, 167n42, 168n58, 169n64, 169n70; transgender visibility and, 119–25; Virginia Tech shootings and, 2–3. *See also* 9/11; safety discourse; terrorism

National Transgender Advocacy Coalition (NTAC), 45–46, 47, 147n53

Nepal, 35, 145n27

Nguyen, Mimi Thi, 161n65

9/11 (September 11, 2001): bathroom bills and, 80; biometric surveillance and, 94–95; Cranbrook lockdown and, 2–3; Guantánamo Bay detention facility and, 4, 60–61, 109, 121–22, 127–28; post-9/11 state surveillance, 2–3, 35–37, 94–95, 145nn27–29, 146n31

no-match policy, 37–38, 41, 43–45, 133–34, 148n65

nondiscrimination ordinances, 79–81, 86–90, 102–3, 157n28

Norma/Normman statues, 74

normative bodies: airport security screenings and, 77–78; anomalies and, 51, 56–57, 74–78; Asian Americans and, 26–27; citizenship and, 9; class status and, 9, 39–40; concealment discourse and, 32–34; disability and, 57; Islamophobia and, 40; race and, 32, 39–40, 61; sexuality and, 39–40; third gender concept and, 35–37, 145nn27–29, 146n31; transgender-identified people and, 39–40; whiteness and, 32; X-ray technologies and, 61

Obama administration, 22, 134–35, 137–38

Orientalist discourse, 4, 5, 70

Paik, A. Naomi, 121

Pakistan, 35–36, 145n128

Passenger Accelerated Service System (PASS), 159n49

passport systems, 25–27, 28, 40–41, 46, 143n3

pat-down procedures, 50–51, 54–57, 63–68, 152n33, 153n51

Paul, Rand, 64

policing systems, 58–59, 61, 101, 110–12. *See also* law enforcement officers

Poole, Mary, 146n34

Pozen, David E., 169n64

prison systems: gender nonconformity and, 121–22; medical necessity frameworks, 53; pat-down procedures and, 66–67; privacy and, 66–68, 152n37; surveillance of law enforcement officers and, 165n14; surveillance technologies and, 110–11; X-ray technologies and, 58–59

privacy: advanced imaging technology and, 61–68; advocacy organizations and, 21, 43–45; airport security screenings and, 21, 51–52, 64, 153n51; bathroom bills and, 103–4, 107, 155n6, 161n76, 162n88, 163n90; disability justice and, 3; gender nonconformity and, 43–49; identity documents and, 41–42; Manning case and, 113–20, 128–29, 156n15; no-match letter policy, 44–45; pat-down procedures and, 63–68; prison systems and, 66–68, 152n37; public bathrooms and, 21, 103–4, 107, 155n6, 157n15, 161n76, 162n88, 163n90; race and, 3, 66; reproductive justice and, 3, 67; right to privacy, 3, 44–45, 152n37; safety vs., 2–4; secrecy vs., 113–20, 128–29, 156n15; sexuality and, 66; terrorism discourse and, 45, 64, 78–79; voluntary surveillance and, 78; whiteness and, 157n15

Proposition 200 (Arizona), 159n45

Prosser, Jay, 158n32

prosthetics, 21, 51–52, 54–56, 72–73

Puar, Jasbir, 18, 71, 147n54, 148n66

public bathrooms: biometric logic and, 21–22, 81, 93–99; citizenship discourse and, 21, 81, 86–93, 99–106; civilizational discourse and, 82–86, 156n16, 157n14; criminalization and, 80–81, 85–86; disability and, 91–93; as gendered space, 83–85; *Goins* vs. *West Publishing,*

Safe OUTside the System Collective (ALP), 143n40, 148n60

safety discourse: airport security screenings and, 21, 50–51, 152n31, 152n33; bathroom bills and, 79–81, 97–98, 102, 103–4, 157n25; criminalization and, 58–59; identity documents and, 40–41; medical necessity framework and, 55; nonnormative gender presentation and, 10; privacy vs., 2–4; public bathrooms and, 79–81, 97–98, 101–4, 157n25; RADAR flashlight, 58–59; voluntary surveillance and, 78. *See also* national security; terrorism discourse

Safetyfest, 143n40

Salter, Mark B., 26

SB 97 (Delaware), 102, 105, 106

SB 1045 (Arizona), 86–87, 90, 97, 157n22

SB 1070 (Arizona), 88, 90, 157n28, 158nn29–31, 161n65

SB 1432 (Arizona), 86–87

secrecy, 113–20, 128–29, 156n15

securitization, 35–37, 145nn27–29, 146n31

September 11, 2001. *See* 9/11

Sex Changes (Califia), 144n19

sexuality, 13–14, 35–37, 66, 87, 137–38, 145nn27–29, 146n31, 166n21

Shine, Jacqui, 165n16

Snorton, C. Riley, 127

Social Security records, 37, 38, 40–41, 44, 146n34

Spade, Dean, 8, 18, 32, 43–44, 127, 165n12, 169n75

Specter, Arlen, 40–41

Stalder, Felix, 146n33

Standing Rock/Dakota Access Pipeline protests, 170n1

Stone, Sandy, 144n19, 147n53

Stryker, Susan, 12, 141n11

suicide bombers, 24–25, 70–71

surveillance: use of term, 17; anticipatory surveillance, 37; biopolitical management and, 19–20, 49, 56–57, 139; construction of gender noncompliance and, 2, 129; gender norms and, 6, 35–37, 145nn27–29, 146n31; lateral surveillance, 124, 165n18; mandatory volunteerism, 148n58; politics of recognition and, 132–34; production of gender nonconformity and, 5–6, 6–14, 110–11, 132–34, 138–40; production of transgender subject, 1–2, 17–18, 20–21, 31–38, 52–53, 139–40, 149n4; public knowledge of, 112, 116, 129; transgender critique of surveillance, 6–14, 22–23, 132–40; voluntary surveillance, 77–78

Sylvia Rivera Law Project (SRLP), 19, 48–49, 143n40, 148n65

terrorism discourse: advanced imaging technologies and, 69–71; airport security screenings and, 46–49, 51, 68; anticipatory surveillance, 37; Antiterrorism and Effective Death Penalty Act (1996), 45; antiterrorism rhetoric, 4, 27, 41–42, 64–65, 69–71, 78, 80–81, 94–95, 106, 108–9, 125–26; bathroom bills and, 80, 99; biometric surveillance and, 81, 94–95, 106; citizenship discourse and, 27–28, 38–43, 80, 148n66; Department of Homeland Security advisory, 24, 38–40, 43–44, 45, 47–48; Guantánamo Bay detention facility and, 4, 60–61, 109, 121–22, 127–28; immigration policy and, 4, 10, 27–28, 37–38, 42–43, 45, 80–81, 94–95, 106, 108–9, 159n51; Manning case and, 108–9, 125–26; militarism and, 70–71, 94–95, 106, 108–9; national identity and, 46–49, 148n66; privacy and, 64, 78–79; race and, 4–6, 45, 69–71, 105; recognition and, 105; voluntary surveillance and, 77–78; whiteness and, 69, 105

Terry, Jennifer, 71

Thurmond, Strom, 94

Title IX, 137–38

Torpey, John, 40–41, 46

transgender: use of term, 10–11, 13, 141nn11–12, 142n15; production of

CPSIA information can be obtained
at www.ICGtesting.com
Printed in the USA
BVHW060835280620
582417BV00009B/376